GETTING BEYOND RACE

GETTING BEYOND RACE

The Changing American Culture

RICHARD J. PAYNE

WestviewPress
A Division of HarperCollins*Publishers*

Copyright © 1998 by Westview Press, A Division of HarperCollins Publishers, Inc.

Published in 1998 in the United States of America by Westview Press, 5500 Central Avenue, Boulder, Colorado 80301-2877, and in the United Kingdom by Westview Press, 12 Hid's Copse Road, Cumnor Hill, Oxford OX2 9JJ

Library of Congress Cataloging-in-Publication Data
Payne, Richard J., 1949–
  Getting beyond race : the changing American culture / Richard J. Payne.
    p.   cm.
  Includes bibliographical references and index.
  ISBN 0-8133-6858-8
  1. United States—Race relations.   I. Title.
E184.A1P36   1998
305.8'00973—dc21   97-51414
                                                                       CIP

The paper used in this publication meets the requirements of the American National Standard for Permanence of Paper for Printed Library Materials Z39.48-1984.

10   9   8   7   6   5   4   3   2   1

To
William J. Brisk
and
Maria Brisk

Friends and mentors who inspired
me to do research

CONTENTS

PREFACE

Viewing contemporary problems through a racial prism is likely to impede the creation of a color-blind society. Given the ideological and deeply emotional nature of race, such an approach to issues of common concern is generally counterproductive. Because race is an issue that is so bound up with personal identity, expectations for an open and honest dialogue on racial issues are frequently unrealized. Most Americans tend to perceive discussions of race as intrinsically accusatory and emotional; consequently, effective communication is virtually impossible, and precious opportunities for breaking down racial barriers are squandered. Problems remain unresolved and continue to incite distrust, fear, and interpersonal conflict. *Getting Beyond Race* maintains that America's success in race relations requires nothing less than the adoption of new ways of thinking about race.

Reframing or changing the way a problem is perceived offers a realistic opportunity to engage in more productive and less confrontational dialogues with the goal of eliminating racial discrimination in American society. Reframing helps to develop new vantage points; it elicits new information, attitudes, and potential solutions. This book posits that reframing problems within the broader context of universal human virtues, and particularly American values, has the potential to further integrate American society. Instead of drawing additional attention to skin color, reframing can help develop a greater awareness of common interests, a common humanity, and a genuine sense of community.

Although race continues to matter, there have been significant improvements in race relations throughout the United States over the past thirty years. An obvious example of this change is the wide public support for Colin Powell's hoped-for presidential candidacy in 1996 (even though he never entered the race) and Powell's standing as a leading contender for the Republican ticket in the year 2000. The central argument of this book is that the emergence of a strong and growing black middle class, the dynamic force of generational change, increasing rates of interracial marriage and transracial adoptions, and profound attitudinal and behavioral changes support the view that America is inexorably moving beyond race.

Blacks and whites have never been closer. They interact daily at all levels of society—from day-care centers to the White House—as individuals and not as monolithic, cohesive white and black communities. Although social proximity has generated conflict as well as cooperation between the two races, it has also eliminated each race's profound ignorance of the other. Furthermore, the growing racial and ethnic complexity so evident in American cities challenges the assumption that America is a society that is neatly divided between blacks and whites. The new Betty Crocker, unveiled by General Mills in early 1996, best illustrates the changing realities of race relations. This newly designed corporate "spokesperson," meant to personify the ideal American woman, is not an unambiguously white American but a computer-generated composite incorporating white, black, Native American, and Asian features.

Getting Beyond Race discusses various strategies for society's continuing evolution in directions in which race no longer matters. It suggests that instead of concentrating on failures, Americans should emphasize their successes. By focusing on what is positive in race relations, Americans create a model for future success. The book argues that, while group identity can be a source of strength, a broader concept of human virtues and a focus on what Americans have in common are ultimately more helpful to disadvantaged Americans in particular and American society in general. Because race relations are ultimately about ordinary people interacting with each other on an individual basis, much of this book concentrates primarily on individuals and small groups whose activities are helping to reduce the significance of race in society.

Now that the legal foundation for racial equality is largely in place, greater emphasis must be placed on individual behavior. The tendency to focus on the big picture of racial issues often obscures the fact that the most important changes in race relations are occurring at the grassroots level. The bottom-up approach endorsed by this book presents a more hopeful and constructive view of race relations than is usual. Based on extensive interviews with ordinary Americans, participant observation, public opinion polls, and exhaustive research, this book concludes that most Americans strongly desire to move beyond race and that they are making significant progress toward that goal.

Chapter 1 discusses the need to reframe racial issues. It suggests strategies for getting beyond the habit of blaming others and the zero-sum approach to race relations. How we choose to perceive others and ourselves directly affects our attitudes and behavior toward them as well as their attitudes and behavior toward us. The chapter further argues that stressing differences instead of common concerns inevitably leads to treating people differently, not equally. Indeed, drawing attention to racial differences can inadvertently make a victim feel responsible for the actions of a victimizer by subtly reinforcing stereotypes of inferiority and superiority based on race. Chapter 1 suggests that by embracing positive American values, building coalitions based on common interests, and negotiating differences, America can continue to make greater progress in race relations.

Chapter 2 examines how race was invented for economic and social reasons. It argues that race is an arbitrary and artificial construct that divides individuals into rigid categories. But, as Chapter 3 shows, the concept of race is being weakened by fundamental changes in American culture. Increased interpersonal contact, the media, religion, family values, sports, generational replacement, and demographic change are playing a major role in this process.

Perhaps the most obvious model of success in race relations is the military. Chapter 4 traces the struggle for racial equality in the military from the American Revolution to the present. Pragmatic considerations as well as idealism eventually led to an integrated military. Not only has the military implemented measures to ensure equal opportunity and fair treatment on base, it has also had an important impact on race relations in the civilian sector.

Affirmative action is one of the most controversial issues in race relations. Chapter 5 discusses the various definitions and public perceptions of equal opportunity and the measures designed to achieve it, the background of affirmative action, and arguments for and against it. Instead of simply accepting or rejecting all aspects of affirmative action, this chapter suggests possible compromise solutions, based in part on the experience of the military with promoting equal opportunity and treatment.

Chapter 6 argues that large-scale immigration from Latin America, Asia, the Caribbean, the Middle East, and elsewhere has complicated the issues of race, racial classification, and racial boundaries. Immigrants bring with them values and beliefs that often challenge American racial perceptions. For example, West Indian immigrants, who come from a culture that places a premium on education and achievement, play a crucial role in challenging racial stereotypes and in building bridges between blacks and whites. Colin Powell, Sidney Poitier, Harry Belafonte, and Shirley Chisolm are among the most obvious examples of how West Indians are contributing to undermining the concept of race.

Because the maintenance of racial boundaries is dependent on racial separation, interracial families directly erode these boundaries. The growth of such families has been facilitated by the abolition of laws against miscegenation. An essential component of maintaining racial barriers is the one-drop rule, which dictates that one drop of black blood is sufficient to make one a black. Chapters 7 and 8 contend that the increasing numbers of interracial marriages and transracial adoptions are weakening the one-drop rule as well as the entire concept of race. Certainly the children resulting from interracial marriages are a direct challenge to the one-drop rule. For example, the growth of a racially mixed group of Americans has led to calls for a multiracial category on census forms and on college and financial aid applications, as well as calls for the abolition of all categories. In late 1997 the Census Bureau responded by allowing Americans to check as many different racial categories as they see fit. A growing public acceptance, especially among younger Americans, of interracial relationships and transracial adoptions is tangible evidence of profound social change.

Getting Beyond Race does not attempt to underestimate the difficulties involved in realizing social transformation, but it reframes the problem of race. The book maintains that Americans will eventually move beyond race by building on positive events, focusing on universal human virtues, and looking forward with hope and a sense of common purpose and destiny. It suggests that America is making steady evolutionary progress toward rendering the social, economic, and political construction of race less meaningful. Racism is in decline, and the very concept of race is becoming increasingly less significant. Demographic and cultural changes, including immigration and the growth of interracial families, are serving to speed up the process.

Richard J. Payne

ACKNOWLEDGMENTS

For more than two decades I have discussed many of the ideas in this book with hundreds of Americans from different backgrounds. Many of them shared information about important aspects of their lives. In a very real way, this book is a collaborative effort. I am deeply indebted to the interviewees whose stories are in the book as well as to those individuals who contributed to my research but wanted to remain anonymous. Several colleagues read parts of the manuscript, raised questions, and offered suggestions. I am particularly indebted to Lucille Holcomb, F. James Davis, Jane Lee, Jeanne Howard, Mary Cunningham, Denis Thornton, Sharon MacDonald, Richard Stivers, Barbara Heyl, Anne Wortham, Denise Davison, Laura Berk, Linda Giles, Cassandra Veney, Maura Toro-Morn, Linda Cummins, Beverly Nance, Gary Klass, Eros DeSouza, David Chesebrough, Wayne Benenson, and Sue Sprecher.

I would like to thank Cari Banahoski, Sinead Rice, Tasha Welch, Richard Ehlers, Jeffrey Taylor, Matthew Nance, and Amy Atchison for helping me with research. I am extremely grateful to Garold Cole, Carol Ruyle, Joan Winters, Pat Werdell, Sheila Hufeld, and Sharon Wetzel at Illinois State University for their invaluable assistance in locating library materials and for their insights on race relations; to Paul Schollaert, Dean of the College of Arts and Sciences, and David Strand, President of Illinois State University, for their support and strong commitment to getting beyond race; to Matthew Nance, Pam Ashworth, and Michele Ganschow for their outstanding word processing skills; and to Paula Goodnight for preparing the index. Leo Wiegman, senior editor at Westview Press, Kristin Milavec, the project editor, and Norman Ware, the copy editor, were very helpful.

Many friends provided useful criticism and helped in many ways. I am indebted to Michele Steinbacher-Kemp, Sherry Wallace, Jo Porter, and Paula Monroe. I am especially grateful to Elaine Graybill for her constant support and encouragement. She served as editor, photographer, and proofreader. I owe a special debt of thanks to my mother, Iris, for teaching tolerance and the importance of education, and to my son, Jason, for helping me to understand how generational change is moving America beyond race.

R.J.P.

1

STRATEGIES FOR GETTING BEYOND RACE

Reframing the Problem

ON THE EVE OF THE TWENTY-FIRST CENTURY, the United States continues to struggle with race, an issue that has had and continues to have devastating consequences for many Americans. But the concept of race, which is defined largely by social consensus, has been steadily eroding. As I will explain in Chapter 2, race is socially, economically, and politically constructed for a variety of material as well as psychological purposes. However, there is only one human race, which is remarkably homogeneous compared to other species.

General racial classifications ignore the obvious biological reality that each individual within the human species, with the exception of identical twins, is genetically unique.[1] Significant developments in science and technology, improved public education, generational replacement or change, and the growing complexity of society, among other factors, have contributed to weakening the social consensus that undergirds the idea of race.

Yet race continues to matter because ideas and beliefs, once they have been institutionalized, can influence public policy and individual behavior even after the interests of their creators have changed.[2] In an environment characterized by various groups attempting to control each other,[3] race is often instrumental in one group's achievement of dominance over another.

However, although race can serve to achieve various objectives, it can also serve as an excuse for personal failure. In a 1993 Gallup poll, 93 percent of Americans with European ancestry and 95 percent of Americans with African ancestry believed that people use racial discrimination as an excuse for their own shortcomings.[4] Thus, in a society as complex and diverse as the United States, race and racism mean different things to different individuals and groups.

Seeing Race

Racism is generally defined in negative terms. It is viewed as any hostile action or belief that subordinates an individual or group based on readily observable physical characteristics such as skin color. A racist ideology, or set of beliefs, encompasses five false assumptions. First is that some groups of people, erroneously defined as "races," are physically superior to others. The second assumption is that some races are more intelligent than others. A third belief is that race and culture are inseparable. The fourth is that race determines personality. The final assumption of racist ideology, that racial mixing lowers the biological quality of superior races, is based on the myth of racial purity.[5] Racists, then, focus on observable differences to exclude others regarded as inferior from access to power, position, and wealth. Racism may be practiced by institutions, groups, or individuals. It has been argued that "whatever black people may do in the way of a racist response, there is no such thing as black racism."[6] However, given their common humanity, all Americans, including black Americans, can be victims as well as perpetrators of racism.

Significant changes in American racial beliefs have complicated race relations. Although many problems are often portrayed in terms of race, the reality is much more complex. A person who might oppose busing to achieve racially integrated schools might also be a strong proponent of racially integrated neighborhoods and workplaces. Opposition to busing can be based on many considerations that have very little to do with race. Furthermore, racial positions are not always fixed and can change depending on the issues and interests involved. People are complex and can hold both racist and antiracist views simultaneously; they may discriminate in some situations and strongly oppose discrimination in others. These apparent contradictions not only reflect major changes in race relations in recent years but also suggest that more positive, less blaming, and less confrontational approaches to racial conflicts might be more constructive than most contemporary methods of addressing racial differences.

A racial prism makes it easier to view almost any conflict between different peoples as racism or any action that gives people of minority races an advantage over whites as reverse racism, without much consideration of specific facts. There are situations in which the term "racism" is not only appropriate but also effective. For example, institutions, groups, and individuals whose actions clearly discriminate against Americans on the basis of race might be induced to change their behavior if they were publicly castigated as racists.

But it is important that only those specific institutions, groups, and individuals should be targeted. Generalizations about people based on specific negative experiences tend to oversimplify complex realities and to offend and alienate many strong opponents of racism. Furthermore, the power of the label "racism" is diminished by overuse; it loses its practical utility as well as its credibility. More importantly, the excessive application of the term "racism" to ordinary human problems can be demoralizing. If racism is so pervasive, then one's ability to effectuate change is seriously limited.[7]

Although short-term psychological gains may result from overusing the word "racism," the more detrimental long-term effect is the nurturing of cynicism, hopelessness, and self-destructive behaviors. For example, blacks who dwell on racism tend to engage in behaviors that sabotage their chances to be successful. If the objective is to get beyond race, then strategies that encourage positive behavior, that cast what are regarded as racial problems in a broader context, and that facilitate coalition building across racial lines are likely to be more productive. For example, behavior that is regarded as racist could be cast in the broader context of human virtues and vices.

Faced with widespread public opposition to overt racism, many ideological racists have adopted a more sophisticated form of racism, as I explain in Chapter 2. They skillfully manipulate racial feelings by using subtle code language, as President George Bush did with his Willie Horton advertisement during the 1988 presidential campaign. Willie Horton, a black man imprisoned in Massachusetts for murder, raped a white woman in Maryland while on a weekend pass from prison. Bush used the advertisement to portray his opponent, Massachusetts governor Michael Dukakis, as being soft on crime and to link blacks with crime. Many middle-class Americans with African ancestry complain about this subtle racism. They tend to see more racial discrimination than do poor blacks, observe less decline in discrimination, and expect less improvement in the future.[8] This perception is undoubtedly influenced by the wide range of contacts middle-class blacks have with whites and by the tendency of some blacks to approach many ordinary problems from a narrow racial context.

Nonetheless, Americans of African ancestry face many forms of subtle racism, scenarios that are so well known they are virtually anticipated. These include being passed up by empty taxis; being subjected to poor service; being under suspicion as a potential shoplifter; and being regarded as a potential criminal in parking lots, on elevators, and elsewhere. According to a 1995 *Washington Post*/Kaiser Family Foundation/Harvard University poll,[9] only 38 percent of whites believed that racism was a major problem in society today, whereas 68 percent of blacks considered racism to be a serious problem.

Divergent perspectives on race relations seem to support the view that America is divided into two separate societies—one black and one white. According to Andrew Hacker, the leading proponent of the two separate nations thesis, the erosion of the civil-rights interracial alliance has occurred principally because Americans with African ancestry have turned away from building racial bridges to shriller forms of politics that seem to indict all whites.[10]

Despite the rhetoric of separatism, blacks are increasingly participating in the mainstream of American life. Many polls refute the two separate nations thesis. According to a 1993 Gallup poll, 52 percent of Americans of African ancestry agreed that the United States is moving toward two separate and unequal societies, and 44 percent disagreed. Among Americans of European ancestry, 33 percent agreed and 63 percent disagreed. Approximately 33 percent of Americans who lived during their country's turbulent years of segregation and overt racism agreed that America is dividing along racial lines; 65 percent of them disagreed. Younger Americans between the ages of 18 and 29 are almost evenly divided, with 47 percent agreeing and 52 percent disagreeing. Those in sharpest disagreement with the two nations thesis are college graduates. Only 27 percent of them agreed with the thesis compared to 70 percent who disagreed.[11]

Whereas 54 percent of Americans of European ancestry believe that race relations are better now than they were twenty-five years ago, only 45 percent of Americans with African ancestry believe that race relations have improved. But only 16 percent of the former and 15 percent of the latter thought that race relations had deteriorated since the 1960s. When asked if there had been significant progress toward Martin Luther King's dream of equality, 64 percent of whites and 62 percent of blacks said yes. But when asked if race relations in the United States are generally good or generally bad, 55 percent of whites and 66 percent of blacks gave the more pessimistic response.[12]

These polls and others clearly indicate both progress and lingering problems; achieving harmonious race relations is a process that is unlikely to move in one direction only or to be entirely smooth. Both conflict and cooperation are integral components of building better race relations. As Roger Fisher and Scott Brown observe, "It would be a mistake to define a good relationship as one in which we agree easily, just as it would be a mistake to define a good road as one that is easy to build. While it is easier to build a good road across a prairie than through mountains, a good road through mountains may be more valuable than one across a prairie."[13]

From Racial Identity Politics to Inclusion

An important barrier to getting beyond race is the idea that race represents a fixed and inflexible identity. Current debates in American race relations have reinforced the view that blacks must be exclusively black and whites must be exclusively white in terms of how they think and how they are identified, despite the growing and complex interactions between blacks and whites.

Instead of embracing a broader humanity and recognizing multiple identities, the politics of racial identity demands an uncompromising and unambiguous loyalty to the myth of a racial group. To know one's racial identity is regarded as tantamount to knowing oneself and is thus hailed as a positive force. The Black Power and Black Aesthetic movements of the 1960s, in an attempt to counteract the dominant perspective that whiteness represented all that was positive and blackness embodied the negative, superseded whiteness by forwarding an equally detrimental and exclusive concept of blackness.

Ironically, this approach is essentially the same that white racists count on to perpetuate the marginalization of Americans with African ancestry from American society. The emphasis on blackness helps to maintain an emphasis on whiteness, thereby joining black and white racists in an unexpected alliance. This approach maintains racial boundaries, promotes attitudes that are more conducive to conflict than to compromise, and assaults the humanity of all Americans. The conceptual scheme or framework that has been adopted has direct implications on America's ability to solve its race-related problems. An emphasis on the "Americanness" and humanness of all citizens will determine the extent to which American society can transcend race and deal effectively with problems that emanate from a racial paradigm.

Identity may be defined as a conception of the self, a selection of physical, psychological, emotional, or social attributes of particular individuals.[14] The self is shaped by many different social, cultural, economic, and political factors. People may see their identity as defined by some moral or spiritual commitment or they may characterize it in terms of nationality, ethnicity, or racial categorization. Identity provides the frame within which people can determine their positions on various issues, on what is right or wrong, on what is admirable and worthwhile.[15] Identity is about having a sense of belonging to a social group.

Specific group identities emanate from shared experiences. The African-American identity has been shaped by the unique experience of slavery, rigid racial segregation, and widespread discrimination. These experiences have contributed to the emergence of a social identity characterized by feelings of community, similarity, and common purpose. Individuals believe that they belong to certain social groups and that such membership has emotional and value significance. Personal identity, on the other hand, entails a sense of individual autonomy. It gives one a sense of location within a community or the larger society because of one's distinctive or unique characteristics.[16]

Believing that race is identity can lead one to overlook the reality of multiple identities, of which race is only one. Each person belongs to numerous social groups simultaneously. One can be a member of a nation, a family, a professional organization, a university, a religious group, an ethnic group, a sports team, or a political party. Consequently, these are multiple conceptions of self: American, mother, daughter, lawyer, coach, and so on. All these groups help to shape the individual's outlook on social, economic, and political issues.

Contrary to the binary view of race in America, which holds that an individual is either black or white, most individuals have a larger number of potential identities by ancestry alone. For example, most Americans with African ancestry also have English, Irish, French, or other European ancestors. Identification with one specific racial group results from a forced or voluntary selecting out from a large number of other ancestors with whom to identify.[17] As I explain in Chapters 6, 7, and 8, more Americans are now rejecting the binary view of race and the idea that the color of one's skin is the dominant, if not sole, determinant of one's identity.

Because identity is about human experience and a sense of belonging, personal as well as group identity change with new circumstances and evolving needs. In a society as dynamic as that of the United States—a country whose self-definition embraces change—identity is far from fixed. The dynamism that characterizes identity in the United States is a function of the interaction of the past and the present as well as the hopes and fears about the future. Identities can die or become fossilized. They can also reappear in a different combination of old elements that come together in a new way.[18] One's work also helps to transform one's identity. Dorinne K. Kondo, in a study of the Japanese workplace, carefully documents how workers transformed themselves in the process of transforming the material world. Kondo argues that human beings create, develop, and enact their identities, sometimes creatively challenging the limits of the cultural constraints that constitute both what we call ourselves and the ways those selves can be crafted.[19]

Identity often functions to draw distinctions between groups to promote group solidarity. Often conflict with other groups is utilized to preserve group identity and strengthen boundaries against the outside world.[20] On the other hand, identity can serve to mobilize and energize individuals and to give them a sense of purpose and direction. Self-esteem and self-confidence can be enhanced by identifying with a particular group. One can derive a feeling of belonging and inclusion. In many cases, group identity is essential to counter alienation from and domination by other groups. Americans with African ancestry provide an excellent example of how a forced group identity ultimately became a tool of survival. But many aspects of the black subculture also encourage self-destructive behavior.

Embracing an identity too tightly, exalting differences, and downplaying similarities with other groups can create serious problems for the alienated group. This strategy risks confining the group to an identity that effectively serves to explain them entirely and simplistically, thereby facilitating efforts to continue to exclude them.[21] Furthermore, depersonalization may result from a very strong identity with one particular group, a development that produces group behavior to the detriment of the uniqueness of the individual. Depersonalization is the tendency to perceive increased identity between self and in-group members and difference from out-group members. One becomes a representative of a social category, identical with others of the same category.[22] Clearly, depersonalization is an impediment to getting beyond race.

Closely related to identity is the categorization of human beings into groups based on race, nationality, class, religion, sex, and other easily identifiable characteristics. Both identity and categorization emphasize differences. Forced categorization, as in the case of blacks, is essential to maintaining a racial hierarchy. Instead of being considered a unique individual, one is first and foremost a member of a category. Members of a category are seen as being essentially the same.[23] For example, many Americans with African ancestry are often frustrated by the tendency of other Americans to perceive them as a homogeneous group. Yet the emphasis on blackness and racial solidarity only helps to strengthen the perception that blacks are all alike.

Many blacks also fail to see whites as individuals. The categorization of people is sufficient to cause intergroup discrimination, with members of the in-group receiving preferential treatment. Andrew Hacker believes that "white people seldom stop to ask how they may benefit from belonging to their race."[24] In other words, they simply assume that they are naturally entitled to certain privileges. Part of the problem is that many Americans of European ancestry do not consider themselves a race. Whites constitute the norm whereas other people form "races." In several interviews, whites pointed out, "I am white and I don't see race." However, Hacker contends that "all white Americans realize that their skin comprises an inestimable asset. It opens doors and facilitates freedom of movement. It serves as a shield from insult and harassment."[25] But many whites, reflecting on their own experiences, regard Hacker's generalizations as wishful thinking.

Group identity and social categorization inevitably lead to an emphasis on differences and an us-versus-them mentality. In a society as competitive as that of the United States, this problem is exacerbated. Gains for whites are often seen as losses for blacks and vice versa. Given that race relations have been based on dichotomous thinking, the us-versus-them approach is deeply entrenched in how Americans perceive racial conflicts in particular and conflict in general. One is expected to take sides based on one's racial identity. A we-they worldview is conducive to blaming the other side, attributing malevolent intentions to its members, projecting our worst fears onto them, and adopting an adversarial approach to problem solving.[26] The growth of black consciousness, the maintenance of a system for distinguishing blacks from whites to monitor race relations and provide equal opportunities for blacks and other minorities, and continuing racial discrimination contribute to the perpetuation of the us-versus-them mentality. But increased opportunities for blacks, resulting in part from the monitoring of race relations, have led to the growth of the black middle class. These middle-class blacks are ensconced in the greater American society and the more frequent and meaningful their contacts with whites, the less likely they are to stress a black identity that emphasizes separation from white identity.[27] This means that the cohesiveness of blacks as a group is weakened and the prospect of collective action becomes largely a fantasy. The development of a strong black middle class, while helping the country to move beyond race, may also sharpen perceptions of class differences among Americans with African ancestry.

The Dangers of Victimology

Historically, what distinguished black Americans from other Americans, with the exception of some Native Americans, is the institution of slavery, rigid segregation in many parts of the country, and discrimination of one kind or another throughout the nation.

African-American history clearly features sustained and systematic victimization. Yet these Americans not only survived slavery and its aftermath, they overcame almost insurmountable obstacles to make major contributions to their country and to achieve personal success. Although black Americans were obviously victims, they were also, and more importantly, courageous and victorious. But instead of highlighting black success, contemporary discussions focus overwhelmingly on black failures, thereby denying or downplaying black achievement. Increasingly, black identity has become intertwined with an ideology of victimhood.

Accompanying the emergence of the Black Power and Black Aesthetic movements of the 1960s was the intellectual argument that "the ideology of blaming the victim so distorts and disorients the thinking of the average concerned citizen that it becomes a primary barrier to effective social change."[28] Such a contention is not without merit. For a group that suffered so much inequality, claiming the status of victim was both historically honest and pragmatic. Lise Noel maintains that "far from reflecting a propensity to complacency and self-indulgent misery, such a demand prevents the dominated from having to beg for a problematical improvement in their condition and instead allows them to demand that justice be done."[29]

Undermining this strategy, however, was the wider society's growing tendency to claim victimhood whenever any of life's ordinary obstacles were encountered. White males complained when they didn't get the job for which a hundred people applied and a minority candidate was chosen. Clearly, only one person could be hired, making all white male applicants victims of reverse discrimination, from their point of view. In many cases the person who is hired becomes the victim of the others' wrath. Political leaders also claim to be victims. For example, in 1996, Enid Waldholtz, a congresswoman from Utah, claimed that she was victimized by her husband, who allegedly stole $4 million from her father to finance her successful race for a seat in Congress. Instead of shouldering some of the responsibility, Waldholtz, like an increasing number of Americans, found refuge in victimhood. As Robert Hughes puts it, "The all-pervasive claim to victimhood tops off America's long-cherished culture of therapeutics. To be vulnerable is to be invincible. Complaint gives you power."[30]

For black Americans, claims of victimhood, although often justified, are not without significant costs. The dilemma facing blacks derives in part from the trivialization of the concept of victimhood by the larger society. If everyone is a victim, then the strength of the claims for justice by legitimate victims of past and ongoing discrimination is substantially diminished. The ideology of victimhood consolidated us-versus-them thinking, thereby hindering prospects for cooperation. Instead of promising inclusion, the ideology of victimhood further alienates victims from the larger society or diminishes their effectiveness when they are included. Victims become problematized either as disadvantaged or unfairly privileged.[31]

To be a victim implies passivity, helplessness, and dependence on the victimizer. Instead of empowering, an ideology of victimhood destroys self-confidence, self-respect, and one's sense of responsibility. In other words, it effectively reduces the ability to influence events that directly impact one's own life. Victimology also affects successful American minorities who are often perceived as betraying the poor. Celebrating success undermines the legitimacy of the victims' most valuable political asset—their supposed helplessness.[32] Taking responsibility for problems and focusing on one's strengths instead of one's status as a victim enhances one's ability to shape outcomes.

Reframing the Problem

Race is a difficult issue to confront directly because for most Americans, regardless of their skin color, it remains an essential component of their self-definition. Race symbolizes advantage and disadvantage, fear and control, exploitation and deception, exclusion and distance, and a fundamental betrayal of the positive Enlightenment values upon which the United States was founded. In other words, there are too many defense mechanisms in place and there is too much anger and pain to enable productive and honest discussions on race. Race symbolizes difference, and what starts out as a dialogue on race often turns out to be a visceral, accusatory, blaming session in which the emotionally loaded charge of racism is likely to surface. Such discussions are generally counterproductive because they are based on a victim-oppressor paradigm in which guilt is supposed to motivate whites to improve relations with blacks, Asians, Latinos, and others.

Talking about race is difficult even in relatively enlightened environments such as college and university classrooms. Denise Beurskens, a white instructor at a large midwestern university, believes that talking about race is an important component of her American and world history courses. But she goes on to say that some white instructors have conveyed that they are nervous when discussing race because of the sensitivity of the issue and because they might say something that might be construed as racist. Having worked closely with African Americans for several years, Beurskens said that she could empathize with their situation. She was aware that when discussing racial issues it was expected that she should say the politically correct thing and not offend anyone. However, she believed that it was important to talk about the problem.[33]

In order to encourage constructive dialogue and to be in a position to take advantage of the opportunities that their society offers, Americans would do well to focus less on race and more on universal virtues and positive American values. Glenn C. Loury contends that "to the extent that we individual blacks see ourselves primarily through a racial lens, we sacrifice possibilities for the kind of personal development that would ultimately further our collective, racial interests."[34] Former chairman of the Joint Chiefs of Staff Colin Powell and former U.S. ambassador to the United Nations Donald McHenry believe that it is a burden to think in racial terms. Both are cognizant of the difficulties facing many blacks and of the existence of racism. But they choose to frame the problem of race in a nonracial way. Powell advises young Americans with African ancestry not to let racism be their problem. "You can't change it. Don't have a chip on your shoulder, and don't think everyone is staring at you because you are black. Let it drag them down. Don't use it as an excuse for your own shortcomings."[35] Similarly, when asked about race, McHenry said: "I don't give it much thought."[36] Both men realize that thinking in racial terms is inherently disadvantageous to many Americans with African ancestry.

Colin Powell's approach has enabled him to transcend race, in the overall view of Americans. Racial thinking inevitably includes internalizing destructive racial stereotypes and diverting attention from underlying problems. Marian Wright Edelman, director of the Children's Defense Fund, recalls that her father, as he was dying in an ambulance, told her that she could be and do anything she wanted; that race and gender are shadows; and that character, self-discipline, determination, attitude, and service are the substance of life.[37] Race for Edelman, Powell, McHenry, and others is a distraction. Most Americans with African ancestry believe that most whites perceive them as "always whining about racism." A *Time*/CNN poll showed that 70 percent of blacks held that perception.[38] Clearly, a new perceptual framework or paradigm is needed to get beyond race.

A frame is essentially a point of view, a way of seeing things. Framing refers to how a problem is conceived, the kinds of evidence that are considered, and the cognitive strategy that is employed.[39] The frame determines to a large extent how we interpret what happens in our environment, what judgments we make, and how we perceive what we regard as reality. Since most of us are sensitive to contextual cues when making decisions, formulating judgments, forming opinions, and taking action, framing is a significant determinant of behavior.[40] Stated another way, framing determines what we deem to be important.

A racial frame influences many Americans to view ordinary human problems in racial terms. For example, two American youngsters who are engaged in an emotional argument might be seen as being involved in a racial conflict if their skin colors are different. Few Americans are likely to see it as a possible dispute between brothers or cousins, because we tend to frame problems literally in terms of black and white. Two white youngsters having a similarly heated argument would not draw the same reaction or evaluation. Instead of a racial incident, their argument would be seen as an ordinary dispute.

Frames are closely related to what Victor Turner calls "root paradigms," or consciously recognized cultural models. He argues that "root paradigms are the cultural transliterations of genetic codes—they represent that in the human individual as a cultural entity what DNA and RNA codes represent in him as a biological entity."[41] But culture is constantly changing and, with time and much effort, the frames through which we perceive the world around us can be altered or at least be challenged by the discovery of alternative frames. Race is only one of several ways of perceiving, interpreting, and dealing with human differences. The habitual use of terms like "race" and "racism" almost guarantees that a racial worldview or perspective will be perpetuated.[42] The stereotypes that are integral components of a racial perspective are often subconsciously accepted not only by those who gain but also by those who are disadvantaged by their existence. This is particularly true of groups in conflict.

Reframing an issue challenges prevailing thinking and the power and advantage that emanate from it. By perceiving the world in nonracial terms, one can be empowered to achieve one's aspirations and to participate more fully in American life. To accept a racial frame is to accept the status quo. The degree to which disadvantaged individuals accept the status quo is a measure of the dominant group's success in controlling the relationship.[43] To become full participants in their society, disadvantaged individuals must change their frame from one that is particular and confining to one that is universal.

Reframing suggests the adoption of a different language when discussing what is regarded as race relations. Language is a powerful agent of change. It influences perceptions, thoughts, and actions in subtle but potent ways. To a large extent, language plays a pivotal role in one's perception of reality. The language used reflects a society's thinking, its values, and its method of structuring human relations. Language defines us; it signals who we are.[44] To say that I am white is another way of saying I am not black and therefore entitled to different treatment. To say I am an American is another way of saying I am similar to people whose skins are a different color. Acknowledging that, as human beings, we share the same potential for good and evil and that, as Americans, we ultimately face a common destiny is essential to building a new framework that can help move American society beyond race. In other words, all Americans must acknowledge the humanness and "Americanness" of each other.[45]

Reframing, like race relations in general, must be the responsibility of the individual. There are numerous examples of how reframing has enabled Americans to transcend race. During World War II, when the U.S. Army in Hawaii was racially integrated, black soldiers of the famous 369th were successful in getting some white soldiers to rethink the racial paradigm by changing the frame from race to military protocol and rank.[46] As will be discussed in Chapter 4, the racially tolerant environment in Hawaii undoubtedly facilitated reframing. In Jackson, Mississippi, highway patrolman Nelson Tate, encountering problems with an eighty-year-old woman who wanted to frame the problem at hand in terms of race, stressed his nonracial identity, namely, that of a state trooper. As he put it, "I am an officer of the state of Mississippi. You were speeding so you are going to be issued a citation."[47] Perhaps Ruth Fisher, an editor from New York, best exemplifies how an individual's frame can help one to move beyond race. She said that she has had as many positive and as many negative experiences with members of other races as she has had with members of her own race. "It isn't that I have had better or worse experiences than anyone else, it is that I, perhaps, perceived the experiences differently."[48] Such a frame grows out of an acceptance of the reality that one finds the best and worst behavior in all groups, regardless of skin color. It is a recognition of a common humanity, which includes a recognition of imperfection, of vices as well as virtues.

From Race to Universal Virtues

Racism is about vices, about the lack of certain universal virtues. In all human societies there is, to greater or lesser degrees, an acknowledgment of fundamental virtues such as treating others in a way that you would want to be treated yourself. Other such virtues include self-responsibility, self-discipline, perseverance, honesty, forgiveness, tolerance, loyalty, lawfulness, justice, and courage. Aristotle believed that some virtues were intellectual whereas others were moral. Wisdom, understanding, and prudence were regarded as intellectual virtues, whereas moderation and good-temperedness were seen as the foundation of moral character.[49] Skin color or physical traits obviously do not determine virtue.

The genius of the civil rights movement of the 1960s was that it embraced universal virtues and emphasized a framework that was inclusive. It inspired people of all colors by recognizing the common humanity of all Americans. Bill Clinton, Jack Kemp, Colin Powell, and Charlayne Hunter-Gault were all deeply influenced by the transcendent message of a movement that framed the despair of Americans with African ancestry in universal human terms. Instead of focusing on differences, it drew attention to common values, thereby allowing blacks, whites, Latinos, Asians, and others to unite for a common purpose. As Roger Fisher and Scott Brown point out, "The greater the extent to which you and I share values and perspectives, the fewer differences we will have and the more easily we will find a basis for dealing with them."[50] Framing racial issues in universal terms facilitates the perception of shared values.

Hard work, discipline, perseverance, and responsibility are universal virtues that have enabled people of every color to overcome barriers. Americans with African ancestry have always embraced these virtues. The civil rights movement focused on them, allowing a marginalized people to take center stage in American politics and enhancing their sense of self-worth and dignity. Blacks and whites who peacefully marched together in an effort to force America to abide by its fundamental values exercised self-discipline. Not only did they prove to be more patriotic than the defenders of segregation in America, they appealed to a common standard of justice and to a basic sense of decency that transcended racial lines.[51]

Anne Wortham, who was born in Jackson, Tennessee, and is now a professor, recalls how her father valued independence, productivity, and self-responsibility. He taught his daughter carpentry and made her learn how to type on a secondhand Underwood typewriter with blind keys. Every day before he left for work, he would type on a sheet of paper, "All good men should come to the aid of their country." Her assignment was to fill the page with that sentence with no mistakes.[52] He had taken charge of his life and taught his daughter to be responsible for her own. Perseverance, which is closely related to self-discipline, involves persisting even in the face of incredible odds. As Edelman writes: "We must not assume a door is closed but must push on it. We must not assume if it was closed yesterday, that it is closed today."[53]

Honesty is a bedrock virtue. It enables one to know oneself, to be genuine, to be truthful, to have self-respect, and to respect others. Honesty entails caring about certain things, being open, and being reliable. Honest people avoid deceitful violations of trust. They feel that such behavior must be shunned because it is wrong and that its wrongness is independent of the results of the action.[54] Racism is about dishonesty. Therefore, one can deal with racial problems in terms of honesty and avoid discussions of race altogether. For example, an automobile dealer who overcharges a customer is dishonest, regardless of whether that customer is Asian, Latino, white, or black. Framing the problem this way encourages the formation of a transracial alliance to prevent dishonesty in the future.

Justice, a primary virtue, is intertwined with trust and honesty. Without justice, societies are eventually weakened by cynicism, arrogance, corruption, and instability. John Rawls believes that justice is the first of social institutions, as truth is of systems of thought, and that "each person possesses an inviolability founded on justice that even the welfare of society as a whole cannot override."[55] An integral component of justice is fairness and equal treatment for all Americans, who are thus regarded as equal citizens.

By honestly applying the same rules to all citizens, society allows each citizen to have an equal opportunity to acquire power, position, and wealth. Each person receives what that person has earned through individual effort and suffers no discrimination. A society founded on justice is one in which no group can legitimately exploit another because of skin color or social status. In a just society, the law is applied fairly and consistently, to the extent humanly possible, to all citizens. By framing racism in terms of injustice, the civil rights movement made impressive steps toward racial equality.

Civility, good manners, etiquette, politeness, and consideration make up the foundation of harmonious social relations and civilized life. In Judith Martin's view, obeisance to etiquette is the oldest social virtue.[56] Good manners and civility are components of a just society, a society in which everyone is treated decently. Civility is essential to effective communication and to the building of a community that is based on trust, respect, and the peaceful resolution of conflicts.

Civility does not imply that we must agree with each other. Rather, it entails a willingness to be tolerant of differences and to listen respectfully to ideas with which we disagree, remembering that we all embrace a common humanity.[57] Such a recognition facilitates practicing good manners and refraining from offensive language in our interactions with others, especially in conflict situations. A customer in a department store, for example, is entitled to proper and decent treatment. In search of civility, many American males with African ancestry bypass suburban malls to shop in neighborhoods where salespersons demonstrate a sense of etiquette and good manners. The lack of good manners may precipitate what could be viewed as a racial problem. Politeness from all involved is likely to improve race relations.

At the foundation of many virtues is courage. Courage plays a pivotal role in the pursuit of other virtues. It takes courage to be responsible for oneself, to have lofty aspirations, to take the initiative in implementing one's objectives, to act on principles, and to participate fully in American society.[58] Courage enables one to speak out against injustice, to stand up against racism, and to face imprisonment as the civil rights marchers did.

Blacks are often disappointed by the lack of courage on the part of most whites, and vice versa. In a *New York Times*/CBS poll, 51 percent of whites and 57 percent of blacks questioned believed that not enough whites publicly opposed white extremists. Also, 56 percent of whites and 43 percent of blacks felt that black leaders do not do enough to oppose black extremists.[59] More important is the exercise of courage by ordinary Americans as they encounter uncivil behavior, dishonesty, and other destructive behaviors in their daily lives. Racism survives partly because ordinary individuals often lack the courage to face up to it.

Compassion, generosity, and kindness are concerned with the well-being of others. These characteristics are found in all human societies and are the cornerstones of most religions. Compassion, in William J. Bennett's view, "is an active disposition toward fellowship and sharing, toward supportive companionship in distress or woe. Compassion thus comes close to the very heart of moral awareness, to seeing in one's neighbor another self."[60] Viewed in universal terms, one's neighbor is any human being.

Of all the virtues, forgiveness is one of the most crucial in the effort to help move American society beyond race. Blacks, whites, Asians, Latinos, and others are challenged to recognize each other's capacity for goodness and adaptability. Forgiveness does not necessarily mean forgetting painful events; indeed, it begins with a remembering and a moral judgment of wrong, injustice, or injury. But forgiveness does require us to focus on the humanity of those who were hateful and hurtful.[61] It requires looking to the future and refraining from seeking revenge. Racism often begets racism when an "eye for an eye" strategy is adopted. Instead of improving race relations, such a strategy is for the most part counterproductive. As Fisher and Brown argue, "If I let my conduct reflect yours, we may never break out of a pattern of hostile interaction. If I react to your bad behavior with actions that are equally bad, I end up accepting the destructive tone you have set."[62]

One of the most dramatic examples of the power of forgiveness is Nelson Mandela's decision to work with white South Africans, who had impris-

oned him for twenty-seven years. Instead of seeking revenge, Mandela focused on how South Africans could build their future together, seeking opportunities to reach out to white South Africans. Another example is Reginald Denny, who was badly beaten in the 1992 Los Angeles riots that
followed the acquittal of white police officers who were videotaped beating
Rodney King, a black man. During the trial, Denny, his face still scarred
from the beating he received, walked across the courtroom and embraced
the mothers of the two men charged with trying to kill him.

Perhaps one of the most unexpected examples of forgiveness in American
politics was when former Alabama governor George Wallace, whose troops
brutally beat civil rights marchers in an effort to maintain segregation and
white supremacy, met with Joseph E. Lowery and others who were participating in the civil rights marches in 1995 to commemorate the 1960s
protests. Many marchers forgave a repentant Wallace, who had himself
previously apologized and begged forgiveness.[63]

Embracing Positive American Values

Just as a framework that positions problems within the context of universal
virtues can assist America in its efforts to move beyond race, embracing
positive American values allows the individual to gain a psychological advantage that comes from a sense of belonging to the larger society. Successful Americans are generally those individuals who, despite their negative
experiences, continue to believe in America's values. Understanding and
cherishing the past does not preclude strongly embracing values that
brighten the future. Stressing the positive qualities of American society and
encouraging each other to build on them can ultimately induce an attitudinal shift that is conducive to nurturing a common humanity.

As in all societies, there are conflicting and inconsistent values in America.[64] But one must choose those values that can be instrumental in bringing
out the best behavior of all Americans. These include values that encourage
openness and friendship, that treat people as individuals, and that promote a
sense of fairness, equal opportunity, and self-improvement. Other fundamental American values include private property, limited government, diversity,
advancement based on merit, and moral equality in the larger society. Disre-
garding or downplaying the importance of these values has consequences not
just for those engaging in nihilistic behavior but also for the entire society.
When some are alienated from society's basic values, they adopt alternative
values and destructive methods with which to propagate them.[65]

At the center of the American value system is the belief that all individuals are imbued with dignity and equal worth; each person is the equal of
every other. Moreover, the goodness of society is judged by how well it
serves the needs and interests of all.[66] From the belief in the sacredness of

the individual and the right to freedom emanates a moral impulse to protect the rights of individuals everywhere. It is therefore not coincidental that from Tiananmen Square to Northern Ireland those who struggle for the dignity and moral worth of the individual turn to American values and sing the American civil rights anthem, "We Shall Overcome." Although individualism coexisted with slavery and racism in the United States, it has also provided a powerful basis for rendering racism illegitimate.[67] It is partly because of this reality that black Americans have strongly supported American values.

Individualism is at the heart of the belief in equal opportunity. Each individual is responsible for the quality of life he or she enjoys. This assumes that each person is free to compete without being burdened by artificial constraints. Not only does equal opportunity promise success depending on one's efforts, it also nourishes faith in the American society.

Most Americans share the American dream and are increasingly supportive of the view that all Americans, regardless of color, should participate in this dream. Despite the prevailing view that whites and blacks are deeply divided, Jennifer L. Hochschild has found that 80 percent of blacks and 90 percent of whites agree that the American dream is alive today.[68] This spirit of optimism indicates not only racial inclusion but also a belief in a common destiny.

Equal opportunity is intertwined with acceptance of diversity. America has been an extremely diverse society for a long time, attracting people from every corner of the earth. But racial and gender barriers, among others, once excluded a majority of Americans from equal access to opportunities. An emphasis on the value of diversity brought about a change in this situation. Although often thought of in terms of difference, diversity is about recognizing individualism as being inseparable from community. Acceptance of diversity implies tolerance, civility, good manners, and a commitment to honesty. It is by listening to diverse views that truth, which is the basis of honesty, has a chance to emerge.[69] The current debates about the value of diversity do not alter the fact that diversity has improved overall race relations.

Focusing on Success, Not Failure

If nothing succeeds like success, then it is equally true that nothing fails like failure. Yet many Americans with African ancestry, who need to emphasize success the most and to build on it, often appear determined to accentuate the negative and to overlook obvious evidence of significant success. Preoccupied with the problems of the so-called black underclass, which makes up approximately 3 to 5 million out of 32 million American blacks, many analysts and commentators downplay or ignore the real story, namely, black success. Little attention is given to black people who fully embrace American values, build strong and secure families, protect their property, get along with neighbors and friends of different races, and provide the best education for their children. Not surprisingly, many successful blacks complain that whites apply the same negative stereotypes to them that they apply to the black underclass. The aberration has become the norm, in the view of many Americans.

Focusing on the positive is not only more likely to produce desirable outcomes, it is also firmly rooted in the American psyche. Few Americans are not infected with perpetual optimism. Telling the disadvantaged that it is hopeless for them to dream of success is tantamount to consolidating negative stereotypes of blacks and maintaining the status quo. Success or failure is closely linked to the attitudes, beliefs, and self-confidence of individuals. Hopelessness breeds cynicism, and cynicism, in Vice President Al Gore's view, "is deadly. It bites everything it can reach—like a dog with a foot caught in a trap. It drains us of the will to improve; it diminishes our public spirit; it saps our inventiveness; it withers our souls."[70] Focusing on the positive counters negative stereotypes and nourishes attitudes that are conducive to success.

Successful blacks, like successful people in general, take responsibility for their own lives, work hard, persevere, and perceive obstacles as challenges instead of barriers. Attitude, more than any other factor, impedes or promotes black success. As I point out in Chapter 6, immigrants to the United States, especially West Indians, face many of the same barriers that are confronted by Americans with African ancestry. Yet West Indians have always been relatively successful in the United States, largely because of their optimism, self-discipline, willingness to work hard, and nonracial approach to difficulties. They don't allow a preoccupation with race to debilitate them.

Successful blacks, although quite aware of racial prejudices, do not see the color of their skin as the problem. Instead, they realize that the problem lies with others' lack of universal virtues. Successful blacks usually don't dwell on race.[71] Baseball legend Hank Aaron embodied this approach. He amassed a record of 755 career home runs in the face of severe discrimination, racist taunts, and threats to his family and to his own life.

Educational achievement has long been regarded as instrumental in overcoming barriers associated with race and class. A strong education is positively associated with income; generally, the more education one has, the higher one's earning power. As the concept of the black underclass gained popularity in the 1980s, blacks were making notable progress in education. Whereas only 51 percent of blacks 25 years old and over had graduated from high school in 1980, by 1994, 73 percent had a high school diploma. In 1995 the high school completion rate for blacks between the ages of 25 and 29 increased to an unprecedented 87 percent, 5 percentage points above the national average and equal to the rate for whites.[72]

College enrollment for blacks has been steadily improving. In the fall of 1994, more than 14 million students were attending America's higher education institutions. This number represented a decline of 26,000 students from 1993. The decrease was due principally to a drop in the number of white, non-Hispanic student enrollments. But the number of Latino, Asian, and Pacific islander students rose by about 7 percent, and the number of black, non-Hispanic students increased by 2.5 percent.[73] The proportion of blacks 25 years old and over who had completed at least a bachelor's degree grew from 8 percent in 1980 to 13 percent in 1994. This is in contrast to an increase from 18 percent to 23 percent for whites. Similarly, the number of Americans with African ancestry receiving doctorates has risen. In 1995 blacks earned 1,287 doctorates, the most since the National Research Council began collecting data on the race and ethnicity of doctoral recipients in 1975.[74] The implications of education for black success are obvious. A 1996 survey by the Illinois Department of Higher Education found that 81 percent of black students who graduated from state universities in Illinois in 1994 found full-time jobs within a year of graduation, a figure that was 3 percentage points higher than that for white graduates.[75]

Success in education has been matched by economic progress and a growing black middle class, whose members are likely to pass on tangible and intangible aspects of success to their children. On the other hand, the proportion of the poorest blacks has also increased, thereby obscuring statistically significant economic breakthroughs for educated Americans with African ancestry, especially among married couples with two incomes. In 1993, black high school graduates 25 years old and over had a median annual income of $18,460. Black college graduates earned a median annual income of $32,360, or 75 percent higher than black high school graduates. In contrast, white college graduates earned $41,090, a figure that was 70 percent higher than that received by whites with high school diplomas.[76]

Census Bureau data show that blacks, especially women, with a college education earn about 86 percent or more of the earnings of white men. In some professions, black women earn about 10 percent more than white women. In cities such as Vineland, New Jersey; Brentwood, New York; Cleveland Heights, Ohio; Southfield, Michigan; Carson, California; and the borough of Queens in New York City, black median household income was greater than white household income in 1989. Growing black economic success is directly linked to educational achievement, as it is for other Americans. An analysis of census data shows that among blacks between the ages of 25 and 44, one in ten classified themselves as professionals in 1970 compared to nearly one in six by 1990. In real numbers, this represents an increase from about 400,000 to nearly 1.3 million.[77]

Comparing blacks and whites as groups often obscures this success, largely because of the growing number of black single parents. In all race groups, married-couple families were generally better off than families with other configurations. Between 1969 and 1993, black married-couple families closed the gap between themselves and white married-couple families. Black median family income increased by 31 percent, from $26,880 to $35,230, or from 72 percent to 81 percent of the white median. However, the overall black family median income in 1993 was $21,550, compared to $39,310 for white families.[78]

Black success in education is matched by success in virtually all other areas of American life. Between 1987 and 1992, black-owned businesses, including manufacturing, finance, retail, construction, and services, grew by 46 percent. The increase for all businesses in America was 26 percent. Total revenue for black businesses rose 63 percent during the same period to $32.2 billion.[79] The potential for future growth remains strong, especially in light of a growing and increasingly more prosperous black middle class. Similarly, black home ownership increased significantly between 1993 and 1996, due largely to market forces and reduced discrimination in lending. Mortgages approved for blacks increased by 38 percent from 1993 to 1994, compared to 30.9 percent for Latinos, 27.1 percent for Native Americans, 17.0 percent for Asians, and 12.0 percent for whites.[80]

Success achieved by individual Americans with African ancestry is impressive by any standard. Oprah Winfrey was the highest-paid entertainer in America in 1996, with an income of $171 million. In 1995 she was one of the four hundred richest Americans, with a net worth of $340 million. In that same year, Michael Jackson made $90 million, Bill Cosby was paid $33 million, and Denzel Washington made $30 million. These individuals were among the forty highest-paid entertainers. In the area of professional sports, blacks have been signing ever-more lucrative contracts and winning more endorsements. Michael Jordan, for example, was ranked the number one athlete in America four years in a row by *Forbes* and earned a total of $44 million in 1994 alone, $40 million of which came from endorsements. Jordan was followed by Mike Tyson with $40 million, Deion Sanders with $22.5 million, and George Foreman with $18 million.[81]

Reginald F. Lewis, whose net worth was $400 million when he died in 1993 at the age of 50, exemplifies how many blacks from modest economic backgrounds have not allowed race to be an obstacle to their success. Born in a working-class family in Baltimore, Lewis literally talked his way into Harvard Law School. He later bought Beatrice International Foods for just under $1 billion. Another example of black success is John H. Johnson, publisher of *Ebony* and *Jet* magazines. Borrowing $500 against his mother's furniture, Johnson created a business empire with annual sales topping $316 million and with a workforce of more than 2,600 people. Lonnie R. Bristow, the first American with African ancestry to head the American Medical Association; Ruth Simmons of Smith College, the first American with African ancestry to become president of an elite, predominantly white college; Ann M. Fudge, president of Maxwell House Coffee; and Vernon Jordan, who is one of the richest and most influential lawyers in America and a close advisor to President Bill Clinton, amply demonstrate black success.[82]

Encouraging a Bottom-Up Approach to Race Relations

Looking at each person as a unique individual, the bottom-up approach to improving race relations recognizes that most ordinary Americans in their own ways and in their everyday struggles attempt to get along with people they encounter, regardless of skin color. This approach is based on a widely held view that emerged in many interviews, namely, that what really counts in getting beyond race is how individuals relate to other individuals with whom they interact in ordinary settings—as they attend their children's athletic or school activities, as they perform their jobs, and as they live their lives. Change will come about, as one interviewee puts it, when one person begins to take responsibility for his or her share. "I find that when you approach a person or a situation at face value, you will automatically block out negative racial tones. Seeing an individual as a person would surely begin the process of change."[83]

The mentor who works quietly with a student or business colleague of a different race is an agent of change. As I show in Chapter 3, Jimmy Carter, Bill Clinton, and Jack Kemp merged their individual experiences into their leadership positions and became agents of racial change. It takes courage for one individual to cross racial boundaries to get to know another individual. It takes courage to say hello to strangers sitting next to you on the train or in the classroom. Although change is often perceived as a top-down endeavor, most meaningful and long-lasting changes begin with the individual. One has greater power to alter one's own behavior than to affect the behavior of others. One is likely to be more influential in one's own neighborhood and community than nationally. Ultimately, race is a local and personal concern. As Sissela Bok contends, "Concentrating from the outset only on the least personal and largest problems imaginable almost guarantees that nothing else will get done."[84]

Numerous examples of grassroots efforts to get beyond race can be found in almost every major city in the United States. When Ku Klux Klansmen opened the "World's Only Klan Museum" in Laurens, South Carolina, in 1996, whites and blacks united in their opposition to it. For many whites, the "redneck shop" was an embarrassment because "it displayed Southerners as ignorant, bigoted people," thereby reinforcing a deeply held stereotype. In a town where blacks make up about 40 percent of the population, more whites than blacks attended protest rallies against the Klan museum.[85] Responding to the burning of many predominantly black churches in the South in 1996, blacks, whites, men, women, Baptists, Methodists, Jews, and Mennonites from Bloomington and Normal in central Illinois drove 800 miles to help rebuild St. Paul's Baptist Church in Lauderdale, Mississippi. Many of these volunteers had participated in marches against racism and were instrumental in getting Bloomington to post signs around the city declaring that racism would not be tolerated.[86] Judy Markowitz, a member of the group that went to Mississippi to help rebuild the church and who has actively opposed racism in Bloomington, was elected mayor of that city in 1997.

Another example of the bottom-up approach to getting beyond race is the formation of the Bensonhurst Redevelopment Corporation in 1990. Following the death of Yusuf Hawkins, a black teenager killed by white teenagers in 1989, Bensonhurst, a Brooklyn neighborhood, became a national symbol of extreme racism. Given the racial, ethnic, and social diversity of Brooklyn, the redevelopment corporation decided to publish a newsletter in five languages to promote greater interracial understanding, held neighborhood conferences, and worked with local schools to help change attitudes and behavior. Individuals also attempted to resolve racial conflicts. Similarly, in 1996, the city of Chicago initiated "the Chicago Dinners," a series of multiracial and multiethnic dinner parties to help facilitate discussions of race relations. Most dinners are held in private homes.[87]

Institutions of higher education are helping to move the country beyond race by taking specific actions. For example, Illinois Wesleyan University in Bloomington, Illinois, encourages students from inner-city Chicago and Detroit neighborhoods to participate in a tutoring-mentoring program that exposes them to college life and provides after-school tutoring to prepare them for college academics. When students from Cabrini-Green visit Bloomington, they are not only exposed to a much more affluent community but they also meet students from different backgrounds. Illinois Wesleyan University and other private colleges offer hope to academically talented inner-city students. As Minor Myers Jr., president of Illinois Wesleyan University, puts it, "What we are saying to these students is clear and simple. Work hard in school, keep your grades up, and 24 campuses across the state of Illinois will make sure the money and academic support are there for you to go to college."[88] Although many problems remain, these examples of bottom-up approaches clearly demonstrate that individuals and small groups are improving race relations quietly and effectively.

Building Coalitions Based on Common Interests

Identifying common interests instead of concentrating on differences makes it easier to eventually deal with perceived and real differences that divide Americans along racial lines. People tend not only to associate with others who have similar interests, they also treat them better than those whom they regard as different. Dissimilarity tends to foster dislike. A racial prism often obscures possibilities for building alliances based on common interests that transcend racial identities.

Framing problems in terms of race often has effects that are contrary to those anticipated. For example, during the nomination of Judge Clarence Thomas for a position on the U.S. Supreme Court, many Americans with African ancestry supported Thomas because he was able to portray himself as an embattled black man who was undergoing a "high-tech lynching." But defending "one of their own" proved to be detrimental to what are generally regarded as black interests, as Justice Thomas's voting record on the Supreme Court underscores. Focusing on interests is likely to bring together blacks, whites, Latinos, Asians, and others who share the same concerns and objectives. By thinking of others as human beings, it becomes more obvious that people share many basic needs and interests upon which positive relationships can be constructed.

Focusing on interests that are conceived of as part of the common or public interest often promotes the inclusion of marginalized others. Blacks, whites, Asians, Latinos, and others are concerned about major public issues such as crime, poverty, unemployment, drug and alcohol abuse, the quality of public education, and broken families. For example, 85 percent of whites and 94 percent of blacks think that crime is a very important issue. Similarly, 87 percent of whites and 83 percent of blacks are very concerned about the economy.[89] Encouraging blacks and whites to see themselves as partners facing their common concerns together is one way to shift the emphasis away from race. Martin Luther King Jr. framed race problems as national problems and admonished Americans that racial conflicts had significant consequences for the country's future and its position in the world.[90] In other words, the interests of the civil rights movement were linked to the general or national interest. This approach makes the emergence of interracial coalitions possible.

Coalitions are by definition cooperative endeavors designed to achieve goals that individual members of the group cannot easily accomplish by themselves. Consequently, they combine their resources and focus on their common interests while downplaying whatever differences may exist among them.[91] Few coalitions are permanent because interests often change or new strategies evolve to obtain slightly different objectives. This implies that skin color alone would not be sufficient to determine the formation and durability of a coalition designed to protect concrete interests. The development of such pragmatic coalitions would clearly indicate an important step toward getting beyond race.

Such interracial coalitions have existed throughout much of America's history. An obvious example is the civil rights movement. Blacks, whites,

Latinos, and Asians; Christians and Jews alike united in their opposition to injustice and hatred. Whites who supported civil rights for blacks braved the same dangers as blacks, and many of them risked being rejected by their families and friends. Two Jews, Andrew Goodman and Michael Schwerner, were killed in Mississippi in the struggle for civil rights. Marching together, blacks and whites overcame racial barriers among themselves while simultaneously inspiring the nation as a whole to live up to fundamental American values. As a matter of fact, Americans of European ancestry have never held a monolithic view on race relations. As far back as the American Revolution, there was opposition to slavery in New England and elsewhere.

There are many examples of blacks and whites working together for the common good. In 1869 there were roughly ten thousand white teachers in the South who were dedicated to eliminating illiteracy in the black community.[92] During the 1880s and 1890s, when declining cotton prices, high railroad freight costs, marketing monopolies dominated by large planters, and steep credit rates threatened the livelihood of small southern farmers, blacks and whites formed coalitions to protect their interests. Although initially divided into the Farmers' Alliance and the Colored Farmers' Alliance, a biracial organization soon emerged from the two groups. Their objective was to obtain higher agricultural prices and lower freight rates and interest charges.[93]

Blacks and whites have often worked together to bring about change when their interests have converged. For example, believing that modifications in race relations were necessary for their businesses to prosper, many southern businesspeople decided to support federally mandated changes in the 1960s. Organizing themselves as biracial pressure groups, black and white businesspeople searched for issues with which to oppose racially extremist elements and state officials who favored the status quo.[94]

There are many examples of contemporary interracial coalitions, both at the individual and group levels. Realizing that they need to diversify their businesses in order to survive and grow, many black business owners are attempting to attract white, Latino, and Asian customers. Citizens Trust Bank, the largest black-owned bank in Atlanta, has adopted this approach. It put up thirteen billboards in English, Korean, and Spanish in minority neighborhoods as well as in predominantly white areas and will for the first time in its seventy-two-year history open branches in predominantly white areas.[95]

Interracial coalitions are increasingly common in politics. Despite claims that race and representation are inextricably linked, blacks and whites often cross racial boundaries to vote for candidates who they believe will best represent their interests. In Minneapolis, which is 78 percent white, Sharon Sayles Belton became the first black mayor in 1993. She was reelected in 1997. In Seattle, with a population that is 75 percent white, Norman Rice, the city's first black mayor, won a second four-year term in 1993. In Dallas, Ron Kirk, who is black, governs with a coalition of blacks and whites and won the mayoral election in 1995 with nearly two-thirds of the vote.[96] Tom Bradley forged multiracial coalitions to become the mayor of Los Angeles, a position he held for two decades. Although race is still used as a wedge issue in many political campaigns, the growing number of blacks who are elected in predominantly white electoral districts indicates significant steps toward getting beyond race.

Ordinary Americans are increasingly aware of the need for members of different races to work together for common purposes. For example, in Pulaski, Tennessee, the birthplace of the Ku Klux Klan, residents recognized that antiracist activities and economic progress were inextricably linked. In 1988, they decided to form a coalition of city leaders, ministers, civil rights advocates, and others who opposed the Klan. Klansmen from around the country gathered in Pulaski to protest the creation of a national holiday for Martin Luther King Jr. Responding to negative national publicity and rising unemployment, residents decided to show their disapproval of the Klan by abandoning the town on the day the Klan was scheduled to march. There were no rest rooms available, restaurants were closed, and the town was draped in orange banners, the international color of brotherhood. Pulaski effectively marginalized the overt racists. Klan activism declined dramatically, the economy improved, and in 1993 Pulaski was named an All-American City by the National Civic League.

Negotiating Differences

Much of the debate on race is counterproductive because those involved pay too little attention to negotiation strategies that would help them deal with differences effectively. Not only do blacks and whites either shout at or whisper to each other when the subject is race, they often fail to honestly communicate their true feelings. Many Americans believe it is better to avoid social conflicts than to address them. But such conflicts are likely to escalate as different races come into increasingly closer contact with each other.

Too many people assume that getting beyond race means that all conflicts will be resolved and blacks and whites will have harmonious relationships forever. Such expectations are clearly unrealistic, judging by the numerous conflicts one finds among members of the same race. The issue, then, is not eradicating conflict but learning how to cope with it.[97] The solution is not to wish for a return to a golden age of racial cooperation, which probably never existed anyway. Effectively managing racial problems begins with the realization that racial progress is often accompanied by racial tensions.

On the other hand, framing conflicts in racial terms erects almost insurmountable barriers to finding solutions acceptable to both sides. Concentrating on race is equivalent to taking a position. Identity politics is about taking positions, and people who are defending their positions tend not to be open to reason. If the dispute is seen to be about specific issues that are independent of race, finding a compromise is much more likely than if the problem is framed in terms of race. When a discussion focuses on principles instead of on specific action, it is unlikely to be productive.[98]

Instead of adopting a coercive, confrontational, position-taking, and blaming approach to problem solving, one should approach problem solving as a cooperative effort and negotiation as a matter of working together to achieve a particular objective. Negotiation that deteriorates into a contest of wills only serves to further strain relations between individuals. By contrast, a cooperative approach often leads to the successful resolution of conflicts. There are several reasons for this. First, a cooperative process facilitates open and honest dialogue between the parties. Shared information can help the parties get to the underlying issues; it also improves understanding and trust. Second, a cooperative process not only encourages mutual recognition of interests but also narrows the range of conflicting interests. Third, such a process leads to greater sensitivity to similarities and stimulates a convergence of beliefs and values.[99] Finally, this approach promotes a "win-win" solution, an outcome that strengthens the foundation upon which future relationships may be built.

An emphasis on negotiating differences avoids the tendency to interpret whatever the other side says or does in the worst light. It also restrains the parties from resorting to blaming each other. Perhaps most importantly, negotiating differences implies a recognition of the other side's humanity. Giving support to the other side reduces confrontation and enhances communication. Consequently, one can be hard on the problem without overlooking the need to be soft on people. Colin Powell has come to be regarded as an individual who has transcended race precisely because he relates to individuals in a positive and humane way. As he put it, "I don't shove race in their face. I don't bring any stereotypes or threatening visage to their presence. Some black people do."[100] Colin Powell doesn't blame others. Even if blaming is justified, it does little to solve the problem at hand. When people are blamed, they usually become defensive, cease to listen, and launch their own counterattacks.[101]

Many whites who are strongly opposed to racism and are committed to moving beyond race find the prevailing approach to racial issues difficult to accept. They believe that coercion and blaming are counterproductive. As an interviewee noted, when whites are labeled the "oppressors of blacks" and made to feel guilty about their dominant white society, this can leave whites with a feeling of resentment. "Although I believe racism has been a major problem in American society, blaming society and whites will not rectify past injustices. It will only inflame animosity presently felt between the two groups."[102] Given the deep emotional nature of race in America, a strategy that acknowledges the painful past but embraces a hopeful future is likely to gain the support of many whites, without whose cooperation blacks cannot achieve their goal of creating a fair and equal society.

Martin Luther King Jr. and other leaders of the civil rights movement clearly understood the pragmatism of looking forward with a purpose and appealing to the best in all Americans to move the country away from the destructiveness of race and racism. Instead of dwelling on the past, King stressed how his dream was deeply rooted in the American dream and expressed the hope that cooperation among Americans as a nation would lead to the realization of the broader American dream.[103] Looking to the future avoids blaming anyone while simultaneously encouraging the formation of interracial coalitions to bring about far-reaching changes.

An important aspect of the negotiation process is the ability to put oneself in another person's shoes, as it were, and to empathize with the other side. Empathy is an other-oriented emotional response based on the perceived needs of another person. It is an attempt to understand another person's experience from the other's point of view. It is the ability to identify with others.[104] One's perception of racial problems is influenced by one's experiences, and it helps the negotiation process to actually feel what the other side feels. When whites are in a minority position, they usually begin to experience what many racial minorities take for granted. Being the only white member on the track team, one of a few whites living in a Latino neighborhood, the only white sister in a black sorority, can contribute to increased empathy among whites for blacks, Latinos, and Asians.

One interviewee, who grew up in the South and lived in Harlem for two years while his father finished his education, recalled how uncomfortable he was being a minority and how the experience heightened his awareness of how painful it often is to be considered a "token." Another interviewee, who was born and raised in an all-white community in Wisconsin, enrolled in a black history course and attended a presentation at the university during Black History Month. Out of approximately one hundred people present, only two were white. As Nancy puts it, "it was an eye-opening experience to be the minority in the room. There was a clear attempt to welcome the 'minorities' to the gathering. I realized that I had rarely been so open with other minorities when I was in the majority."[105] Finally, when whites themselves experience discrimination from other whites, they are more likely to develop greater empathy toward others who are discriminated against. For example, the great number of Jews active in the civil rights movement was largely due to the fact that many Jews also faced discrimination. A white woman whose son was born without a left hand became more determined to challenge prejudice as she and her son endured stares and pointing by other whites.[106] Putting oneself in another person's shoes helps improve race relations, partly because it enhances communication and feelings of empathy.

An essential step in the communication process is trying to understand the other side's perceptions, their fears, and their aspirations. The idea of trying to know more about the other side first instead of trying to be understood is often neglected in discussions on race. Too often, one side is too intent on convincing the other to accept a particular interpretation of the facts or on formulating a reply to what is being said instead of listening to what is being said. Few people in so-called dialogues on race listen closely enough to understand the other side. A more constructive approach involves assuming the need to learn more about those with whom we are attempting to communicate.[107]

Prejudice on both sides leads to the view that there is no need to gain additional knowledge and insights about the other side. Many blacks assume that they simply need to convince whites to change their behavior, a task that can be accomplished, in their view, by getting whites to understand them instead of trying to get to know individual whites. That understanding others is a prerequisite to trying to persuade them is contrary to how most Americans approach race relations. People tend to listen better if they believe an attempt is being made to learn more about them, not as a group but as individuals who are imperfect human beings.

Building Trust and Social Capital

The issue of trust is at the heart of race relations. Building trust between blacks and whites is difficult, partly because there are many historical, as well as contemporary, experiences in which trust was destroyed or never allowed to develop. Trust is based on information about particular individuals, groups, and organizations. It is the expectation of regular, honest, and cooperative behavior, based on commonly shared norms.[108] Although trust is generally perceived to be an integral part of a community, it is ultimately about individuals and how they interact with each other. Trust is an individuating process that develops from a lengthy series of mutually positive experiences.[109]

Trust is the product of activities that help to create a sense of common identity. People who work together for a common purpose often strengthen their identification with each other and, consequently, develop trusting relationships. Cooperation under similar circumstances over an extended period of time helps to create shared values, beliefs, and attitudes—all of which facilitate the development of interpersonal trust based on the perception of predictability, which is confirmed by actual behavior that is consistent over time. The U.S. military provides an example of how cooperative behavior and mutual dependability encourages the development of trust among members of different racial groups.

Building trust involves taking risks. To avoid taking risks, many blacks and whites prefer to continue distrusting each other. However, the choice is not between trust and distrust; there is usually a combination of trust and distrust in most social situations. Indeed, it is nearly always problematic for one person to trust another, largely because the trustee often has a choice between keeping the trust or breaking the trust.[110] On the other hand, this choice is sometimes constrained by the costs that result from not maintaining trust. In addition to tangible costs such as loss of business, exclusion from various activities, and deterioration of relationships, distrust and strategies based on it can be psychologically burdensome. Distrust usually drains one of energy, decreases one's ability to objectively evaluate the environment, and reduces one's opportunities for learning to effectively manage that environment in beneficial ways.[111] Trust, on the other hand, increases the possibilities for experience and action. It helps to create and sustain solidarity in social relationships and in society in general.[112] In this sense, trust is an integral component of social capital.

Social capital refers to connections among individuals that encourage co-operation and trust. The more people connect with each other, the more they trust each other, which, in turn, facilitates increased joint action. Social capital, like other forms of capital, is productive. It makes possible the achievement of objectives that would not be attainable without it.[113] Robert D. Putnam argues that most forms of social capital are moral resources—that is, resources whose supply increases rather than decreases through use and that become depleted if not used. For example, the more people trust each other, the greater their mutual confidence.[114] Conversely, the relative absence of trust leads to suspicion, hatred, and fear.

People who trust each other are willing to cooperate to achieve mutually beneficial goals. West Indians, Asians, Africans, and other immigrants often enjoy significant economic success in the United States because of their ability to form rotating credit associations from which members borrow to develop small businesses or to finance college educations. Members of credit associations are socially connected and trust each other. Social capital leads to the formation of economic and human capital. People share information and skills in the process of working together. Social capital in general and trust in particular also function to improve community life. When trust is established, communities are safer, businesses cost less to operate, and people develop better relationships. Building trust, together with the other strategies discussed in this chapter, is essential for getting beyond race.

2

INVENTING RACE

The Social and Scientific Construction of Reality

SOCIAL AND SCIENTIFIC CHANGES as well as broader cultural changes are directly challenging the concept of race, an idea that has profoundly influenced how Americans relate to each other. Whereas the emphasis on race inevitably draws attention to readily visible and superficial differences and endows those differences with functional meanings, the growing consensus in America is that race should not matter and that our commonalities and "Americanness" are far more important than variations in skin color.

As I will show in Chapter 3, a new generation of Americans with higher levels of education, more contact with people from diverse backgrounds, and constant exposure to ideas that contradict the essential premises of racism increasingly find the concept of race unacceptable. This does not mean that race no longer matters. However, even though race continues to matter, it is systematically being eroded by deliberate efforts to get beyond it and by far-reaching social, technological, and demographic changes in American society. These developments help transform an emphasis on race from an asset to a liability, thus weakening its socially constructed usefulness.

Common Origins

Race as a meaningful concept is also being challenged by the scientific community, although use of the term has not been abandoned. Race has always been an arbitrary label that was wrapped in pseudoscientific doctrine to legitimize socioeconomic and political power. In the process of exaggerating small and highly selective differences among people, such as different skin color, pseudoscientists ignored the fact that the classification of human beings into races is in the end a futile exercise. Evidence that all human beings have a common origin in Africa is widespread and widely accepted. Walter Gilbert, the Carl M. Loeb University Professor at Harvard University and Nobel laureate, documented a relatively recent origin for the first Homo sapiens and all humans alive today. His Harvard research group took snippets from a gene on the y chromosomes of hair and cell-line samples they had collected from around the world. After careful examination revealed no differences in the DNA among the sample of thirty-eight men, Gilbert concluded that descent from a common ancestor is the most likely explanation for his findings.[1]

In the most comprehensive scientific study of human genes to date, L. Luca Cavalli-Sforza, Paolo Menozzi, and Alberto Piazza collected genetic material from tens of thousands of individuals from approximately five hundred ethnic groups. They concluded that the superficial characteristics that form the foundation of the concept of race can be explained by different environmental conditions. Based on these physical differences, they further concluded that the number of distinguishable races can range from three to sixty, depending on the criteria used.[2]

On the other hand, genetic arguments for racial differences are *not* supported by scientific evidence. There is ample genetic variation in all populations, even in relatively small ones. Furthermore, the differences among these small groups are insignificant when compared to differences within the major groups called races. This is partly due to the fact that, contrary to the fiction of a pure race, human beings have been mixing for many centuries. "Whatever genetic boundaries may have developed, given the strong mobility of human individuals and populations, there probably never were any sharp ones, or if there were, they were blurred by later movements."[3]

Narrow studies of so-called racial groups often obfuscate common characteristics of different races. For example, the widely held belief that high rates of hypertension among Americans with African ancestry is due to racial differences ignores the stressful conditions under which many of them live. People of African descent in the Caribbean, Latin America, and Africa itself have extremely low rates of hypertension. (Few tourists would describe people of the Caribbean as highly stressed.) A racial explanation is therefore misleading.

There are numerous examples demonstrating that people who are classified as racially different have many genetic similarities. Equatorial Africans, Italians, and Greeks could be regarded as one race, because they all carry the sickle cell gene. Asians and the San or Bushmen of South Africa have similarly shaped eyes. Asians, Native Americans, and Swedes have similarly shaped teeth. Norwegians, Saudi Arabians, and the Fulani of northern Nigeria could fall into the same racial category because they are lactose tolerant. Depending on the traits selected, Swedes, the Fulani, the Xhosa of South Africa, the Ainu of Japan, and many Italians could be regarded as a single race.[4] In other words, racial classification is an extremely arbitrary cultural construct that is not scientifically valid. Genetically, there is no valid scientific evidence that races are inferior or superior to each other. This indicates that the very concept of race has been socially and scientifically constructed.

The Social Construction of Race

Whereas Canadians are divided by language and the Irish by religion, Americans have used race to distinguish among those who are regarded as belonging to the dominant cultural circle and others who are excluded, different, and culturally distant. Distinctions based on superficial facts acquire deeper significance when deliberate efforts are made to make social, economic, and political reality conform to ideas embodied in the theory of racial divisions among human beings. Consequently, although race is a scientific fantasy, it is an unfortunate, socially constructed, fact. But this social fact is highly dependent on acceptance of the assumption that, biologically, race is fixed, measurable, concrete, and objective.

Race, unlike gender, cannot be defined biologically with objective measures and innate characteristics. Whereas a female in America remains a female in Brazil, a person who is defined as black in America could be regarded as white in Brazil. The offspring of someone defined as black and someone defined as white in South Africa is labeled "colored" in South Africa but "black" in the United States. Race, unlike gender, is variable—relative to location and historical period. For example, southern Europeans, Jews, and the Irish were classified as nonwhite in the nineteenth century. Although their gender remained constant with the turn of the century, their racial designation changed. Crucial to the social construction of race is the belief that skin color is of pivotal importance to social relations and that what is regarded as "racial" cannot be classified as part of some broader category or conception.[5]

The social construction of race is facilitated by obvious superficial differences and concerted efforts to treat those regarded as "others" in such a way that their behavior and way of life conform to what amount to self-fulfilling prophecies. For example, the belief that some races are not as intelligent as others is followed by the allocation of resources in ways that help to make this assumption true. An essential aspect of the social construction of race is the creation of institutions that perpetuate the socioeconomic and political order. In other words, even though race is believed to be a natural phenomenon, maintaining the status quo cannot be left to chance. Race becomes an institutional fact that cannot survive without a conscientious effort to sustain it.[6]

Of course, the social construction of race depends to a large extent on its acceptance by both those who benefit and those who suffer from it. To accomplish this objective, both groups must be enculturated to regard this artificial social arrangement as natural, as reality. Schools, families, churches, clubs, and peer groups play a vital role in conditioning members of society to accept race as reality. For a variety of reasons, everyone learns the rules of racial classification and internalizes race as social identity. As time passes, race becomes common sense—a way of comprehending, explaining, and acting in the world.[7] Those who created the racial system as well as those who are constrained by it cooperate to maintain much of the status quo until challenged by new conceptions of reality.

Variations in skin color were clearly noticed by ancient Greeks and others. Blacks, primarily Ethiopians, were known to the Greeks as early as the second century B.C. and were mentioned by Homer. The peoples around the Mediterranean traded and fought with each other and, in the process, developed certain attitudes toward each other. The peoples the Greeks regarded as barbarian had lighter as well as darker skin color. Unlike the racial ideologies that developed as western Europeans conquered parts of Africa, Asia, and the Americas, the Greeks did not view skin color and cultural sophistication as being connected. Consequently, the Greeks were willing to consider as fully civilized the Nubians of the Nile valley, who were among the darkest people they had encountered.[8]

The interactions of Mediterranean peoples were accompanied by a growing presence of blacks in many parts of Europe. Blacks, for example, served in the army of Septimius Severus, the Roman emperor born in Africa. Severus, who was protective of his soldiers, provided the black soldiers who accompanied him to Britain and elsewhere with the same advantages and treatment as other Roman soldiers. Consequently, many blacks were physically assimilated into the population of the Greco-Roman world, since there were no institutional barriers or social pressures against black-white unions.[9] Skin color alone did not determine social status.

Race as a hierarchical divider of human beings and a determinant of cultural differences did not emerge until the spread of European colonialism and the development of slavery in the Americas. When the Portuguese sailed along the west coast of Africa in the 1400s, they did not believe in the cultural incapacity of the Africans they encountered. On the contrary, the Portuguese, like the Spanish, actively sought to convert Africans to Christianity, a religion that recognizes the equality of all human beings. Their religious definition of human equality made it more difficult for them to be racially prejudiced. Instead of rationalizing their ruthless conquests in racial terms, they believed that killing or enslaving the heathen was serving the highest purpose of God.[10] Like the ancient Greeks and Romans, the Portuguese and Spanish integrated converted Africans into their societies, a pattern that continued in the Americas.

Early racial theories in Europe were closely connected to nationalism and class distinctions among people with essentially the same skin color. In addition to designating Africans and Asians as separate races, European intellectuals as well as commoners accepted the idea of three different European races, namely the Teutonic (Nordic and Germanic), the Alpine (Celtic), and the Mediterranean (Iberian and Latin).[11]

Theories of racial superiority in Europe were strengthened by the French diplomat Comte Arthur de Gobineau between 1853 and 1855. His objective was to fight the rising democratic spirit in Europe and to preserve the nobility. It was in Germany, with its growing nationalism, that de Gobineau's view that the future of European civilization depended on the dominance of the Aryans found a receptive audience. Richard Wagner introduced de Gobineau's theories to his circle, and they were soon given new applications by his son-in-law, Houston Stewart Chamberlain, and eventually by Adolf Hitler and other German Nazis.[12]

In the United States, the issues of slavery and territorial expansion played a pivotal role in the social construction of race. The English who settled what would later become the United States of America were relatively isolated from people with different skin color. Their reaction to Native Americans was much more negative than that of the Spanish, Portuguese, and French. English culture had conditioned the English to see ugliness and evil in black, a perception that inspired both fear and hostility.[13] This background helped to pave the way for the adoption of a racial prism that would become central to American society. By 1850, America's economic success and its expansion westward were seen as evidence of the innate superiority of the American Anglo-Saxon branch of the Caucasian race. The concept that whites were superior to other races became more firmly entrenched. European racial theories were more tightly embraced. Europeans acquired greater interest in America as a laboratory in which they could observe blacks and Native Americans to gather evidence to support their own racial theories.[14] By the middle of the nineteenth century, the assumption that skin color determined culture and virtue was established as fact throughout much of American society. Skin color and social attributes were now believed to be inseparable.

If Europeans perceived themselves as belonging to races that coincided with national identities as opposed to merely white and black, how did white and black come to be central to Americans' self-definition and identity? The term "white" was used to distinguish European explorers, traders, and settlers from the Africans, Asians, and Native Americans with whom they came into contact. Whiteness and blackness were socially constructed to include people who were regarded as socially and economically privileged and to exclude those who were seen as beyond the cultural circle of those designated as privileged, respectively.

Prior to the American Revolution, European Americans who worked on plantations in the colonies as indentured servants and as ordinary laborers showed little interest in a white identity. In many cases, they made little distinction between themselves and blacks. The American Revolution, which led to the decline of apprenticeship, indenture, and imprisonment for debt, and the growth of slavery in the South contributed to the social construction of whiteness as representing freedom and entitlement. Blackness, on the other hand, was equated with slavery.[15]

Whiteness was socially constructed to unify previously divided Europeans who now lived together in America, a country where enslaved Africans made up a large proportion of the population in some southern states. Whiteness became an asset. To be white meant that one belonged to an advantaged group. Poor Europeans, who had very little understanding of the concept of whiteness, were promoted to the "white race" and endowed with unprecedented civil, social, and economic privileges vis-à-vis enslaved as well as free Africans. These privileges required those designated as white to oppress and exclude those designated as black.[16] Whiteness and blackness became central components of American culture.

Systematic efforts were made to strengthen racially constructed boundaries by downplaying differences among whites and highlighting differences between whites and excluded groups, especially those designated as black. During the late nineteenth and early twentieth centuries, the United States accomplished the cultural homogenization of whites through social reform movements, education, and a combination of incentives and disincentives.[17]

How the Irish became white in America clearly demonstrates the social construction of whiteness as a privileged category. Much of the terminology used to describe blacks was employed against early Irish immigrants to the United States. They were seen as lowbrow, savage, groveling, bestial, lazy, wild, and sensual.[18] To be called an Irishman was tantamount to an insult in many parts of the United States. Some Americans viewed the Irish as part of a separate caste or dark race, possibly originally African. In the early years, Irish settlers were often referred to as "niggers turned inside out[;] the Negroes, for their part were sometimes called smoked Irish."[19] As the Irish gained the status of "white," they were included in the privileged group. This meant that Irish laborers were freer to compete for jobs in all areas of the economy and that Irish entrepreneurs could operate outside a segregated market. Their new status as whites accorded them social, political, and economic rights enjoyed by others designated as white.[20]

So effective has been this social construction of race that many white Americans seem largely unconscious of the benefits that accrue from their skin color. Consequently, getting beyond race involves whites' recognition of how whiteness is inextricably intertwined with blackness in an obverse relationship and what it means culturally to be designated as white. Ruth Frankenberg contends that when white people look at racism they tend to see it as an issue others face and not as a problem that involves them. She argues that to speak of whiteness, to name whiteness, is to assign everyone a place in the relations of racism. Racism shapes white people's lives and identities in a way that is inseparable from other facets of daily life.[21]

That whiteness is still regarded as preferable to blackness is demonstrated by the fact that few whites are willing to trade places with blacks, despite accusations by some whites of reverse discrimination. Peggy McIntosh states that she has come to see white privilege as an invisible package of unearned assets that she could count on cashing in each day but to which she was expected to remain oblivious.[22] Ironically, many black Americans' acceptance of race as their principal identity inadvertently enhances the ability of many whites to retain their racial identity and the privileges that accompany it. The social construction of race was deliberately designed to justify the institution of slavery, to promote white solidarity, and to create entitlements and advantages for Americans categorized as white.

Economic Interests and the Construction of Race

Ironically, it is in America, the embodiment of freedom, that slavery and skin color became permanently intertwined. In ancient civilizations as well as in premodern western Europe, there was no obvious link between slavery and skin color. Captured Africans in Greece and Rome were not assigned a fixed inferior status in those societies. There does not appear to have been much prejudice against Africans because of their skin color in either Greece or Rome.[23] Slavery flourished throughout southern Italy and Sicily. German, Celtic, Jewish, Gallic, and North African slaves were treated more or less the same by their Roman masters. In some cases, slaves were both darker and lighter in terms of skin color than those who enslaved them. Similarly, slavery in ancient Egypt encompassed a wide range of skin colors, and slaves and slaveholders often traded places as their fortunes changed due to wars and other factors.[24]

Slavery in Europe and Africa was not based on skin color. In Dahomey, for example, the economy depended on slavery to such a great extent that annual raids and military expeditions against neighboring groups and villages were conducted primarily for the purpose of securing men, women, and children for sale, a practice that helped make the transatlantic slave trade easier for Europeans to initiate.[25] In none of these societies—ancient

Rome, Greece, and Egypt and more recently western Europe—was skin color equated with a permanent form of servitude. In many cases, former slaves rose to join the elites. Freed slaves, while frequently relegated to low social status, were accepted as members of the societies in which they had previously been enslaved.

Dominated by religious thought and practice, western Europeans initially viewed the enslavement of captured Africans and Native Americans as part of the process of rescuing lost souls and heathens. In this regard, Europeans were similar to Muslims, who distinguished between believers and nonbelievers in their system of slavery. This meant that nonbelievers who converted to Christianity could claim their freedom. The idea of a Christian slave was unacceptable in the early period of European interaction with the newly discovered lands of Africa, Asia, and the Americas.

The activities of Catholic missionaries clearly frustrated the slave traders, whose interest in making money was of paramount importance. Unlike the Catholics, who colonized areas under the aegis of their monarch and the Catholic Church to which that monarch was committed, Protestants tended to enjoy greater freedom to pursue private enterprise without much interference from religious or political institutions. Consequently, the practice of freeing slaves who professed Christianity soon ceased in countries under Protestant control.

In the United States, economic interests challenged religious convictions, with the latter soon being subordinated to the former. Racial ideas that the British brought with them to North America were transformed as European settlers interacted with both Native Americans and enslaved Africans. A product of the Enlightenment, the United States became at once the most religious and the most secular society. The secularization of American society helped to undermine the view of the unity of mankind that is central to Christian thought. Furthermore, a growing demand for labor in the colonies directly affected the status and treatment of both indentured Europeans and enslaved Africans. In order to attract more European settlers to the colonies, the term of indentured servitude was shortened and the treatment of servants improved. Enslaved Africans, on the other hand, experienced harsher treatment and fewer opportunities to gain their freedom.[26]

When the first shots of the American Revolution were fired in Lexington and Concord, Americans believed that they had been heard around the world, thereby bestowing universal significance upon them. But most importantly, the shots were heard at home by enslaved Africans, by free Africans who fought in the American Revolution, and by many Americans of European descent who believed that their new country's commitment to freedom applied to the slaves.

Confronted by the glaring incongruity between America as a beacon of freedom and America as a slave society, those with an economic interest in perpetuating the institution of slavery made a concerted effort to demonstrate that the concepts of freedom and natural equality of mankind were not applicable to enslaved Africans. Therefore, if all men were created equal and endowed by their Creator with certain unalienable rights, then enslaved Africans could not be men. Americans with African ancestry were not only perceived to be outside the boundaries within which whites lived and enjoyed freedom, they had to be seen as not fully human.

This combination of America's position as a bastion of liberty in a world characterized by oppression on the one hand and Americans' strenuous efforts to protect an economic system based on the enslavement of Africans on the other helped generate an extreme form of racism. Thomas Sowell observes that "in despotic countries no special ideology needs to be invoked in defense of slavery. Although racial arrogance and racial oppression occurred throughout Latin America, it never approached the pervasive fanaticism reached in the United States."[27]

White opposition to slavery before and after the American Revolution triggered extreme racial views and practices, especially in the South. Many Americans believed that their nation's self-definition made it necessary to treat blacks and whites equally. New Englanders, motivated by moral and religious convictions and not encumbered by economic dependence on slavery, were inclined to view Africans and Native Americans as fully human and therefore entitled to freedom. Southerners, in contrast, not only were economically dependent on slavery but also needed to maintain the institution as an integral part of their self-definition.

By 1850, northern abolitionists, led by William Lloyd Garrison and others, argued that slavery was evil and demanded that blacks be granted their freedom and equal rights as Americans. But, as George M. Fredrickson argues, once the abolitionists had thrown down the gauntlet, proslavery apologists had two choices: They could either reject egalitarianism altogether or they could deny the humanity of blacks and reserve the egalitarian, natural-rights philosophy exclusively for whites.[28]

Having psychological as well as economic interest in denying the humanity of blacks, many whites in both the North and the South articulated the view that Africans were slaves by nature, just as whites were naturally free. To support this economic construction of race, blacks *had* to be denied freedom. Whites without an apparent stake in slavery would not only enjoy the psychological benefits of whiteness, they would also feel protected from the slaves held in permanent bondage. As a result, a distinction had to be made not just between the slave and the free person but also between blacks and whites, two groups that were deemed to be inherently incompatible.[29]

The foundation of a racial hierarchy and the permanence of slavery had been established in virtually every British colony before the American Revolution. Laws were enacted to restrain a slaveholder's power to release slaves. A slaveholder was sometimes required to ensure that a freed slave would not become a public burden. In many cases, the slaveholder had to prove that slaves had earned their freedom through meritorious service. By the 1850s, at the height of the development of racial doctrines in America, the slaveholder who wanted to free slaves was forced to rely on legal ingenuity and subterfuge.[30] In North Carolina and elsewhere, some free blacks were able to obtain freedom for their families by buying them and keeping them as slaves. Despite differences among the laws related to freeing slaves in the various states, on the whole it was much more difficult for a slave to gain freedom in North America than in Latin America.

That these historical factors greatly contributed to current race problems in American society can be seen by comparing American slavery with the institution of slavery in Latin America, a region that does not suffer as many sharp racial divisions and tensions as the United States. The significant differences between slavery in the United States and in Latin America, especially in Brazil, can be traced to the customs and religious views of the southern hemisphere's colonizing powers, Spain and Portugal. Both countries had a long history of interacting with Africans and were much more tolerant of racial differences than was England. Furthermore, Spain and Portugal had themselves been occupied by the Moors, a fact that had far-reaching cultural consequences for them. And, finally, both countries were Catholic.

The voyages of Portuguese navigators around Africa between 1445 and 1488 propelled Portugal to the forefront of the African slave trade, first to Europe itself and later to the Americas. Having maintained a system of slavery long after the rest of western Europe had ended the practice, Spain and Portugal did not require the institution of racial differentiation to justify human bondage. Jews, Moors, black Africans, and even Spaniards themselves were enslaved both in Spain and in the New World. In other words, slavery was a long tradition, one that had little relation to skin color.

Unlike Americans, citizens of Spain and Portugal did not enjoy significant political freedom. Liberalizing influences such as the Magna Carta in England and the Protestant Reformation in much of northern Europe did not significantly affect Spain and Portugal. The institution of slavery was supervised by both the Catholic Church and the Crown. The general consensus was that the status of the slave was not permanent, and the distinction between slavery and freedom was perceived to be a result of misfortune. Thus, a free person could just as easily have had the misfortune to be a slave.[31]

From the Catholic viewpoint, slaves were free and equal in God's sight, and their souls were as important as those of free people. The slaveholder had no greater moral status than the slave. Slaves attended church on Sunday together with slaveholders and other free persons; they were married in the Catholic Church, and the banns were regularly published. Unlike in the United States, where slaveholders exercised absolute control over slaves, throughout Latin America in general and in Brazil in particular slaves were free to marry even against the slaveholder's will, and married slaves could not be separated.[32]

Because the Catholic Church did not regard slavery as a permanent condition based on skin color, and because Brazilians generally believed in the equality of all human beings in God's sight, enslaved Africans could more easily obtain their freedom in Brazil than in the United States. In fact, manumission was strongly encouraged by the Catholic Church. Freeing one's slaves was regarded as an honorific tradition, one that was practiced on happy occasions such as the birth of a first son or the marriage of one of the master's children.[33] Furthermore, opportunities for slaves to purchase their freedom were more frequent in Brazil than in the United States. Whereas 90 percent of the black American population was enslaved in 1860, in Brazil more than half of the black population enjoyed relative freedom.

This gradual freeing of slaves, together with efforts not only to include slaves in the fabric of society but also to nurture their moral worth as genuine human beings, contributed to greater racial harmony in Brazil than in the United States. Visitors to Brazil during the period of slavery found relatively good relations between whites, blacks, and racially mixed people. There was no rigid segregation in trains, restaurants, or places of entertainment.[34] Brazil's relatively egalitarian racial attitudes, despite the harshness of slavery, promoted the building of bridges between blacks and whites.

Racial Classification: Strengthening the Boundaries

One of the most interesting aspects of race relations in the United States is the degree to which both blacks and whites have accepted the rigid categorization of people into distinct racial groups. In a society where Africans and Europeans have lived in close physical proximity, the dominant assumption of separate racial groups remains largely unchallenged by the majority of whites and blacks. Both groups generally accept the racial classifications they have been assigned by proponents of slavery and inequality who lived centuries ago. For many Americans, race *is* identity; it is who they are in a very real sense.

In 1977, Susie Guillory Phipps, who believed she was white and had been enjoying the privileges that accompany the status of being white, obtained her birth certificate in order to apply for a passport. The significance of racial classification was vividly demonstrated by her reaction upon learning that according to her birth certificate, recorded in Acadia Parish, Louisiana, her parents had been designated as "colored." This meant that she was, in contemporary terms, an African American.

Shocked and actually physically sickened by this revelation, Susie Guillory Phipps spent approximately $40,000 attempting to change the racial designation on her birth certificate. The Fourth Circuit Court of Appeals concluded that Phipps would have to change her parents' racial designation in order to become white by law. Pointing out that an individual may not change the racial designation of another person, the court refused to classify Phipps as white. She was black because her great-great-great-great-grandmother had been a slave.[35] Such a case would not have arisen in any other society, including South Africa.

Under the racial classification system developed in the United States, "one drop of black blood" makes an individual black, regardless of physical appearance. This so-called one-drop rule is what Susie Guillory Phipps encountered. To remain a member of white society, she had to maintain the fiction that she had never breached these insurmountable walls that separate blacks from whites. One-hundred percent racial purity, which has always been a fantasy, was the essential ingredient of racial classification.

The Phipps case shows that in the United States, unlike in Latin America, racial categories involving blacks and whites are dichotomous, fixed, and inflexible. One is either black or white, despite obvious racial mixture. It also illustrates America's refusal to recognize an intermediate racial category, which would have the potential to bring together blacks and whites, as is the case in Brazil and elsewhere. Finally, it documents the fact that one cannot transform or transcend one's racial status, largely because such status is ascribed rather than achieved. Race has been constructed as a symbol of social status: It functions to marginalize individuals who are classified as less advantaged and as being outside the privileged racial circle.[36] To blur distinctions between black and white by accepting the fact that many blacks and whites are biologically related to each other would frustrate racists and render less effective the social construction of race. Extremely rigid racial classification for blacks and whites—more rigid than for other groups—became the cornerstone of race relations in America. Remove these classifications and the now insurmountable wall of the "one-drop rule" will collapse, as American society continues to move beyond race. The 1997 decision of the Census Bureau to allow Americans to check more than one racial category underscores this change.

Economic interests and psychological needs conspired to institute the one-drop rule. As I explain in Chapter 7, the one-drop rule was meant to ensure that offspring of slaveholder and slave would be undeniably slave—and, consequently, have no legal claim to an estate or freedom. Applied *only* to Americans with any African ancestry, the one-drop rule, although widely accepted by blacks and whites, defies all logic. Under this rule, a white woman can give birth to a black child, but a black woman cannot give birth to a white child. Any offspring of an interracial relationship is automatically black.

Another obvious reason for constructing the one-drop rule was to increase the number of slaves, which included children fathered by slaveholders. The status of children of black and white parents was directly linked to the definition of slavery. A large free population, half-black and half-white, obviously contradicted the dichotomous view of race that rigidly separated Europeans and Africans into categories of black and white, slave and master. As early as 1662 in Virginia and in 1663 in Maryland, the courts had decided that the status of children should follow that of the mother, who was almost invariably a slave.[37]

In addition, the one-drop rule was designed to deny the Americanness of people who could trace several generations of American-born ancestors. No matter how long their relatives, black and white, had been in America, Americans with African ancestry were always considered outsiders. This was indeed a ludicrous notion given the wide range of skin colors found within the group classified as "black." Noel Ignatiev contends that "the hallmark of racial oppression is the reduction of members of the oppressed group to one undifferentiated social status, a status beneath that of any member of any social class within the dominant group."[38] The one-drop rule, then, was also designed to secure the privileged social status of members of the white group, no matter how poor they were or how recently their families had arrived in the United States. The one-drop rule diminished the possibility of conflict among Europeans who had come from places often warring with each other to settle in America by creating the artificial bond of skin color, while forcing individuals with African ancestry into another largely undifferentiated group. But differences among Americans with African ancestry have always existed. There has always been a relatively privileged black group—largely the descendants of "house slaves" who were more likely to be light-skinned and educated.

Although distinctions between black and white were clear enough, variations in skin color within the black group led to the creation of a hierarchy of subcategories: black, mulatto, quadroon, and octoroon. For example, in 1860, 13 percent of blacks were classified as mulatto or racially mixed. But as the one-drop rule was more rigorously enforced, the mixed race category was eliminated, and by 1900 the distinctions among blacks were downplayed. The need to divide blacks had declined due in part to increased European immigration. Whites were now more confident of their ability to "impose biracial domination over a black-brown minority."[39]

Confronted with these relentless efforts to relegate them to a permanently inferior social category, Americans with African ancestry, some of whom had blonde hair and blue eyes, responded by burying their differences and accepting the one-drop rule to forge a united front. Although variations in skin color had been a source of intragroup conflict, the new strategy was to generate pride among all those who could trace African ancestry.[40] By so doing, Americans with African ancestry adopted the one-drop rule, which had originally been invented by whites to protect their own economic and social interests. As I will discuss in Chapter 7, many

Americans with African ancestry see their acceptance of the one-drop rule as advantageous; they are as reluctant as most whites to recognize the obvious racial mixture within their group.

Race, Science, and Intelligence

The social construction of race was augmented by the development of pseudoscientific theories purporting to prove innate biological differences among people of different races on the basis of readily observable superficial characteristics. Science, by seeming to be objective, impartial, and verifiable, legitimized racial theories in the eyes of many Americans who were otherwise inclined to believe in the equality of all human beings. However, science is not a neutral activity that is entirely divorced from the socioeconomic and political environments in which it is conducted. Science is influenced by society as much as it influences society. Undergirding the power of scientific theories in American society is a predisposition toward science as representing the ultimate truth.

Yet, because they are products of their culture, scientists are limited by prevailing assumptions and patterns of thought. Scientific facts usually are not pure and unsullied pieces of information, because dominant cultural values help to determine what is seen and how it is seen.[41] In most cases, results tend to support predictions; scientists usually find what they are looking for while ignoring, trivializing, or carelessly explaining away contradictory evidence.

Given scientists' personal and psychological investment in emotionally loaded racial classifications, scientific objectivity in this area was compromised from the beginning. Thomas S. Kuhn observes that "an apparently arbitrary element, compounded of personal and historic accident, is always a formative ingredient of beliefs espoused by a given scientific community at a given time."[42] Thus, social and scientific constructions of race reinforced each other, thereby strengthening the arbitrary element in the scientific process.

Unfortunately, science often functions to consolidate and institutionalize ideas that are consistent with society's dominant interests. Science is a particularly powerful instrument in this endeavor because it purports objectivity. Its conclusions are supposedly based on accurate observations of natural phenomena rather than deriving from ordinary human struggle. Its explanations and pronouncements are often regarded as true in an absolute sense for all times and all places. Science is powerful because average citizens cannot understand it; its esoteric language must be explained by scientists themselves.[43] Therefore, scientific language is considered to be authoritative. Because of these factors, science has profound social and political consequences for race relations.

Most urgent among the scientific studies of race was the need to demonstrate innate and fixed natural differences—especially in relation to intelligence—among socially constructed races. In a society that is based on meritocracy instead of ascription, on the concept of fairness instead of historical entitlement, how does one explain glaring contradictions of these fundamental principles? Science answers this question by advancing the doctrine of biological determinism, which continues to be at the heart of contemporary controversies on the connections between race, intelligence, and achievement.

Richard J. Herrnstein, coauthor of *The Bell Curve,* in recent years has been one of the most ardent supporters of modern ideologies of natural inequality. Biological determinism, or the view that people assume their natural level in a meritocracy, is composed of three ideas. The first and most important is that human beings possess varied abilities because of innate differences rather than because of environmental influences. Second, these innate biological differences are genetically inherited and cannot be mitigated by environmental factors. Finally, human nature guarantees the formation of a hierarchical society.[44] From this perspective, whites (rightly) should dominate society because they are naturally more intelligent than blacks, Latinos, Asians, and Native Americans, whose positions in society are determined by innate deficiencies. The social construction of race as fixed was clearly consistent with these scientific theories, the net result being a perpetuation of the status quo.

During the first half of the nineteenth century, scientific evidence was marshaled to strengthen arguments that favored the continuation of economic, political, and cultural control of America by "the older American stock" of Anglo-Saxon origin. In other words, nationalism and racial theorizing became inseparable. Both the English and Americans of European ancestry were convinced that their phenomenal economic, political, and technological achievements were directly related to their racial characteristics. Democracy, freedom, political stability, territorial expansion, and economic prosperity were perceived as evidence of the racial superiority of the Anglo-Saxon race. Racial mixing, especially between blacks and whites, threatened to dilute this power.

Immigrants from other European nations were also seen as contributing to the weakening of the European-American racial stock that was already established in the country. Jews, Poles, Italians, and others were thought to be less intelligent and, therefore, undesirable. In his preface to Madison Grant's book *The Passing of the Great Race,* Henry Fairfield Osborn argued that the greatest danger to the American republic was the "gradual dying out among our people of those hereditary traits through which the principles of our religious, political, and social foundations were laid down and their insidious replacement by traits of less noble character."[45] So deeply ingrained were these ideas in American thought that legislation was passed to exclude immigrants who were believed to be racially inferior, and concerted efforts were made to prevent interracial relationships from developing.

Preoccupied with finding differences among socially constructed races, scientists from the 1820s onward examined virtually every aspect of bodily structure and function as well as mental aptitude. Phrenologists and others were searching for evidence that would support the socially acceptable view of inherent racial differences and the belief in superior and inferior races. They carefully examined the texture of hair, the size of the cranium, the shape of the nose, the color of the skin and eyes, the shape of the head, the age of sexual maturity, the sexual organs, the distribution of blood types, and many other anatomical and physiological features. Based on their measurements, they reached the general conclusion that whites as a race were inventive, creative, and powerful; blacks were docile and ignorant; and Native Americans were savage and intractable.[46]

Although significant differences were found among whites as a racial group, they remained a separate and distinct scientific category. The fact that the differences within socially constructed racial groups were found to be greater than those among racial groups was ignored. In the final analysis, scientific findings confirmed the dominant cultural view of racial groups in American society. Racial characteristics were innate and not greatly affected by education, circumstances, opportunities, or the general social, political, and economic environment; consequently, altering the status quo was deemed to be impossible.

Perhaps the best example of how science corroborated the integral components of the social construction of race is the development and use of intelligence tests. More than anything else, racial ideologies assume that races regarded as inferior are naturally and irredeemably less intelligent than those regarded as superior. However, strenuous efforts made to prevent enslaved Africans from learning to read and write undermined the validity of such beliefs in the minds of many whites; these efforts seemed to suggest that many whites themselves had serious doubts about the validity of their own beliefs. Although America has made significant progress in getting beyond race, intelligence tests are still regarded by many Americans as reliable indicators of the innate intellectual differences between various racial groups, especially between blacks and whites.

At the beginning of the twentieth century, Alfred Binet, director of the psychology laboratory at the Sorbonne, was asked by taxpayers in France, who believed that their money was being wasted on attempts to educate "retarded" children in regular classrooms, to devise a test that would enable teachers to separate children according to intellectual abilities. From 1905 to 1911, Binet endeavored to measure natural intelligence as opposed to acquired knowledge. Although he developed a test, Binet concluded that intelligence is too complex to be representable by a single indicator.[47] In 1916, Lewis M. Terman of Stanford University modified Binet's test to suit American academic conditions, thereby inaugurating the Stanford-Binet Test of Intelligence. In 1923, Carl Brigham, who became secretary of the College Entrance Examination Board, further developed intelligence testing in the United States. In his book *A Study of American Intelligence,* Brigham expressed concern about the dangers of "incorporating the Negro into our racial stock." He believed that "the decline of the American intelligence will be more rapid owing to the presence here of the Negro."[48] Racial admixture was thought to be a major cause of America's decline.

Conducted in an environment pregnant with deeply rooted hostility toward Americans with African ancestry and with strong beliefs in the virulent stereotypes of them, intelligence tests invariably mirrored both prevailing racial attitudes and the existing social structure. Blacks' performance on the tests was not as good as that of whites, and groups that were better off economically achieved higher scores than groups from modest or poor economic backgrounds. The examples given below underscore the ideological influences on intelligence tests. The practice of giving positive interpretations for whites and negative interpretations for blacks when their performances on specific tests were essentially the same was widespread.

When G. R. Stetson found at the turn of the nineteenth century that Americans with African ancestry generally performed better than Americans of European ancestry on memory tests, he explained that blacks' superior performance in such tests was directly linked to their relative primitiveness. Yet ten years later, when an English researcher named Cyril Burt found that upper-class boys displayed complete superiority over working-class boys in memory tests, he concluded that a disciplined memory was characteristic of greater intelligence.[49] Research showing that blacks had a quicker reaction time than whites was seen as evidence of the inferiority of blacks because faster reflexes were surely characteristic of lower intelligence. When later research demonstrated faster reaction times for whites, this was accepted as evidence of white intellectual superiority.[50]

Similarly, research findings were manipulated to corroborate that immigrants were intellectually inferior to native-born Americans. In 1913, when a leading American psychologist, Henry H. Goddard, administered intelligence tests to recent immigrants at Ellis Island, he found that 83 percent of Jews, 80 percent of Hungarians, 79 percent of Italians, and 87 percent of Russians were feebleminded.[51] A consistent finding of American intelligence testing was that immigrants were less intelligent than native-born Americans, with the most recent crop of immigrants invariably being the least intelligent ever, a verdict that undermines the earlier assumption that intelligence is fixed and virtually unaffected by environmental factors.[52]

Arguing that differences between the races in measured cognitive ability have been detected ever since intelligence tests were first devised, Richard J. Herrnstein and Charles Murray, in their book *The Bell Curve*, essentially confirm what the early intelligence tests concluded: namely, that whites are inherently more intelligent than blacks and that intelligence is genetically inherited and basically fixed. Although they question what it means to be black in America in racial terms, and acknowledge that some people whose ancestry is more European than African are designated as "black" in America, they nonetheless attempt to build a scientific argument for differences in intelligence among socially constructed races or ethnic groups. In a feeble attempt to disguise the methodological weakness upon which their scientific theory is constructed, they decided "to classify people according to the way they classify themselves."[53] However, given the widespread racial mixture in the United States among both blacks and whites as well as the acceptance of the one-drop rule by many Americans of African ancestry who could just as easily classify themselves as white, *The Bell Curve*'s arguments are largely invalid because its essential premise is flawed.

A widely recognized problem with intelligence tests is that they are often more closely correlated with environmental factors than with genetics. Furthermore, intelligence tests are limited in their ability to measure many qualities that are essential for success in American society. Test scores are influenced by a number of nongenetic factors including prenatal care, access to adequate public schools, a supportive learning environment at home, family income, intensive coaching for taking tests, and what Claude M. Steele calls "stereotype vulnerability." Black students' performance on intelligence tests is believed to be affected by their own acceptance of the stereotype that blacks as a group are not as smart as whites.[54]

That intelligence is not simply a function of genetics is clearly demonstrated by the unwillingness of middle-class parents, regardless of their racial identity, to trade places with poor people. For example, if education and environmental factors do not matter in relation to intelligence, why are parents across the United States so concerned about the quality of the schools their children attend? If race determined intelligence, then trading places would not significantly affect test scores. Few parents are willing to take the chance of changing their children's environment. Programs such as Prep for Prep in New York, which successfully prepares minority children to attend the nation's most prestigious private academies, support the view that a combination of genetic and environmental factors determine intelligence and success.

Obvious inconsistencies and contradictions in the scientific study of races play a major role in rendering the entire enterprise unacceptable to serious scholars and the educated public. Arnold J. Toynbee, for instance, asserted that the so-called racial explanation of differences in human performance and achievement was either an ineptitude or a fraud.[55] The development of academic fields such as cultural anthropology, in which cultural influences on human behavior are closely studied, further weakened the credibility of scientific race theories. As the ethnic composition of the country changed, the scientific community became more diversified and members of groups deemed to be inferior began to have a greater influence in science. Immigrants, women, Jews, and others provided scientific data to refute claims of their own inferior qualities.[56] The intellectual prowess of these new groups provided incontrovertible evidence of the fallacy of early racial scientific findings.

Economic, social, educational, and military changes in society also challenged the old order. The Great Depression reduced previously successful Americans to poverty, thereby shattering the belief that heredity and biological characteristics determined one's position in society. The rise of Nazism in Germany further demonstrated the consequences of allowing race theories to carry through to their logical conclusions, just when the confidence of the middle class in biological determinism was being undermined.[57]

During World War I, the U.S. Army helped to discredit the belief in the innate intelligence of different races. Army testers found that black recruits from the northern United States were far superior to black recruits from the southern states. More importantly, their tests showed that blacks from some states in the North were superior in their performance to many southern whites.[58] Environmental influences could no longer be discounted. Finally, greater educational opportunities for ordinary Americans provided increased understanding of world history and culture.

History shows that no single race has dominated international affairs indefinitely. A deeper understanding of history has also enabled Americans to realize how civilizations interact and influence each other. Western civilization borrowed from the Chinese, the Egyptians, the Arabs, the Persians, the Moors, and others. Fundamental cornerstones of European civilization were often borrowed from other races. Steel was invented in either India or Turkistan; and gunpowder, printing, and paper in China; advanced mathematics was imported from the Arab, Moorish, and Asiatic peoples.[59] If intelligence is hereditary and fixed, how could Europeans, who were less technologically advanced than many other civilizations, rise to global prominence in the sixteenth century? How do racial theories explain the emergence of Japan as an economic superpower or the decline of Britain's economic might?

Race as Magic, Myth, and Totem

Race as a pseudoscientific construction is magic, myth, and totem. Irrational beliefs and behavior are parts of virtually all societies, from the most technologically primitive to the postmodern. Technological and scientific advancements do not necessarily destroy the myths upon which many contemporary perceptions are based. The persistent centrality of race in American society is evidence of how magic and science can coexist.

Magic, the religious form of our ancestors, is generally defined by our society as an irrational attempt by human beings to directly influence the behavior of nature as well as of other humans, for good or for ill, by their own power, as distinct from appealing to divine powers through sacrifice or prayer.[60] People rely on magical rituals and beliefs to achieve specific rational objectives. Race in America, as a pseudoscientific construction, fits the dominant culture's definition of magic. For example, race was first constructed for economic and social purposes, but the idea and practice of racism are irrational. In other words, race is an irrational means of achieving what are perceived to be rational objectives. From Max Weber's viewpoint, "magical behavior or thinking must not be set apart from the range of everyday purposive conduct, particularly since even the ends of magical actions are predominantly economic."[61]

In the sense that there is no causal connection between the instruments of magic and the desired outcomes of the practice of magic, human attempts to effectuate social control through magic are irrational. But magic can be perceived as rational because it often engenders in those practicing it a sense of confidence, competence, and control, which is instrumental in the achievement of specific rational goals.[62]

One of the most obvious examples of the connection between race and magic is the belief that skin color determines performance. Whites often perceive themselves to be competent when compared to blacks mainly because of irrational racial classifications. Skin color can create a sense of confidence, competence, and control. The positive values associated with white skin contribute to white success, and the lack of such confidence in black skin is an important factor in black failure. Focusing on skin color is conducive to being influenced by race magic. This belief in race as magic is reinforced by evidence of the success of those whose skin color is thought to be the embodiment of extraordinary power. Recognition of black success helps to limit the negative psychological as well as practical effects of race magic.

What makes race magic highly effective is the ubiquitous nature of race in American society. The racial worldview, like the magical worldview, is an almost complete worldview, one that explains virtually anything and everything in terms of race. Failure and success, criminal activity and lawfulness, personal virtues and vices, domestic relations, employment histories, and religious practices are all frequently attributed to race even by sophisticated scholars. A magical worldview explains everything in terms of magic, failed magic, or magical conspiracies.[63] Similar to a magical worldview, a racial worldview sees skin color as influencing many facets of society and as permeating every aspect of culture.

Many studies of race are generally regarded as scientific and therefore beyond the realm of magic. Yet the pseudoscientific basis of racial classification renders science that assumes the existence of specific races akin to magic. Magic and science are similar in the sense that both have specific aims and both are based on the belief that if one performs a specific set of activities, one will accomplish desired objectives. But whereas science is based on the normal universal experience of everyday life and is governed by observation and reason, "magic is based on specific experience of emotional states in which man observes not nature but himself, in which truth is revealed not by reason but by the play of emotions upon the human organism."[64]

Race is the product of fears, emotions, and efforts by human beings to enhance their status and control others. Whereas theories of science are determined by logic, those of magic are dictated by the association of ideas that emanate from the human desire to achieve specific economic and social objectives.[65] Race, like magic, is therefore pseudoscience. Neither is based on logic. For example, the one-drop rule, which applies only to Americans with African ancestry, classifies someone with blue eyes and blond hair as black because a distant ancestor was of African origin. Logically, such a rule would also imply that a person with one drop of white blood would be classified as white. But race isn't about logic in a scientific sense.

Closely connected to the conception of race as magic are social myths. Myths, the explanations behind magic, are faulty assumptions that reflect certain beliefs. Beliefs are themselves largely unexamined ideas. Myths and beliefs are therefore closely intertwined. Myths reflect beliefs and give sanction to the actions of society while simultaneously providing the forms upon which belief and conduct are molded.[66] Myths explain why things are a certain way. They are the historical statements of those events that vouch for the truth of a certain kind of magic and how the magic came into the possession of a community.[67]

Aware of differences in skin color, some theologians trace the origins of races to Noah's three sons. The Europeans, Asians, and Africans were endowed with specific myths of origin. Europeans, the most favored group, were descendants of Japhet, who represented the nobles; the Asians were the children of Shem, who represented the clerks; and the Africans came from Ham, the ancestor of the serfs. The Hamites occupied the lowest level of this hierarchy and were condemned to serve their cousins as slaves because of a mysterious curse.[68] These myths undoubtedly helped to influence the social and scientific construction of race during the period of European expansion and the growth of slavery in America.

Myths, like magic, play important roles in all societies, to varying degrees. Myth functions to preserve the status quo, to provide continuity in society, and to justify contemporary socioeconomic conditions by evoking precedents. Myth helps to strengthen tradition by linking it to an inaccessible, unknowable, and unverifiable higher supernatural reality of initial events. From this viewpoint, races exist and are inferior or superior because of God or nature. Myth is also employed to rationalize extraordinary privileges and duties and to account for egregious social inequalities.[69] Myths designed to justify social differences to satisfy the needs of particular groups often have the force of law and often directly influence the legal system. The very nature of myths and their centrality to human existence make them almost impervious to rational thought. Because they are built into the structure of social relationships, racial myths usually help create reality. These irrational views are nurtured by obvious superficial biological differences. Apparent differences in skin color facilitate the tendency of myths to make clear thinking about the social construction of race unnecessary.[70]

In addition to conceptualizing race as magic and myth, race can also be viewed as performing the function of totems. The term "totem," literally taken from the Ojibwa American Indian word *ototeman,* means "he is a relative of mine." Totemism is both a mode of social organization and a system of religious beliefs and practices.[71] Totems are symbols that represent particular clans, usually associated with animals such as eagles, bears, tigers, and coyotes. The underlying purpose of the totem is to provide a sense of identity with and belonging to a group that claims a common ancestor. Totems are visible reminders of the group's common bond. Clan members are distinguished by their totem.

Race is akin to totemism in the sense that skin color is perceived by many Americans as an identity, as an indication of who belongs to which group. Race is often regarded as a basis of social, economic, and political solidarity. Ruth Benedict, in her book *Race and Racism,* first published in 1922, contends that "according to racism we know our enemies, not by their aggressions against us, not by their creed or language, not even by their possessing wealth we want to take, but by noting their hereditary anatomy."[72] Race is an obvious social marker that creates a perception of familiarity between individuals with the same skin color, even when they are complete strangers.

3

THE CHANGING AMERICAN CULTURE

Challenges to Race

PREOCCUPIED WITH RACIAL DIVISIONS and the politics of identity, many Americans have overemphasized those aspects of American culture that perpetuate racial antagonism and misunderstanding while overlooking those components of American culture that are conducive to getting beyond race. Furthermore, the tendency to focus on blacks and whites ignores the growing numbers of Americans of Latin American and Asian heritage and the greater visibility of multiracial Americans who are actively seeking to change rigid racial classifications. Perhaps the most potent challenges to race are generational replacement, demographic changes, and extensive, ongoing interactions among individuals from different racial backgrounds in all areas of American life. In this chapter I examine the general concept of culture and the complex nature of American culture. I argue that family, interracial contacts, multiculturalism, religion, the media, and sports are changing the racial component of American culture.

The Concept of Culture

Culture is a complex, nebulous concept. In this chapter, culture is understood to be a set of shared values, beliefs, perceptions, attitudes, modes of living, customs, and symbols. Although discrete and often contradictory aspects of culture exist, they function together to form an interrelated and integrated whole. The connections among different components of culture infuse culture with meaning.[1] These connections also contribute to the ambiguity, dynamism, and complexity that are essential characteristics of culture.

Emile Durkheim, in his book *Division of Labor,* articulates the view that as societies become more complex, cultural consensus is weakened. Divergent attitudes and values develop, and beliefs and attitudes are modified in ways that are significantly different from those prescribed or proscribed by the collective conscience or defined by moral consensus.[2] By promoting skepticism and innovation, pluralism challenges established traditions, values, and beliefs. Revolutionary technological changes that link individuals around the world and across the country to each other combine with growing diversity and generational change in American society to weaken the consensus undergirding the social, economic, and scientific construction of race.

Cultural values, beliefs, attitudes, and symbols are passed from one generation to the next by parents, schools and colleges, religious institutions, the mass media, political and social organizations, friends, and peer groups. These agents of cultural transmission, or enculturation, can work together or at cross-purposes, thus making the conveyance of culture inconsistent, unpredictable, and sometimes difficult. In many cases, the outcome is the opposite of what was intended.

Enculturation, no matter how thorough, does not create complete uniformity of behavior, for several reasons. First, human beings are strongly influenced by biological as well as environmental factors. Biological factors invariably cause innate differences in mental, physical, and behavioral capabilities. Whereas some of us absorb racial beliefs and behavior without much scrutiny, others are likely to reject race because they plainly see its inherent inconsistencies and superficiality. In other words, individuals are likely to respond differently to enculturation. Second, information transmitted through enculturation varies from family to family and from institution to institution. Even within families there are divergent views on race. Third, enculturation is an ongoing process, part of which sometimes occurs outside one's culture. For example, Americans living and traveling abroad often confront views that modify their racial attitudes. Finally, individuals tend to maneuver within their cultures, choosing courses of action to satisfy their personal interests as well as the demands of their society.[3]

Although culture provides the environment within which one must function, it does not automatically determine how most individuals respond to particular situations. Individuals and groups constantly challenge cultural symbols and meanings, thereby contributing to the dynamism inherent in complex cultures such as that of the United States.

Race and American Culture

Given the historical perceptions of race as the equivalent of culture, an American culture that recognizes its diverse components strongly demonstrates significant progress toward moving beyond race. The inclusion of Americans with African ancestry into the mainstream of American life also indicates an acknowledgment of the role blacks have played in shaping American culture. The social, economic, and scientific construction of race deliberately exaggerated differences between the values, attitudes, and beliefs of blacks and whites. American culture was seen primarily as a European-derived culture, and Americans were defined as individuals of European ancestry. Non-Europeans were regarded as distant others who were not part of American culture.

One of the most articulate statements about who is an American was written by J. Hector St. John de Crevecoeur, a French-born naturalized American. In his *Letters from an American Farmer,* written in 1782, Crevecoeur described the new American as "either a European or the descendant of a European; hence, that strange mixture of blood, which you will find in no other country. Here individuals of all nations are melted into a new race of men, whose labors and posterity will one day cause great changes in the world."[4]

An equally articulate view of how the social construction of race and perceptions of American nationality affected Americans with African ancestry was advanced by W. E. Burghardt Du Bois in 1903 in *The Souls of Black Folk.* In sharp contrast to Crevecoeur, Du Bois included Americans with African ancestry in the American cultural circle, but expressed frustration with the fact that blacks had "a double-consciousness, this sense of measuring one's soul by the tape of a world that looks on in amused contempt and pity."[5] Unlike an American with European ancestry, an American with African ancestry was believed by Du Bois to feel "his twoness—an American, a Negro; two souls, two thoughts, two unreconciled strivings; two warring ideals in one dark body, whose dogged strength alone keeps it from being torn asunder."[6] These contradictions were not desired by blacks.

The Myth of Separate Black and White Cultures

Contemporary debates on the centrality of Western values in American culture clearly indicate a struggle between old and new definitions of what makes up American culture, with most advocates of new definitions stressing the need to include non-European contributions. Yet the refusal of many Americans of European ancestry to accept other Americans as full and equal citizens sharing a common culture initially contributed to a reluctance among many non-European Americans to embrace a common American culture. Ironically, the emphasis on black culture, for example, only sharpened the polarization of black-white perceptions and relationships. Being culturally black required both participation in antiwhite activism and the denigration of white society and what are seen to be white values.[7] Nonetheless, there is a major shift away from equating race with culture. The changing American culture is characterized by greater recognition and inclusion of the divergent but integral components of American society.

Because cultural differences, or perceptions of differences, are essential to keeping individuals within separate groups, the social construction of race depends on widespread acceptance by both blacks and whites of two distinct, separate, and incompatible cultures. An indication of the changing nature of American culture is the growing willingness to recognize that the belief in the existence of separate black and white cultures is as much a myth as is the idea of pure races. Since the first twenty Africans arrived at the Jamestown settlement in Virginia in 1619 as indentured servants, blacks and whites have been intimately involved in creating a common American culture. What it means to be black and what it means to be white are inextricably linked in a symbiotic relationship. One does not exist apart from the other.

For more than 375 years, blacks and whites have fashioned their common culture. The institution of slavery could not have existed without the daily interaction of slaves and slaveholders. C. Vann Woodward believes that "the supervision, maintenance of order, and physical and medical care of slaves necessitated many contacts and encouraged a degree of intimacy between the races unequaled, and often held distasteful, in other parts of the country. The system imposed its own type of interracial contact."[8] Both groups influenced each other in profound ways on a daily basis. Europeans and Africans together created a unique culture that is distinct from European as well as African culture. Europeans made Africans into Americans and Africans made Europeans into Americans. Influence flowed in both directions, as it does in any intimate relationship.

Many outstanding characteristics of American culture are products of black and white interaction. Slavery and freedom, the Declaration of Independence and the Constitution, the concepts of whiteness and blackness, the Civil War, the American preoccupation with race, music and art, agriculture and industrial production, education, and religion all are shaped to greater or lesser degrees by relations between blacks and whites. Black feminists such as Sojourner Truth, Ida Wells-Barnett, and Fannie Lou Hammer played critical roles in the advancement of women's rights; Sojourner Truth, in particular, was a prominent leader who helped shape the feminist agenda in the 1800s.[9] There is virtually no aspect of American culture that has not been affected by race, directly or indirectly. Contacts between whites and blacks in all areas of American life make the idea of separate black and white cultures an obvious fallacy.

Differences exist between individuals and groups within any culture. In England, Oxford likes to distinguish itself from Cambridge. Yale is certainly not the same as Harvard. The states of California and Illinois have never been thought to share the exact same culture. Variations among whites are as real as variations among blacks, with many blacks and whites having more in common with each other than with individuals who happen to share their skin color. Regional differences are often more pronounced than purely racial differences. Blacks and whites in the South are in many ways different from blacks and whites in the North. The Italian section of Boston could hardly be mistaken for South Boston, where many Americans of Irish descent live. Religious fundamentalists, black and white, are not the same as Episcopalians, whether the latter are black or white. Differences clearly exist among Americans, but these variations do not exclude the existence of a shared common American culture.

Both whites and blacks share a common African heritage, which has become an integral part of American culture. Many aspects of what is regarded as white culture are influenced by African culture. Various ethnic groups in Africa had developed expertise in the areas of wood carving, weaving, and forging metals. These skills were transferred to America with enslaved Africans, who constructed many of the antebellum mansions in Charleston, Mobile, and New Orleans, embellishing them with decorative handwrought grilles and balconies.[10] The workmanship of these mansions illustrates the fusion of European and African culture that became American culture.

African culinary influences also are amply evident in America. Jambalaya, gumbo, and other popular New Orleans dishes exemplify the fusion of African and American cultures. Okra, a crop native to West and Central Africa, is an important part of southern cuisine for both blacks and whites. Sorghum, black-eyed peas, and other crops from Africa became important agricultural products in America. Just as Europeans helped to shape Africans' cooking abilities, Africans also influenced European cooking.[11] With regard to American folklore, members of ethnic groups such as the Wolof of Senegal and the Hausa and Fulani of Nigeria who came to America as slaves brought stories about Brer Rabbit, Brer Wolf, Brer Fox, and Sis' Nanny Goat with them. These stories, like other stories from Europe, are interwoven in the fabric of American culture.[12]

This symbiosis of African and European culture is evident in jazz, the quintessential and universally recognized American music. Although jazz developed as a distinct musical genre around the end of the nineteenth century in the southern United States, its origins can be traced back to both Europe and Africa. Jazz combines many musical and nonmusical, religious and secular traditions that were connected to the institution of slavery. Black work songs, field shouts, dirges, hymns, spirituals, and simple melodies that were predominantly African in origin combined to form jazz.[13] When adopted by white orchestras and bandleaders such as Benny Goodman in the late 1930s, jazz was embraced as legitimate entertainment. Ragtime, which is part of the jazz tradition, also illustrates the blending of European and African influences. Scott Joplin's success was derived in part from his ability to combine aspects of European music with African music.

Rock and roll, which emerged in the 1940s from a combination of rhythm and blues, country music, and jazz, is regarded throughout the world as American music and not just as African-American music. Despite efforts to segregate blacks and whites, technological developments facilitated communication between them. The radio made rhythm and blues records accessible to most Americans. Commercial radio stations could profit only by playing music potential customers wanted to hear. Parents could not effectively monitor what their children listened to on the radio.

The trend toward eliminating racial barriers in music was strengthened by the growth of countrywide competitive television networks. By 1956, music performed by Americans with African ancestry was now available to all Americans. Many musicians of European ancestry borrowed generously from black American music. For example, Elvis Presley's commercial breakthrough in 1956 came with the song "Hound Dog," which had been released three years earlier by the blues singer Willie Mae Thornton.[14] Elvis brought together different elements of American culture.

Evidence of the changing American culture is also found in the widespread recognition by many Americans of the fusion between traditional black music and contemporary country music. In a 1996 television documentary, simply titled "American Music: The Roots of Country," country and western legends proclaimed their debt to black music. Brenda Lee, for example, credited black gospel music as her source of inspiration for a country music career. Hank Williams Jr. believed that country music was inseparable from the blues. Johnny Cash credited what was called "race music," especially black gospel and blues, for helping him write "Blue River" and other popular songs. All of these musicians benefited from the close proximity of blacks and whites in many rural areas of the South.[15]

Increasingly, Americans with African ancestry, such as Wynton Marsalis and Jesseye Norman, are accepted as Americans who happen to play classical music or sing opera. When Bobby McFerrin conducts the New York Philharmonic at Avery Fisher Hall as well as other orchestras around the country, he is an embodiment of the changing American culture. Similarly, Awadagin Pratt's performance of Grieg's Piano Concerto at the Philharmonic and the fact that he was awarded the Naumburg Prize for classical music represent small but significant changes in race relations in America.[16] The growing recognition that blacks and whites share a common culture is a direct challenge to the social construction of race.

Multiculturalism: A Two-Edged Sword

In sharp contrast to the view that Americans share a common culture, multiculturalism emphasizes the cultural uniqueness of different racial and ethnic groups. But multiculturalism also calls attention to the contributions made by groups that have been deliberately and systematically excluded from full participation in American life. American culture is composed of many cultures, both European and non-European. The social and scientific construction of race inevitably stressed cultural separateness and group identities instead of integration and individual identities. However, major changes in race relations have been occurring since the end of World War II, and mainstream society has itself been altered by numerous and powerful social, economic, technological, and political forces. Although some Americans of European descent still desire to maintain racial segregation, they are a distinct and declining minority.

Multiculturalism that encourages balkanization on the basis of racial group identities seriously impedes the process of racial inclusion. On the other hand, multiculturalism that highlights different historical facts, ideas, and approaches to problems within the framework of a common culture strengthens efforts to move beyond race. Yet the advocacy of multiculturalism as well as the strenuous resistance to it indicate major shifts in American culture.

In a positive sense, multiculturalism represents a pluralistic view of American culture, in which ethnic groups can maintain separate identities but simultaneously embrace common American values. However, American culture also elevates individuals above groups and focuses on the uniqueness of each person. If multiculturalism's objective is to foster respect for members of ethnic groups as individuals, then it is consistent with fundamental American values. Paradoxically, while many Americans of European ancestry complain about multiculturalism's tendency to elevate group identity above individuals, many Americans with African ancestry express frustration at being regarded by white Americans as a group instead of as individuals. The irony is that both groups contribute to what they regard as a problem. Some blacks call for black solidarity and the promotion of African-American culture, thereby consolidating the tendency among many whites to see black individuals as inseparable from the group.

Multiculturalism that promotes separate group identities and discourages individuals from exercising their freedom of association with people from diverse racial and ethnic backgrounds becomes an impediment to getting beyond race. From Amy Gutman's viewpoint, "The survival of many mutually exclusive and disrespecting cultures is not the moral promise of multiculturalism, in politics or in education. Nor is it a realistic vision."[17] Multiculturalism that promotes a greater understanding among Americans of those parts of their history and contemporary society that are generally ignored or not accurately addressed is beneficial to society as a whole.

Although new interpretations of familiar historical accounts are bound to encounter resistance, disagreements that occur within the context of a shared culture can be instrumental in creating the awareness necessary to improve race relations. Multiculturalism that is aimed at getting national recognition of contributions made by non-European Americans and that teaches how to diminish racial discrimination is consistent with building a common national culture and identity. This kind of multiculturalism can help to decrease racial antagonisms among all Americans.

Opposition to multiculturalism as an agent of cultural change emanates partly from a pervasive view that American culture is essentially Western culture. Efforts to include the cultures of Africans, Asians, Native Americans, and others are often perceived to be threatening to American culture. Part of the problem is a narrow view of culture by both advocates and opponents of multiculturalism. Culture is increasingly global in nature, primarily because of revolutionary communications technologies. The worldwide emphasis on Western culture does not have to preclude an appreciation of other cultures. But a multicultural approach that dwells on our differences without calling attention to our similarities creates misunderstanding and greater racial divisions.

Multiculturalism is often perceived as an insistence on ethnicity as identity. Instead of encouraging Americans to move beyond race, this approach embraces race as a source of self-esteem and self-definition. Living with members of one's own racial group and practicing its distinctive culture are regarded as providing a sense of security and comfort.[18] From this viewpoint, multiculturalism carries the dangerous potential of further dividing American society and weakening a shared American culture. Moreover, multiculturalism is believed to be an instrument of intimidation, a tool for limiting discussion of controversial issues, and an attempt to rewrite history. As Richard Bernstein puts it, multiculturalism "sanctions a cultivation of aggrievement, a constant claim of victimization, an excessive, fussy, self-pitying sort of wariness that induces others to spout pieties."[19]

Divergent views of multiculturalism reflect its potential to further polarize different racial groups as well as its ability to increase understanding, tolerance, and respect for others who are perceived to be outside mainstream culture. Given the centrality of culture to racial divisions, multicultural debates seem almost inevitable. But although proponents and opponents of multiculturalism project a perception of irreconcilable differences among various ethnic groups, the reality is that blacks, whites, Asians, Latinos, and others are being assimilated into American culture even as they wrestle to find their positions in it.

The Family as an Agent of Change

A consistent theme in almost all the interviews conducted for this book was the family's pivotal role in shaping racial attitudes and behavior. This is largely because the family is the first and usually the most important agent in the enculturation process. Individuals internalize cultural values, beliefs, feelings, and attitudes that are prevalent in their immediate environments. In most cases, they attempt to construct identities that are consistent with parental values.[20] But many children adopt values that are inconsistent with those of their parents. In other cases, parents' verbal messages may contradict their own behavior. For example, a father in Montana whose own views were prejudiced against non-Europeans insisted that his children treat his Mexican farm workers decently. His daughter, Mary, focused on the latter, more tolerant image of her father and downplayed the former.[21] The process of enculturation is complex; it is difficult to generalize about how families influence their children's racial attitudes and behavior. Nevertheless, the family is an essential part of the bottom-up approach to getting beyond race.

Contrary to the general view of blacks and whites as monolithic groups, each family wrestles with the question of how to relate to people of different races. Although racial discrimination has always been an integral component of American society, it competes with values that are opposed to racial prejudice. In other words, many of the values passed on by parents to their children directly challenge racism. Marilyn Boyd, for example, grew up in a family in which both parents taught values and engaged in practices that fostered open and tolerant racial attitudes and behavior. Her father, a rancher's son from Idaho who moved to Olathe, Kansas, embraced the American belief that one should succeed on the basis of one's talents and should be judged as an individual. He told his children positive stories about Native Americans, and in the 1950s sponsored an Indian friend for membership in the Episcopal Church.

Marilyn's mother, who was raised in Minnesota and was a schoolteacher, also believed in and taught racial tolerance. Both parents were "Roosevelt Democrats" who were strongly committed to social justice and were opposed to racism in any form. Marilyn embraced these values. She later supported open housing laws in Illinois, worked at a black orphanage (which her children visited several times a week), and now directs an international program at a major midwestern university. Her daughter became a Peace Corps volunteer in the Central African Republic and has worked with American children in disadvantaged urban areas.[22] Values acquired from Marilyn's parents have been passed on by Marilyn's daughter to others around her.

Sheila Welch, an author of children's books who grew up in the Pennsylvania Dutch region in the 1950s, had similar experiences. Sheila's grandparents disagreed on racial issues. In contrast to her grandfather, who had once saved a black child's life, her grandmother would cross the street to avoid walking next to a black person. Sheila's parents, who lived a few houses away from a black family in a rural area, strongly discouraged the use of racial slurs. Sheila, who is white, made friends with her black neighbors; they played at each others' homes and put on summer shows together, with the support of their parents. When an insurance agent visited Sheila's home to inquire about the neighbors, he asked if they were "colored." Sheila's mother replied that she didn't really know or care but that they were the best neighbors they had ever had.[23] These childhood experiences undoubtedly played a role in Sheila's decision to adopt six children with African ancestry, thereby directly contributing to efforts to get beyond race.

Families who faced prejudice or other disadvantages themselves seem to empathize with people from different racial and ethnic backgrounds. Kelly Keogh, a high school social studies teacher, recalled his experiences as an Irish Catholic in Protestant Nashville, Tennessee, in the 1960s. Aware of his own minority status, he has always been sensitive to the plight of other minorities. His father, who felt that he was treated unjustly because of his religion, stressed the importance of building bridges to people of different races. Kelly's parents were close friends with a black family who gave Kelly his first job and who became a second family to him.[24]

Similarly, Arthur C. Sanders III, member of the Urban Bankers Forum of Chicago, credited his parents for helping him to deal effectively with people from different racial and ethnic backgrounds. An American with African ancestry, Arthur was raised in an environment that brought him into close contact with many different people. His father, a medical doctor, and his mother, the head reference librarian at a major university, taught him to appreciate different viewpoints. He says, "I was constantly encouraged (admonished, really!) to keep an open mind to differences."[25]

Teaching by example is facilitated by living in racially mixed neighborhoods. Patricia Fowler strongly believes that her parents' close relationships with non-European Americans during World War II enabled them to realize that there are "good people" and "bad people" of all races and that being white does not necessarily make a person "good." Consequently, they raised Patricia in an environment in which she learned to judge people for who they are.[26]

Jane Liedtke also emphasizes that her family's interaction with diverse groups of people laid the foundation for her own close relationships with people of different races and ethnic groups. Jane's grandparents were German immigrants who worked as sharecroppers their entire lives. They had no wealth and no more than a high school education. Her father, who never even attended high school because his parents died young and he had to earn a living, taught Jane to be kind to others. Her mother was a postmaster and had an ethnically diverse workforce. Jane grew up among black children in the 1960s. Her parents never expressed prejudice. Jane, now a professor, has an interracial family.[27]

Family members' personal experiences with prejudice also help to shape relations with individuals from different racial backgrounds. Angela Dreessen, a senior at a major midwestern university, recalls how her mother, who grew up in Peoria, Illinois, encouraged others to adopt a nonracial approach because of her own formative experience. During a brief stay in Mississippi in 1963, her mother, who is white, walked over to the "colored" side of the segregated train station. Whites in the train station made derogatory comments and stared rudely at her because she had crossed the racial boundary. Shaken by what happened, she vowed to raise her three children not to be racist. Two of them have had interracial relationships; Angela was the first white woman to join a black sorority at her university.[28]

But not all families share these views on race relations. Some parents are prejudiced, yet believe that each person should be treated as an individual. In many cases, one parent is prejudiced and the other favors racial harmony. Children in such families more often than not seem to adopt the values of the racially tolerant parent, especially if they have positive experiences with people from the out-group. Donna Richter, for example, was convinced that her father's negative perceptions of black people were wrong when, as a nine-year-old, she was introduced to a black missionary from Africa who was visiting her church.[29] On the other hand, unprejudiced people may become prejudiced if their encounters with members of another race have been negative.

Ruth Fisher, an editor who lives in New York, believes that she could have gone either way in terms of racial attitudes. Whereas Ruth's father was prejudiced, Ruth's mother had acquired egalitarian attitudes from her own father. Ruth describes her grandfather as a man with an eighth-grade education who was a voracious reader. He was a coal miner in Colorado during World War I and worked with blacks and Mexicans. Ruth states: "Skin color mattered little to him. Why should it? He spent the larger part of his day black and his hands were tattooed by the coal he mined." Ruth taught her own children to practice her grandfather's egalitarianism. Her daughter, a graduate of Harvard Law School, rejected lucrative job offers and instead went to work on an Indian reservation. Ruth lives in a racially integrated neighborhood and has friends from many different backgrounds.[30]

Many Americans from small towns and urban areas that are not racially diverse acquire tolerant values in other ways. Some observe or experience class-based discrimination and are able to see people as individuals who should be judged by their behavior. In towns with little or no racial diversity, many parents teach their children religious beliefs and American ideals that support equality. Linda Giles, for example, talked about such an environment. She pointed out that her parents had exposed her to children's books and educational materials about people from various cultural backgrounds. When she encountered prejudice during her junior year in high school, she found it contrary to her upbringing and rejected it. She is now a professor of cultural anthropology and works with students from all races.[31]

Interpersonal Contacts

An underlying assumption of segregationists was that essential aspects of American race relations would undergo fundamental change if blacks, whites, Latinos, Asians, and others freely interacted as individual members of society. Extensive contacts between members of various racial categories are evident throughout the United States, a development that not only underscores significant changes in American culture but also indicates that these contacts will increase and deepen in the future. If preventing interpersonal contacts strengthened racism, increased interaction among blacks, whites, Latinos, and Asians contributes to eliminating old racial boundaries as well as to eroding the premises upon which race is socially constructed.

Intimate and personal relations have always played a decisive role in human affairs. President Harry Truman's connections with Jews, for example, were crucial in the U.S. decision to recognize the new state of Israel. Close personal relations between blacks and whites during slavery were instrumental in obtaining freedom for slaves in some cases and may have helped weaken the institution of slavery. Friendships among ordinary individuals, given the openness of America's democratic society, gradually undermine racial boundaries.[32]

Gordon Allport, in *The Nature of Prejudice,* articulated the view that prejudice may be reduced by equal-status contact between majority and minority groups in pursuit of common goals. He believed that social norms, laws, institutional supports, and environments that engender trust, respect, and friendship were essential to this endeavor.[33] Eventually, close contacts often give rise to the realization that individuals from socially constructed categories share a common humanity and the same basic human needs.

Extended intimate contact encourages the development of empathy: the ability to feel another's suffering and to put oneself in another's shoes. Contact characterized by ongoing cooperative activities often promotes improved interpersonal communication and attraction, trust, greater feelings of similarity, and a growing tendency to help one another. In their "robbers cave" experiment, Muzafer Sherif and his colleagues found that noncompetitive cooperative activities and functional interdependence encourage members of two or more groups to develop positive reciprocal attitudes.[34]

Extensive positive interaction among individuals from various racial categories often leads to perceptions of individuals as unique human beings. The more contacts that blacks, whites, Latinos, and Asians have with each other in a range of different circumstances, the greater the chances are that they will make distinctions among individuals who belong to a racial group. In other words, at first they will not automatically see individuals as members of a racial group but as persons with unique attributes. This personalized interaction influences individuals to focus on specific information about each other instead of using category identity to determine the character of their interactions.[35]

But negative experiences that emanate from contacts with members of another racial group usually serve to strengthen stereotypes of the entire group. Victims of crime, for example, generally regard any member of the victimizer's racial category as a potential criminal. Significant departures from universal virtues and American values often elicit responses that do not contribute to efforts to get beyond race. Jonathan Rieder documents how the Jews and Italians of Canarsie in Brooklyn responded to what they regarded as antisocial behavior by Americans with African ancestry. Many whites in Canarsie perceived black street slang as a sign of blacks' refusal to observe the most basic proprieties. Instead of being drawn closer to blacks, whites became more negative toward them. Many Jews and Italians had themselves encountered prejudice and had worked hard to improve their lives. Rieder contends that the legendary sacrifices of Jewish and Italian immigrants nourished contempt for poor blacks, who seemed unwilling to work hard to succeed.[36]

In general, however, Americans have become more tolerant of each other as contacts have increased. There is more socializing among members of different races than at any other time in American history. An argument frequently heard is that whites and blacks go their separate ways after being together at work. But this limited social interaction between blacks and whites after work, when placed in a broader societal context, does not appear to be exceptional. Most Americans describe their lives as busy and few seem to have time for friends and neighbors, black or white. Furthermore, automatic garage door openers, televisions, and computers have induced Americans to become even more isolated from each other. Nevertheless, approximately 68 percent of Americans live in at least partially integrated neighborhoods, and 66 percent of whites have black friends, compared to 80 percent of blacks who have white friends.[37] These personal contacts play a much greater role in helping move the country beyond race than is generally acknowledged. Consistent with the bottom-up approach to race relations is the view that each individual's behavior can either improve or set back race relations.

Personal contacts with members of different races had a profound impact on Martin Luther King Jr., Jimmy Carter, and Bill Clinton. They, in turn, moved the country closer to its ideal of being a color-blind society, thereby dramatically changing American culture. Martin Luther King had a white playmate from when he was three years old to about age six. However, the friendship was terminated by the white boy's father. When King was informed by his playmate that their relationship had to end, he discussed the problem with his parents and first became aware of racism. King stated: "I did not conquer this anti-white feeling until I entered college and came in contact with white students through working in interracial organizations."[38]

Jimmy Carter was raised in the predominantly black town of Archery, Georgia. Carter's playmates and best friends were black. They worked in the fields together and played like all normal children. Black parents had complete authority over Carter when he was in their home. Due to the work schedule of his mother, Lillian Carter, who was a registered nurse, Carter was raised by Annie Mae Jones and other black women. They cooked for the Carter family, saw the children off to school, and met them when school ended. These contacts influenced Carter's later life, including his decision not to join the White Citizens Council in Plains, Georgia, even though he was threatened with a boycott of the family peanut business.[39]

Bill Clinton, both as a young man and as president, has demonstrated how influential early contacts with blacks have been on his life and subsequently on his formulation of national policy. When Clinton's father died, his mother moved to New Orleans to pursue a degree in nursing, leaving her one-year-old son with his grandparents, Eldridge and Edith Cassidy. The Cassidys taught Clinton to respect people of all races. His daily contacts with blacks enabled him to develop strong personal relationships with them. These contacts continued throughout his life. While attending Georgetown University, Clinton volunteered to work for the Red Cross in inner-city Washington following Martin Luther King's assassination. This assignment was dangerous enough to force Clinton to wear gloves, a hat, and a scarf to conceal his skin color.[40]

Ordinary Americans have also stressed the importance of personal contacts in their attempts to move beyond race. Some have cited attending parties with people of different races, driving a school bus, meeting teachers and students of different races, playing golf in mixed-race groups, volunteering in the inner city and on projects such as Habitat for Humanity, and attending workshops. When asked what experiences had helped her improve relations with people from various racial backgrounds, Denise Beurskens, who is white, emphasized interpersonal contact—getting to know people on a personal basis. She believes that her personal contacts reduced her reliance on stereotypes in assessing people of different racial backgrounds. She states: "I was able to better understand that there were as many differences among blacks as there are among whites. The more experiences one has with people of different races and cultures, the more comfortable one feels with the relationship. One can then judge whether one likes or dislikes a particular person based on the human characteristics of that individual, rather than his or her racial identity."[41]

Diana McCauley, who is black, also noted that her personal interactions with whites from elementary school through graduate study enable her to get along with people from diverse backgrounds. Both social and professional interactions helped enhance her relations with and understanding of people from various racial groups.[42] Diana is the president of a predominantly white school board in Illinois. Finally, Don Bernaducci credits living in lower-income apartments as a child for helping him to develop racial tolerance. Having played with black children, he is easily comfortable with black adults as well. Bernaducci had a black college roommate, whom he describes as a "wonderfully kind and intelligent human being."[43]

Fraternizing at College

With the exception of the military, college campuses provide the most numerous opportunities for students to develop interpersonal contacts and to transform those contacts into lifelong relationships. Colleges, universities, and other institutions of higher education bring together students from diverse backgrounds, many of whom had never interacted with individuals of other races prior to arriving on campus. They are away from home, many for the first time, in an environment that is designed to encourage risk taking and open-mindedness. They often find their ideas clashing with different perspectives. Most college freshmen are like new recruits in the military: They have to learn many new things just to survive on campus. It is therefore relatively easy for them to make contact with members of different races who are either students themselves or members of the faculty and staff. Colleges bring students into situations where cooperation is required. They room together, visit each other's homes, eat in the same cafeterias every day, participate in study groups, study on the same floor of the library, play sports together, and engage in many of the same extracurricular activities.

Colleges and universities, as microcosms of the larger society, are inevitably arenas of conflict as students adjust to the new realities of living with people from diverse backgrounds. Students, whether in America or China, are in the forefront of social change. Some students form coalitions based on their personal interests, and many of these coalitions are multiracial. In the process of coping with different perspectives, they learn how to negotiate, how to resolve conflicts. Students also learn about racial issues from each other and their professors as they engage in intellectual discussions.

Kelly Keogh, for example, believes that one of the most beneficial experiences he had in terms of improving his view toward different racial groups was the opportunity to study historical and sociological relations between races. The idea of judging someone based on the content of that person's character became paramount in his outlook.[44] This view is consistent with the finding that education diminishes prejudice. The liberalizing effects of education are demonstrated by the tendency of educated people to embrace fewer negative racial stereotypes than those with less formal education.

College professors, especially those who participated in the civil rights movement of the 1960s, tend to make an effort to expose students to new perspectives. Many professors bring to the campus values that they practice in their own lives. Eric Welch, an American of European ancestry who adopted six children with African ancestry, exemplifies the tendency to connect life in the ivory tower to life in the real world. He tries, when teaching college orientation classes, to make students aware of what stereotyping means and how it affects each of them. He also attempts to teach himself and his children that individuals need to treat others as individuals and to avoid speaking of "them or they" but rather of "him or her" so that characteristics are assigned to individuals rather than groups.[45]

Students are often required to take multicultural or other courses that integrate diverse perspectives on various issues. Linaya Leaf, a professor at Rocky Mountain College in Montana, discusses how the college curriculum has been revised to include multicultural courses. Interdependence of knowledge is now part of the college's mission statement. All incoming freshmen read a multicultural text before arriving on campus and then spend the first week of orientation discussing these issues.[46]

But the most important interpersonal contacts and learning occur beyond the classroom. Jim Pruyne recalls how he shared a college room with a Mexican-American student at Grinnell College in Iowa in the early 1950s. In 1957, he took a group of white students from a large midwestern university to Westpoint, Mississippi. They were the first group of whites to work with blacks in Westpoint since Reconstruction. In 1962, he took another group of white students to Savannah, Georgia, to help organize voter registration. These students stayed at black Americans' homes while in Savannah. Pruyne worked closely with Donald McHenry, who was then a college student, to integrate on-campus as well as off-campus housing.[47] McHenry later became the U.S. ambassador to the United Nations during the Carter administration.

Universities such as Notre Dame, Stanford, Yale, and Harvard encourage their students to participate in programs that serve minority communities. At Yale, for example, Richard C. Levine, the university's president, created the President's Public Service Fellowship, a multiracial program designed to help alleviate some of the problems in New Haven's poorest neighborhoods.[48] Many college students serve as mentors and tutors for disadvantaged children.

Many students are made aware of racial discrimination for the first time in college. Susan Smith, who is white, grew up in Nashville and had early contact with Sarah, a black woman who worked in her home once a week. Although Susan developed a close relationship with Sarah, it was not until graduate school that she moved beyond her otherwise racially segregated world to interact with black students as an equal. She learned from a black student that although he could check out books at the public library, he could not sit at a table there. She was obviously surprised by the extent and pervasiveness of racial discrimination. She later taught at a predominantly black college for seven years and got to know students and professors on a personal level.[49]

Similarly, Linda Giles, who is white, believes that college provided numerous experiences that helped shape her feelings and behavior in relation to race. Through joining the International Student Association on campus, tutoring grade school children in the inner city, and working in the university cafeteria, Linda made significant and long-lasting contacts with students and others from diverse backgrounds. Having been involved in many student political and civil rights activities in the 1960s, she became sensitized to and angry about the prejudice and hardships that blacks faced. These experiences motivated her to participate in the March on Washington in 1963. She also spent a year in Volunteers in Service to America (VISTA) working with low-income white, black, and Latino communities in the south Chicago suburbs.[50]

Despite many positive interactions among students from various racial backgrounds, there is widespread concern about balkanization along racial and ethnic lines on many college campuses. White students complain about the tendency of black students to segregate themselves in cafeterias and elsewhere. Many racial minorities feel that white students create an unfriendly atmosphere on campus. In an attempt to feel safe, many minorities have persuaded colleges and universities to create separate "theme houses" for their own specific groups. At the University of California at Berkeley, where white students are now a minority, Asian, Latino, and black students have their own separate dormitories. This is also true of Stanford, Cornell, Wesleyan, Brown, and other universities.

In caving in to pressure from students who favor racial segregation, colleges and universities have diminished their chances to help move American society beyond race. Many black, Latino, and Asian students often overlook the facts that colleges belong to the students who attend them and that learning is not a safe, risk-free enterprise. It is through living with people from different backgrounds and confronting their feelings that students obtain an education in the broader sense, one that will enable them to skillfully navigate an increasingly racially diverse America.

Balkanization on campuses, the training ground for America's leaders, contributes to perpetuating segregation in society. During the period when racial minorities favored integration and many whites did not, college campuses were instrumental in forcing society to become more tolerant and humane. Friendships across racial lines, which are essential to getting beyond race, can only materialize through interaction. People are usually not changed by statistics; they are changed by interpersonal relations.

The Media and Cultural Change

Leaders in France, Canada, Australia, and many other countries have voiced fears concerning the power of the American media in their own cultures and societies. Even as many groups around the world are newly assertive of their ethnic and racial identities, cultural boundaries are crumbling in significant ways. It could be argued that asserting ethnic and racial identity is a manifestation of cultural insecurity, brought on by the growing standardization of cultures within countries as well as by the globalization of American culture. Images of race relations in general, and of blacks and whites in particular, that are created or reported by the media influence perceptions of different racial groups not only in America but also abroad. It is therefore of great importance to examine the media's role in America's changing culture in relation to race.

It was evident during the civil rights movement that the media were central players in race relations. Police brutality was shown by the media to an astonished nation. These pictures fundamentally altered many Americans' perceptions of racial discrimination and helped to hasten passage of long-delayed civil rights legislation to guarantee all Americans the promise of equal rights. The media have made incidents of racial hostility public and have, on the whole, made Americans more aware of racial inequality and its consequences.

But the widespread belief is that the media are, for the most part, too eager to concentrate on the most negative aspects of race relations. Radio, television, and newspapers are replete with negative images of America's racial minorities, especially Americans with African ancestry. Blacks are portrayed as dependent, lazy, self-destructive, and antagonistic toward other Americans. Welfare mothers, pregnant teenagers, and violent young black men are characterized as representative of the black community. In truth, many of these negative images accurately represent a pervasive reality of American life for all races, not just for blacks. Separating blacks from the larger society and reporting on them without providing the broader context conveys the message that blacks are symbolic of welfare dependency, teenage pregnancy, crime, and hatred. Many of these negative images are reinforced by prominent black Americans who also dwell on the worst aspects of their communities while neglecting to direct attention to the majority of blacks who work hard; who are successful, honest, and law-abiding; who get along with people from different racial backgrounds; who pay taxes; and who die for their country.

Yet the media have also brought many examples of racial cooperation to the viewing public. Although Stanley Crouch has argued that the press is insensitive and that many reporters do not understand very much about their country,[51] what is often overlooked is that the media also report on the activities of Jesse Jackson's Rainbow Coalition and the willingness of whites in Iowa, Wisconsin, Arizona, and across the nation to work with blacks, Latinos, and Asians to achieve various economic and social objectives. The media are instrumental in drawing attention to issues that concern many black Americans by inviting black intellectuals and others to write articles or appear on television and radio programs.

Many of these intellectuals are regarded by the media to be the representatives of the black community, which is often viewed as monolithic. The reality is that the black community is diverse. Furthermore, the lives of many black intellectuals are far removed from those of ordinary Americans, regardless of skin color. A law student at an Ivy League university who was raised in a small midwestern city was somewhat surprised to learn from a leading black intellectual that as an American of European ancestry she was closely associated with "the man," or the white power structure. From her perspective, this leading Ivy League professor was "the man," regardless of skin color.

Radio, television, and newspapers have heightened awareness of race as one of the most important issues facing Americans. To some extent, the media have been responsible for making people think about ways in which they can help diminish racial tensions. However, frequent reports of racial hostility discourage those who hope to build coalitions similar to those that effectively fought for civil rights during the 1950s and 1960s. According to public opinion polls, both blacks and whites believe that the media are largely responsible for making race relations seem worse than they are. In a *New York Times* poll conducted in 1990, 55 percent of blacks and 55 percent of whites agreed that newspapers and television news programs have been detrimental to race relations.[52]

This perception is confirmed by interviewees, most of whom see the media as reinforcing racial stereotypes. They say that music videos, popular music in general, special television programs, news broadcasts, and newspapers do not reflect the reality around them. Incidents of racial conflict and controversial individuals and groups receive too much coverage, especially when racial issues are seen within the broader context of significantly improved race relations over the past thirty years.

Television programs such as *The Cosby Show, Law and Order, ER,* and *Touched by an Angel* are generally regarded as examples of how the media are changing American culture in positive ways. *The Cosby Show* highlights black middle-class life without making race an issue. Instead, issues of individual character and universal human values are emphasized. In *Law and Order,* a Latino detective and his white partner report to an African-American woman. Teams of black and white doctors, nurses, and technicians cooperate to save lives on *ER. Touched by an Angel* features three spirits—a feisty middle-aged black angel and two gentle young white angels—working together to save souls. In sharp contrast to most television programs, which do not have racially mixed casts or audiences, *ER, The Cosby Show, Touched by an Angel,* and *Law and Order* are among the favorite programs of both black and white audiences.[53]

Movies such as *To Sir with Love* and *Guess Who's Coming to Dinner* (both 1967) not only marked a breakthrough for blacks in film but also tackled some of America's strictest taboos. The subsequent progress made by blacks in the movie industry has helped to change some of the more negative images of blacks. In 1995, it was clear that there had been a significant transformation in the film industry. Black actors and actresses are no longer marginalized in all-black films; they are playing leading roles in mainstream movies. In 1995, blacks had prominent roles in only 24 percent of the summer's thirty-eight major films. By 1996, blacks played leading parts in 45 percent of the summer's forty-two major movies. Six of the most financially successful movies that year featured black stars. Actors and actresses such as Denzel Washington, Samuel L. Jackson, Whoopi Goldberg, and Whitney Houston are increasingly playing color-blind roles in mainstream films.[54] Black influence on the evolution of American culture is evidenced by the fact that while Jesse Jackson and others were picketing the 1996 Academy Awards, claiming that there was not enough black representation in the movie industry, black performers like Whoopi Goldberg, Vanessa Williams, and Kareem Abdul-Jabbar were participating in the Oscars program and Quincy Jones, an American with African ancestry, was producing and directing it.

Despite continuing problems, the media play a significant role in changing American culture in regard to race relations. Although newspapers and television are criticized for not hiring more racial minorities, progress has been made. However, focusing on the negative aspects of race relations and portraying the most negative images of racial minorities on television and in newspapers are widely regarded as detrimental to efforts to build bridges among racial groups. But in the process of concentrating on the media's failures, the positive contributions of the media are often downplayed or ignored.

Religion and Cultural Change

Religion, which has always been at the heart of American culture, has been used to justify segregation and enslavement on the one hand and to advocate the recognition of a common humanity and freedom for all Americans on the other. Among the most outspoken opponents of slavery were the Quakers, who eventually found it difficult to reconcile slavery with their Christian faith. In 1774, on the rising tide of the American Revolution, the Pennsylvania–New Jersey Friends (Quakers) decreed that disownment (or banishment from the community) would be the penalty for selling or transferring slaves for any reason but to set them free.[55] The influx of indentured servants into Pennsylvania, many of them impoverished immigrants of German origin, undoubtedly made the Quakers' abolitionist work easier. On arrival in Philadelphia, many of the immigrants "were sold off as so much cattle, or blacks. At times for the lack of money parents had to sell their children."[56] But the Quakers' commitment to abolishing slavery and the concept of a common humanity was evidenced by their willingness to teach former slaves to read and write and to help them establish themselves as free people. However, it was not common for Quakers to fully embrace blacks as equals, despite the 1796 decision of the Philadelphia Yearly Meeting to "entertain applications for membership without distinction of color."[57]

Churches, many of which were in the forefront of the civil rights movement in the 1960s, are now both conforming to significant changes in race relations and attempting to unite different racial groups around common interests and a common humanity. The greatest changes have occurred in many white Southern Baptist churches, precisely because of their long resistance to racial integration. Since the early 1990s, religious conservatives have called for racial reconciliation, a sharp departure from their staunch opposition to racial healing.

Ralph Reed, the former leader of the conservative Christian Coalition, argues that white evangelical churches carry a shameful legacy of racism, and he advocates a repudiation of racism and bigotry "in all its ugly forms."[58] More than 130 years after President Abraham Lincoln signed the Emancipation Proclamation, the Southern Baptist Convention proclaimed that slavery is sinful and asked forgiveness from blacks for its historic role in defending segregation and discrimination. To show their sincerity, at a 1994 meeting in Memphis, a coalition of twenty-one white Pentecostal groups decided to unite with black coreligionists and held a foot-washing ceremony, with whites and blacks washing each others' feet.[59]

One of the principal reasons for religious opposition to racial discrimination is political pragmatism. Racism is becoming more of a liability than an asset for many national religious organizations. Given the country's general repudiation of racism, in theory if not always in practice, groups such as the Christian Coalition, which hope to influence the political process by seizing the moral high ground on issues such as abortion and out-of-wedlock births, lose both their credibility and their effectiveness if they are believed to support racism. Furthermore, there is now greater recognition of diversity within the black community. Increased interpersonal contacts between white and black Christian conservatives reduce the tendency to look at blacks as a monolithic group. Moreover, alliances with conservative blacks like Clarence Thomas, Alan Keyes, and Representative J. C. Watts are seen as helpful to the Christian Coalition's social and political agenda.

Churches in the South and elsewhere are providing the leadership essential to moving the country beyond race. But many Americans still believe that churches are among America's most segregated institutions. An extreme and atypical example of this segregation is the attempt by the Barnetts Creek Baptist Church in Thomasville, Georgia, to disinter the body of a mixed-race baby who was buried in the church's all-white cemetery.[60] Yet many churches are striving to become more racially integrated, and there is ample evidence of change.

Examples of majority white churches that are not only racially integrated but are led by blacks are the United Methodist Churches in Charlotte, North Carolina; Birmingham, Alabama; Augusta and Columbus, Georgia; and Greenville and Clemson, South Carolina. Black priests preside over Roman Catholic parishes in Atlanta and in Boone and Hickory, North Carolina. Black pastors also lead predominantly white congregations in the Evangelical Assembly of God in Chicago; the First Baptist Church of Vacaville, California; and the Riverside Church in Manhattan.[61] In many churches throughout the country, blacks and whites worship together, despite the general perception of racial segregation in churches.

Catholic churches and schools have brought individuals from different racial backgrounds into situations where mutual respect and racial tolerance are expected. Some interviewees stressed how their Catholic upbringing taught them to take seriously the idea of a common humanity and to treat people decently. As Sharon Stanford, who is white, puts it, "I had a Catholic private school background. I believe that God created us all, not favoring one or the other. That is not to say I don't experience negative prejudices. However, intellectually it is very difficult to justify sustained feelings, so you work them out."[62]

Jews, Muslims, Buddhists, and others are also committed to improving race relations. Close cooperation between Jews and blacks has often resulted in meaningful social, political, and economic reforms in the United States. Despite current tension in the black-Jewish alliance, cooperation continues in a less systematic manner and at reduced levels. Individuals who are affected by their religious experiences also become agents of racial change. Patricia Fowler, for example, joined a Buddhist peace organization and was exposed to people from various racial backgrounds. Her interaction with blacks, Asians, and others taught her that "every person has human needs and sorrows. We all feel the same joys and pains, and often have the same experiences."[63] Feelings of similarity engender empathy and facilitate the promotion of efforts to get beyond race.

Personal experiences with people from different racial backgrounds often intersect with religion to give rise to powerful movements that aim to transform society as a whole. The rise of the Promise Keepers is an example of this phenomenon. No religious group has been more explicit and passionate about racial reconciliation than the Promise Keepers, an organization founded by Bill McCartney, a former football coach at the University of Colorado. McCartney worked closely with racial minorities in sports, one of the truly integrated areas of American society. A predominantly male organization, Promise Keepers exhorts men to be more accepting of racial diversity. Promise Keepers actively encourages black, Latino, Asian, and Native American membership.

One of the group's seven guiding principles, or "promises," directly addresses the achievement of ethnic and racial diversity as a major organization objective. Another "promise" is a pledge to "reach beyond any racial and denominational barriers to demonstrate the power of biblical unity."[64] Although the Promise Keepers remains largely a white group, it is succeeding in attracting more racial minorities. Black Americans, for example, are in leadership positions in cities such as Chicago and Dayton. Although the group's exclusion of women and homosexuals raises many questions about the universality of its message, it does manifest positive results in the area of race relations. The passion and enthusiasm one hears from white members of the Promise Keepers underscore a significant shift in racial attitudes and offer hope for the future.

Sports: A Unifying Force

In a country as diverse as the United States, sports play an integrative role and serve as a vehicle of upward mobility. Baseball, for example, has been instrumental in Americanizing immigrants. Since sports embody many cultural values, individuals who participate in them are generally exposed to fundamental American values. The cooperative nature of sports guarantees that members of the team, in order to ensure the team's success, have to trust and protect each other to a large extent. Players on integrated sports teams follow the same rules, thereby developing common values and a shared understanding not only of the game but of the larger society. Sports demonstrate to mainstream Americans that racial cooperation is possible.

It is generally assumed that sports help improve race relations by bringing players from diverse backgrounds into close contact with each other. Although many southern universities had integrated their classrooms by the 1960s, integrating athletic teams took longer, partly because segregationists understood that close contact between the races would foster the development of deep friendships and feelings of equality, thus shattering the myth of racial superiority. Both the 1996 Republican vice presidential candidate Jack Kemp and former Senator Bill Bradley of New Jersey credit sports with bringing them into close contact with blacks and exposing them to the prejudice many of their teammates experienced in even the most mundane human interactions.

Significant changes in race relations in the South are widely believed to be the direct result of school integration in general and the integration of sports specifically, especially football. Greg Knox, an American with African ancestry who coaches football players and is a recruiting coordinator, believes that sports foster harmonious race relations. He points out that "you see so many pictures of black athletes hugging white athletes after a victory, whites consoling blacks after a loss. They hold hands. They see each other as a group, as a unit."[65]

Sports motivate blacks and whites to accept each other on and off the field. The desire to win submerges, and perhaps erodes, negative racial attitudes and unites blacks, Latinos, Asians, whites, and others behind a common objective. As in the military, teams must cooperate to win. It is in the interest of a team and its fans that the athletes encourage and motivate each other by accentuating the positive. Tommy Tuberville, head football coach at the University of Mississippi, argues that "sports is the number one reason that people in the South have started accepting each other, because they're fighting for a common goal: for the university to be successful. If it hadn't been for sports, things would still be 15 to 20 years behind."[66] This close contact encourages athletes to face up to stereotypes as they get to know each other as unique individuals.

Like soldiers, many athletes develop deep social bonds. The coach, like the drill sergeant, becomes the common focus of attention. White and black players often room together partly because coaches group players according to their positions on the team. These intimate experiences, when positive, help destroy prejudice on both sides. Coaches often counsel players on personal matters, acting in many instances as substitute parents. Coaches, as well as coaches' family members who become involved with the team, see the human side of players and often empathize with them as individuals and not just as athletes. Many interpersonal relationships that develop because of sports usually draw in relatives and friends, thereby expanding the number of individuals who are confronted with racial stereotypes—their own as well as those of others.

Sports also promote equality by leveling the playing field and stressing achievement instead of skin color. Playing with talented athletes diverts attention away from skin color to ability, a measure of the individual and not race. Coaches who select players based on racial criteria alone will eventually destroy the team, especially when such selection criteria become obvious to the athletes. The intense competition that characterizes sports influences coaches and others to favor racial equality. Furthermore, the basketball or football programs at major universities such as Georgetown, Minnesota, Ohio State, Southern California, Temple, Arkansas, and Tennessee have black coaches. Blacks in leadership positions help destroy racial stereotypes. Many of these coaches command respect from all races as positive role models.[67]

Finally, sports command a wider societal influence. Outstanding athletes are regarded by Americans of all ages and races as role models and idols. A Gallup poll conducted in October 1993 shows that 94 percent of whites and 92 percent of blacks think that black athletes are very important or somewhat important as role models in the black community.[68] Children of all races have their favorite players, and race does not seem to be a major consideration in which athletes become most popular. Performance and character are what fans of all ages regard as important. Athletes such as Michael Jordan and Earvin "Magic" Johnson are admired across the racial spectrum. Their ubiquitous exposure by advertisers is based on the knowledge that they help sell products because they have transcended racial lines.[69] In other words, although sports cannot eliminate prejudice, they help to move the country toward the goal of getting beyond race.

Generational Replacement and Demographic Change

Generational change is one of the most potent challenges to racial inequality based on the social construction of race. The fact that a majority of Americans in many parts of the country grew up with segregation is bound to influence the overall racial climate. Older Americans exercise considerable power in many of America's institutions, decide who will be hired and promoted, and play a crucial role in shaping public policies. On one hand, their enculturation could be viewed as being conducive to perpetuating the status quo in race relations. On the other hand, many older Americans have seen the scars of racism and have become, if they were not already, active agents of social change.

Older Americans often recognize the superficiality of race and generally have accumulated enough experiences with individuals from different racial backgrounds to realize that skin color does not determine character. Moreover, other factors play a greater role in the lives of these older Americans as they face more pressing personal issues. They are likely to have friends of different races in the workplace and in retirement communities. In other words, they are not immune to the effects of social changes. Influence in race relations, as in other areas of life, flows in more than one direction. Many grandparents and parents learn from their grandchildren and children that race is not always their most important concern, if it is a concern at all. Younger Americans often make close friends across racial lines and then force relatives from an older era to confront their prejudices. Children often help parents gain new perspectives on these issues.

Accompanying generational change is an unmistakable demographic shift that is altering the racial composition of the United States. Such a development can be seen as strengthening minorities vis-à-vis Americans of European descent. But it can also be seen as diminishing the significance attached to skin color. The wide range of colors and outlooks will render race less meaningful. I will discuss these ideas in Chapters 6 and 7.

Data from the Census Bureau show dramatic changes in America's racial and ethnic composition. As blacks, Native Americans, Latinos, and Asians increase in proportion to the total population, the white proportion of the population will obviously decline. By the turn of the century, non-Hispanic whites will make up 71.5 percent of the population, blacks 12.5 percent, Latinos 11 percent, Asians and Pacific islanders 4 percent, and Native Americans 1 percent. By 2050, the non-Hispanic white population is projected to decline to about 52.7 percent; 16 percent of the population will be black, 20.1 percent will be of Hispanic origin, 10 percent will be Asian and Pacific islander, and 1.2 percent will be Native American.[70] America's growing racial and ethnic diversity is leading to increased interpersonal contacts and more complex race relations. Under these new conditions, old concepts such as race are bound to be challenged and will diminish in significance.

In addition to generational replacement and demographic shift, in the years to come more Americans will be better educated. The computerization of society has hastened the dissemination of information and made access to knowledge much easier. These developments are augmenting an ongoing trend. Since 1972, the proportion of adult Americans with under twelve years of education has decreased from 40 percent to 18 percent. The proportion with more than twelve years of education has risen from 28 percent to 50 percent.[71] The implications of these changes are of major importance for race relations. Education tends to promote greater tolerance, understanding, and appreciation of racial diversity. Racial categories are more likely to be questioned, and more individuals are likely to cross racial boundaries and blur the distinctions among various groups.

President Clinton demonstrates how interpersonal contacts with individuals from different racial groups, together with generational change, directly reduce racial tensions and help move the country beyond race. As mentioned earlier, Clinton grew up with blacks. During his second year at Yale Law School he roomed with William Thaddeus Coleman, an American with African ancestry.

Ignoring both the black and white attitudes that promoted racial barriers, Clinton at one point sat down with a group of black law students in the law school cafeteria. Despite their derogatory racial remarks, Clinton continued to eat and talk with the black students. Clinton's presence at the blacks' table became so habitual that soon even the most militant black students would ask about his whereabouts on those few occasions when he could not join them.[72] Clinton's commitment to promoting racial inclusion and treating blacks as individuals was evident in many of his actions when he became president. He appointed a racially diverse cabinet, increased minority representation throughout the government, astutely defended affirmative action programs, and embraced blacks in their churches, homes, and in his administration.

Like President Clinton, young Americans acknowledge the existence of racial problems and the reality that America is not a color-blind society. But they believe that the future will be characterized by racial equality and integration. Most Americans in their twenties have never experienced officially approved segregation and many are visibly horrified to learn of past segregation and discrimination. They are increasingly uncomfortable with racial categories and often refuse to classify themselves racially when required to do so by schools, colleges, and universities. Their friends are from diverse racial backgrounds, their teachers are more sensitive to racial concerns, and in many cases their parents supported the civil rights movement.

In polls conducted by Peter D. Hart Research Associates and *USA Today,* young people between the ages of fifteen and twenty-four have attitudes that are conducive to getting beyond race. For example, 85 percent of black youths, 84 percent of Latinos, and 79 percent of whites say that they are comfortable with the idea of being roommates with someone of a different race. Ninety-three percent of whites, blacks, and Latinos indicate that they would be willing to work for someone of a different race. Approximately 72 percent of young Americans believe that there is nothing wrong with people of different races dating each other. Fifty-seven percent of teenagers who date have dated interracially. Only 28 percent believe that their parents would oppose interracial dating, whereas 23 percent said that their parents would disapprove of such relationships but not admit it. About 62 percent of the parents of teenagers say that they would be "totally fine" if their children dated interracially.[73]

Generational replacement and demographic change combine to dramatically alter not only race relations but also the very concept of race itself. Although young people realize that discrimination remains a problem in American society, their own attitudes and beliefs work against the continuance of racial inequality and racial categories. As they assume leadership positions, their values are likely to have a positive effect on race relations.

4

THE MILITARY

A Model of Success
in Race Relations

AMERICA'S MILITARY REPRESENTS A MODEL of racial equality for the rest of American society. No other national institution has managed to make such impressive progress toward getting beyond race in such a relatively short period of time after racial integration was accepted as official policy. Americans in the army, navy, and air force practice racial equality. Compared to civilian society, which tends to elevate race above achievement, the military is an organization in which achievement determines rank, which, in turn, determines how one is treated.

Given the strong commitment of Americans with African ancestry to the military, especially after that organization was desegregated following World War II, many whites find themselves being commanded by blacks of higher rank. On military bases, blacks, whites, Latinos, Asians, and others enjoy equal treatment in such facilities as post exchanges, swimming pools, chapels, barber shops, and housing. Charles Moskos notes that "military life is characterized by an interracial equalitarianism of a quantity and of a kind that is seldom found in other major institutions of American society."[1]

America's military combines many factors essential to getting beyond race. The army, in particular, is undoubtedly the largest and most racially and ethnically diverse organization in the country. It brings together many Americans from poor backgrounds who regard military service an opportunity to improve themselves. Their socioeconomic similarities are reinforced by their shared willingness to shed blood for their country. In other words, they show a genuine commitment to their country and its fundamental values. Having common objectives, most new recruits realize that military rules require them to cooperate to achieve these goals.

From basic training to the most sophisticated activities, the army focuses attention on the importance of teamwork. Consequently, individual members of different races have to communicate with each other, share sleeping quarters, and experience close interpersonal contacts under common conditions. Their survival both in training and in war depends on their sense of confidence in each other, their trust, and their cooperation. These are the essential ingredients of social capital. The very nature of the military forces them to assume new identities that are not based primarily on race. Racial identities, although important, must now compete with emerging new identities that are an integral part of military life. This shift away from a purely racial identity to one shaped by common experiences and cooperative behavior diminishes the significance of racial considerations.

Like other American institutions, the military has wrestled with issues of racial integration and exclusion. However, decisions concerning the integration of the military were rendered more complex than those in the civilian sector, partly because of the unique mission of the armed forces. The waging of war, from the beginning, has played a pivotal role not only in creating America but also in establishing and safeguarding the freedom that America embodies.

The military's missions to secure independence for the colonies during the American Revolution; to make the world safe for democracy in World War I; and to fight Nazism, racism, and territorial expansion in World War II were obviously inconsistent with the practice of racism at home, especially in light of black participation in all of these conflicts. Many Americans realized that fighting for one's country was the ultimate measure of patriotism; they also knew that blacks who fought for the freedom of others would demand freedom for themselves and that such demands would challenge America's cultural and political foundations. Furthermore, segregationists recognized that the racial integration implemented by foreign armies, especially those of France and Great Britain, would directly challenge the existing racial order in the American military establishment.

But maintaining racial segregation has collided with military needs throughout America's history, thereby complicating the relationship between blacks and the military on one hand and blacks and the larger American society on the other. During the early colonial period, blacks and whites were required to protect various settlements from attacks by Native Americans and Europeans. However, in 1639, the colony of Virginia, worried that free black militiamen could incite slave revolts, implemented a policy of excluding blacks from military service. Massachusetts and Connecticut followed Virginia's example in 1656 and 1661, respectively.[2] Yet the need to defend the colonies, to expand westward, to gain independence, to maintain national unity during the Civil War, and to stop international aggression in the twentieth century eventually led to the recruitment of blacks into the military. Their permanent participation as equal citizens, however, was delayed until after World War II.

Several factors combined to influence the United States to fully integrate Americans with African ancestry into the military. So deeply ingrained in American culture is the belief that shedding one's blood is the ultimate test of patriotism that the continual shedding of blood by blacks, even though they were still denied full equality, raised serious questions about the country's fundamental values. Moreover, organized civil rights activities by blacks and whites during the 1940s and 1950s had serious political implications, particularly for the Democratic Party. The chasm between America's rhetoric about "making the world safe for democracy" and the country's simultaneous refusal to practice democracy at home in relation to blacks and other racial minorities was not lost on either America's allies or its enemies. France and Great Britain, for example, treated their black servicemen and women decently, in sharp contrast to American racial policies. But the most important factor contributing to the integration of the military was the desire to achieve military efficiency. Unequal treatment and the segregation of blacks proved to be an increasingly costly policy. Because black servicemen's accomplishments on the battlefield were easily measured, although often slow to be recognized, white military personnel who believed in fairness as well as in military efficiency were able to argue convincingly for equality in the military. The ease with which the link between military inefficiency and racial discrimination was demonstrated, together with the liberalizing tendencies that were spreading throughout American society, facilitated changing racial policies in the military.[3]

Racial equality in the military has direct consequences for the socially constructed hierarchy of race in American society. Successful race relations in the military effectively strengthen arguments for racial integration in civilian society by demonstrating that members of different races can live and work together. Engaging in cooperative activities, facing common danger, and living together in unfamiliar locations all serve to promote the development of close interpersonal relations. These bonding experiences often help to change the racial attitudes and behaviors of military personnel. Many of the military's beliefs about racial equality are transferred to civilian society by members of the armed forces.

Having gained greater self-confidence and a new perspective from which to view human relations, military men and women who are members of racial minority groups are less likely to tolerate discrimination in civilian life. Their greater sense of entitlement to the full benefits of American citizenship serves as a catalyst for social change. Finally, the integration of the military directly affects communities around military bases. The military, by insisting on equal treatment for all military personnel both on- and off-base, establishes new standards for the neighboring civilian population.[4] Given the respect commanded by the military, racial equality in that organization becomes a model for civilian society to emulate.

Blacks in the American Revolution: The Quest for Freedom

Having proclaimed the universal right of all men to life, liberty, and the pursuit of happiness in defense of freedom from British control for the American colonies, the leaders of the American Revolution faced a dilemma. The incompatibility between slavery and the new American ideals of freedom and egalitarianism posed a serious challenge to those Americans who opposed black efforts to secure their freedom by supporting the revolution. Early in the conflict, the Massachusetts legislature decided that free blacks would be permitted to serve as soldiers in the state militia. However, large slaveholding states such as Virginia and South Carolina insisted that black men should not be recruited for service in the Continental Army. Their objections were supported by General George Washington. During a meeting in Cambridge, Massachusetts, where revolutionary troops were encamped across the Charles River from British forces in Boston, Washington and his staff unanimously agreed to prohibit the enlistment of both enslaved and free blacks in the Continental Army.[5]

But military realities soon encouraged pragmatism in relation to recruiting blacks. The eventual participation of free as well as enslaved blacks in the Continental Army and Navy as soldiers and laborers was allowed principally because of military needs. Approximately 5,000 blacks, most of them from New England, served in the American military during the revolution, many of them in integrated units. Practiced in the strategy of dividing and conquering, the British took advantage of America's apprehension about including blacks in the military by offering freedom to slaves who joined royalist forces and by recruiting free blacks. Confronted with the possibility of a large exodus of blacks to the British side as well as with the direct challenge posed to America's revolutionary ideals of freedom and equality by British promises to grant freedom to slaves who managed to escape from bondage, Americans were forced to reconsider their own exclusionary policies.[6]

In response to the British strategy and to the increasing military difficulties faced by his own forces, Washington authorized the recruitment of free blacks in December 1775. Two years later, the severe winter of 1777–1778 at Valley Forge, which was accompanied by widespread illness and suffering, inadequate food and clothing, high rates of desertion, and the possibility of mutiny, forced American military leaders to reassess their policy of not recruiting slaves. In order to defeat the British, more soldiers were needed. Consequently, the Continental Army accepted all volunteers, including slaves who managed to escape. Rhode Island, Massachusetts, and Connecticut allowed their state militias to include slaves.[7]

Like the Continental Army, the Continental Navy also needed more men to accomplish its objectives. Despite Britain's preoccupation with problems elsewhere in its global empire, the naval force that it sent to the American theater was formidable. Meanwhile, living conditions on most American ships were extremely difficult, and brutal treatment of sailors by their superiors was commonplace. Under these circumstances, it was difficult to find many volunteers for naval service. Americans who were already in the navy deserted in large numbers. The manpower shortage resulting from desertion and the low levels of recruitment necessitated reliance on blacks to help man the ships and provide coastal defense.[8]

Blacks also served in the military as substitutes for those whites who had decided to avoid the fighting. Many enslaved blacks substituted for slaveholders, a practice that was widely accepted. It was also illegal. Free blacks, however, could legally take the place of a white male who did not wish to join the military. Thus, when a slaveholder decided to send a slave as his substitute, he had to confirm that the substitute was actually a free person under the law. As a result, many slaves who served in the military as substitutes were able to obtain their freedom when the war ended.[9]

For most blacks, fighting for America's freedom in the Revolutionary War was indistinguishable from fighting for their own freedom. Many Americans of European ancestry also supported black participation in the war because they believed that the fundamental values boldly proclaimed in the Declaration of Independence were applicable to both blacks and whites. The revolution inspired and strengthened American humanitarianism among those who found it difficult, if not impossible, to reconcile the aims of the war with the continuation of slavery. Public opinion in the North eventually supported antislavery efforts during the war. The abolitionist movement, strongly influenced by the Quakers, grew dramatically. States such as Vermont, Pennsylvania, Massachusetts, and Rhode Island abolished slavery between 1777 and 1784.[10]

From the beginning of the American republic, war was closely associated with freedom and equality for blacks. Unlike most Americans, blacks quite literally had to shed their blood to enjoy the rights promised to all by the American Revolution. The majority of the five thousand black soldiers and sailors who fought during the revolution gained their freedom and enhanced their standing in their communities. Their individuality and humanity were recognized by other Americans. The Revolutionary War gave rise to the strongly held belief among Americans with African ancestry that military service, especially in wartime, results in greater freedom and equality of opportunity in peacetime.[11]

The Civil War and the End of Slavery

From the beginning of the American Civil War, both the North and South depended heavily on black labor. Forming the foundation of the South's economy, blacks were crucial to the Confederate attempt to gain independence. Without blacks, the grain needed to feed the South's army and navy and the industrial products essential for the war effort could not have been produced. Throughout the conflict, Confederate authorities forced enslaved blacks to construct fortifications. States such as Virginia required slaveholders to permit the government to "lease" slaves for military purposes when necessary. Similarly, the North employed as many as 200,000 of the approximately half a million black men and women who had escaped from slavery and crossed over Union lines. They worked as teamsters, carpenters, cooks, nurses, laborers, and scouts. Their intimate knowledge of the South made them excellent guides and invaluable informants. Many of them provided the Union army with information about Confederate troop movements, conditions in the South, and the quality and quantity of enemy supplies.

Nevertheless, the freedom for blacks that would emanate from their full participation as soldiers and sailors in the Civil War had serious implications for both the North and the South. With increasing numbers of immigrants arriving in the North, many whites systematically suppressed any perceived threat that blacks posed by competing for available jobs. Furthermore, many Americans in the North who believed in the natural and innate inferiority of blacks understood that the social status of blacks would be improved by their participation in the war. Abolitionists had long argued that blacks could obtain freedom and equality by demonstrating their willingness to die for their country. The idea of recruiting blacks for military service, as soldiers and sailors, was rejected by the North because of its long-term effects on the socially constructed racial hierarchy of American society.

But just as military realities had forced the Continental Army and Navy to reverse their opposition to enlisting blacks, mounting casualties in the long Civil War in which neither side seemed to enjoy a decisive military advantage eventually convinced Union authorities to seriously consider allowing blacks to join the military. The belief in black inferiority predominated in both the North and the South. Yet the high cost of the war in human lives, disagreements among the states over burden sharing, the growing reluctance of white men to endure the inconvenience and danger integral to war, and increasing social and political unrest in many northern cities by workers who opposed the draft and who feared losing their jobs if conscripted contributed to the decision to recruit blacks. In January 1863, President Abraham Lincoln issued the Emancipation Proclamation, which officially authorized the enlistment of black troops in the Union army. Pragmatic considerations forced Lincoln's administration to focus on winning the war and lay aside fears about alienating the border states, which also enslaved blacks. More than 186,000 blacks, roughly 10 percent of all Americans who fought for the North, served in the Union army.[12]

Due in part to a perennial shortage of manpower, the navy also allowed blacks to join. In fact, the U.S. Navy had been integrated since the American Revolution. With a tradition of recruiting blacks, the navy did not face the same public opposition to racial integration that the army was experiencing. Severe problems caused by a shortage of white sailors were exacerbated as the navy expanded during the Civil War to blockade southern ports. The North also increased the number of river gunboats and mortar boats in an effort to prevent the Confederates from operating along the rivers. By the end of the Civil War, approximately 30,000 blacks had served in the Union navy, out of a total Union naval force of 118,000 men. Comprising one-fourth of the navy, blacks were inevitably thrown together with whites on ships and riverboats.[13]

Compared to the navy, the army remained largely segregated, with white officers commanding black troops. Initially, Union officials, believing that blacks would be inferior soldiers, confined many of them to garrison duty. But as blacks demonstrated great courage and fighting skills in bitterly contested engagements such as Fort Wagner and Port Hudson, Union authorities began to reassess their original faulty assumptions. The bravery of blacks and their military contributions to the Union army were not lost on the Confederacy. After struggling with the very serious political and societal implications of recruiting blacks, the South belatedly decided to draft blacks to serve in its own army.

To a large extent, blacks' participation in their country's wars generally resulted in improvements in race relations, although not always immediately after the conflict. By behaving in a manner that was inconsistent with widely held expectations, blacks were able to change white attitudes from being overwhelmingly negative to being somewhat positive. For example, when the Civil War began, cartoonists and caricaturists portrayed blacks as invisible men and as hardly human. Following emancipation and the enlistment of a large number of blacks in the Union army, artists began depicting blacks with distinctive, recognizable human features. Clearly demonstrating their belief in a racial hierarchy, these artists began to sketch black soldiers with Nordic profiles.[14] But this also demonstrated that some whites now regarded blacks as part of American society.

World War I:
Fighting for Democracy at Home and Abroad

Military policies concerning the participation of Americans with African ancestry in the armed services at the beginning of the twentieth century did not differ significantly from previous practices, with the exception that blacks could join the military under the Selective Service Act. Like the American Revolution and the Civil War, World War I was perceived by proponents of equality and freedom for blacks as a catalyst for change in American society. Given Americans' reluctance to involve themselves in World War I, a seemingly distant conflict over issues that many did not fully understand, opposition to black recruitment, primarily in the South, was insignificant compared to earlier conflicts. As the war progressed and news of extremely high casualties resulting from trench warfare and new military technologies reached the United States, draft boards often did not require whites to join up. Blacks, on the other hand, were not frequently rejected.

Racial attitudes in the United States were so strongly set against social equality for blacks that the government, and the military in particular, enforced a policy of strict racial segregation. About 200,000 Americans with African ancestry went to Europe during World War I, and 160,000 of them were assigned to menial jobs. Many black soldiers unloaded transport ships; built roads, railroads, and storage depots; transported material to the front; and served as servants, drivers, and porters for white officers.

Toward the end of the war, when the British and French wanted Americans to replace some of their own units, General John J. Pershing, the commander in chief of the American Expeditionary Forces in France, agreed to a request from Henri Pétain, the French general, to give the 93rd Infantry Division, composed of black soldiers, to the French army as a replacement for some of their units. White Americans, on the other hand, resisted fighting under the command of foreigners. Also attached to the French army was the 369th Coast Artillery Regiment or "the Harlem Hellfighters," an all-black group.

In sharp contrast to America's policy of segregating black and white soldiers, France integrated blacks into its army. Many blacks distinguished themselves in war. The 369th Coast Artillery Regiment, for example, fought with the French in the Meuse-Argonne offensive. Their courage under fire was recognized by the French, who awarded the Croix de Guerre to the 369th regimental colors and to approximately 150 soldiers. When they returned home after the war, these soldiers were honored by many black and white Americans in a parade on Fifth Avenue in Manhattan.[15]

American racial attitudes and behavior clashed sharply with French cultural values that strongly supported racial equality and inclusion. Blacks who fought alongside the French were treated as equals, an experience that pleasantly surprised blacks but was strongly resisted by white Americans. In an attempt to impose their racial beliefs on the French, American officials admonished French officers not to interact with blacks on an equal basis. An American document sent to French officers and civilians stated that "the number of blacks in America would be a menace of degeneracy if it were not for segregation." Americans resented any familiarity with blacks by whites and considered it an affront to their national policy.[16]

Confident in the presumed superiority of their own culture, the French not only rejected American pressure but also angrily protested against American racial beliefs and practices. The French people accorded black soldiers a measure of respect and decency that they had never experienced in the United States. Despite American anxieties over racial mixing, it is estimated that there were nearly two thousand marriages between French women and black American soldiers.[17]

The experiences of blacks as well as whites in Europe had obvious implications for race relations in American society. Serving in the military has always played an important role in defining who is an American. The American military uniform and flag have always been potent symbols of patriotism and inclusion in American society. For whites who embraced hostile racial attitudes, blacks in uniform represented a serious threat to their views of blacks as outsiders and subordinates. Thirty-eight blacks were lynched in 1917 and fifty-eight suffered the same violent death in 1918. The Ku Klux Klan was rejuvenated as a terrorist organization in the South and spread its activities to other parts of the country.

After the war, many whites deeply resented the returning black soldiers. They believed that the blacks had been corrupted by the humane treatment they had received in Europe. Mobs of angry whites accosted black soldiers and tore their uniforms from them. More than seventy black veterans were lynched during the first year of the postwar period, many of them still in uniform. These lynchings were followed by race riots in many American cities, a development that signaled a change in how blacks would now respond to racial violence.[18]

World War II: Moving Toward Racial Integration

Between the first and second world wars, the United States and the world had undergone changes that made the continuation of America's policy of racial segregation in the military counterproductive and inimical to America's vital national security interests. Furthermore, racial practices widely accepted at home encountered opposition among America's allies and were used effectively as propaganda against the United States by Nazi Germany. Equally important, more Americans were themselves rejecting racism.

Germany's own concept of racial superiority, which was used to justify systematically killing more than 6 million Jews in the Holocaust, made racism a central issue in World War II. American war propaganda emphasized German racial policies, thereby inadvertently drawing closer attention to America's own views of white supremacy. Because Adolf Hitler had stressed the superiority of the Aryan race, the United States attempted to mobilize popular support for the war against Germany by distancing itself from arguments extolling white superiority. Americans, in the process of defeating Germany, were also undermining the foundations of racial discrimination and segregation at home.

Americans with African ancestry, as products of American culture, shared their society's attitudes of patriotism and loyalty despite their realization of the chasm between the rhetoric of war and their own continuing mistreatment at home.[19] Reinforcing blacks' positive attitudes toward the war was their belief that by proving their loyalty and fighting ability, they would be rewarded with fuller recognition of their Americanness.

Operating in a society that had grown comparatively more receptive to racial equality, black political organizations and their white allies pressured the government to end racial discrimination. In early 1941, the Brotherhood of Sleeping Car Porters, under the leadership of A. Philip Randolph, began to mobilize black support for a march on Washington, which was scheduled to occur on July 1, 1941. Increasingly cognizant of their growing political power within the Democratic Party, thousands of blacks prepared for a massive demonstration.

Recognizing how devastating such a march would be on America's war propaganda against Germany, President Franklin D. Roosevelt and his administration pressured Randolph and other members of his organization to cancel the demonstration. One week prior to the scheduled march on Washington, Roosevelt decided to issue an executive order outlawing racial discrimination in war industries. In response, Randolph and his supporters did not demonstrate.[20]

Executive Order 88021, issued on June 25, 1941, put the issue of racial discrimination within the broader context of the war effort. It states:

> Whereas it is the policy of the United States to encourage full participation in the national defense program by all citizens of the United States, regardless of race, creed, color, or national origin, in the firm belief that the democratic way of life within the Nation can be defended successfully only with the support of all groups within its borders; and whereas there is evidence that available workers have been barred from employment in industries engaged in defense production solely because of considerations of race, creed, color or national origin, to the detriment of workers' morale and of national unity, I do hereby reaffirm the policy of the United States that there shall be no discrimination in the employment of workers in defense industries or government because of race, creed, color, or national origin.[21]

The executive order also outlawed racial discrimination in government vocational and training programs for defense production. The Committee on Fair Employment Practice was established in the Office of Production Management to receive and investigate complaints of discrimination and to redress valid grievances. Although Roosevelt did not integrate the armed forces, a key demand of blacks, this executive order marked a major step toward desegregation.

Determined to end discrimination and segregation in the armed forces, blacks continued to pressure the Roosevelt administration to go beyond the steps taken in Executive Order 88021. With growing self-confidence and increased political power, blacks decided to support political parties and individual candidates based on their positions on discrimination and segregation in the military. In June 1944, the Republican Party included in its platform a pledge to conduct a congressional investigation to determine if mistreatment, segregation, and discrimination against blacks in the military undermined morale and reduced efficiency. With the 1944 presidential election in mind, the Roosevelt administration was persuaded to endorse reforms to gain the support of black voters.[22]

Leaders at the highest levels of government and a growing number of ordinary Americans who had become sensitized to racial problems through war propaganda that portrayed the United States as the embodiment of freedom and equality supported integration. Increased contact and cooperation between blacks and whites in the war industries and elsewhere in society also encouraged this process. Returning troops who had experienced cultures that were not defined primarily in racial terms contributed to the creation of a climate that was conducive to integrating the military. This radically altered environment facilitated the acceptance of arguments advanced by proponents of racial equality.

The gap between America's creed and its practice, magnified by the war, was disturbing to many Americans who strongly embraced their country's liberal democratic values and respect for individual rights and human dignity. After the war, violent racial conflict was caused partly by returning soldiers' challenges to the status quo on one hand and by deep resentment of black progress by white supremacist groups that believed in many tenets of Nazism on the other. This conflict heightened awareness on the part of many Americans of the need to challenge racism at home as they had done abroad during the war.

President Roosevelt's death in 1945 led to Harry Truman's rise to the presidency. Even as Truman dropped two atomic bombs on Japan to end World War II, another war was developing between the United States and the Soviet Union, allies in the war against Germany. The outbreak of the Cold War and Truman's articulation and implementation of a policy of containment vis-à-vis the Soviet Union had deep ramifications for race relations in the United States. Emerging as the undisputed global superpower, the United States was increasingly forced to reconcile its racial policies with its rhetoric of being the world's bastion of democracy and beacon of freedom.

The ideological nature of the Cold War meant that ideas were the principal weapons of this new struggle for the hearts and minds of people around the world. Just as domestic factors had influenced American foreign policy, international realities were now shaping American domestic politics and race relations. Because of these external pressures, President Truman was now in a stronger position to implement policies advocated by blacks and an increasing number of influential whites to bring about greater racial equality.

Black and white proponents of equal opportunity and treatment for all Americans took the initiative to persuade Truman to act. During the 1946 congressional elections, many blacks either backed Republican candidates or simply refused to vote, thereby helping the Republicans to gain more power in Congress. Motivated in part by the growing power of black voters, Truman issued an executive order creating the Presidential Civil Rights Committee to investigate and make recommendations to him on all aspects of racial discrimination.[23]

Facing an extremely tight race in the 1948 election, Truman was confronted with an independent third-party challenge from Henry A. Wallace and his Progressive Party, which included in its platform a promise of a presidential proclamation to end segregation and discrimination in the military. Sensing the appeal of the Progressive Party to civil rights advocates, black and white, Truman took the advice of Special Counsel Clark M. Clifford and gave racial problems greater priority.

In July 1948, President Truman issued Executive Order 9981, which established the Presidential Committee on Equality of Treatment and Opportunity in the Armed Services. Pointing out that the armed services had to maintain the highest standards of democracy with equality of treatment and opportunity for all who serve, the president declared that his new policy would promote "equality of treatment and opportunity for all persons in the armed services without regard to race, color, religion, or national origin."[24]

The presidential committee was authorized to examine the rules, procedures, and practices of the armed services to determine what changes would be necessary to carry out the new policy. Recommendations were made to the president and the secretaries of the army, navy, and air force. Whereas the secretaries of the navy and air force strongly opposed segregation, the army was the most reluctant to support racial integration.

Integrating the Navy

As previously discussed, blacks served in the American navy as early as the revolution. However, during the early 1900s, as Jim Crow laws were vigorously enforced, blacks made up little more than 1 percent of the navy's personnel. In 1920, the navy adopted a policy of total exclusion of blacks. This policy was amended slightly in 1932 to allow blacks to join as stewards in the messman's branch.[25] Segregation in the navy was obviously more difficult to enforce than in the army. Nonetheless, it was accomplished through separation based on assigned duties.

America's participation in World War II and the crucial role of the navy in that conflict demonstrated that segregation was a liability. Many individuals within the Department of the Navy who believed in ending racial discrimination and promoting equal opportunity and treatment for all Americans actively lobbied for modifications in the navy's practices. Others supported equality from a more pragmatic point of view. From their perspective, racial discrimination prevented the efficient utilization of America's human resources during wartime. Adlai E. Stevenson, a special assistant to Secretary of the Navy Frank Knox, advocated racial integration. This trend was strengthened by President Roosevelt's order in 1942 to the navy to use blacks for assignments from which they had previously been barred. Further modifications were made in 1944 when Secretary Knox undertook the unprecedented step of allowing two ships of the fleet to be manned by all-black crews. A small number of black sailors were integrated into white crews on oceangoing vessels. When James V. Forrestal succeeded Knox as secretary of the navy in 1944, he made a radical departure from segregationist policy by approving a plan for integrating the crews of twenty-five auxiliary ships of the fleet.[26]

Special branches of the navy, such as the marines, also began to integrate. Prior to World War II, there had been no black marines, although this organization had been created in 1774 by the Continental Congress and was established in its current form in 1798. In 1942, blacks were permitted to join the Marine Corps; however, they served in segregated units as laborers, ammunition handlers, and antiaircraft gunners. In 1949 and 1950, Marine Corps training units were racially integrated.

Black women, like women in general, faced an even more daunting challenge in being integrated in the navy. Although white women had been given restricted roles in the navy, black women were not allowed to join until 1945, at which time Forrestal's determination to end discrimination ensured their admittance. Forrestal recommended to President Roosevelt that the navy treat black women exactly as it treated white women,[27] although women in general were still not given the same opportunities as men.

Integrating the Air Force

As in the case of the navy, a combination of political pressure, obvious military needs, and courageous individuals eventually led to the integration of the air force. Throughout the late 1930s, the National Association for the

Advancement of Colored People (NAACP), black newspapers, and various civil rights organizations pressured the War Department to accept blacks into the air force. In 1939, sensitive to the growing political potency of black voters, Congress approved the creation of civilian pilot training schools for Americans with African ancestry, from which pilots could be recruited in the event of America's involvement in the escalating conflict in Europe. Although the air force sponsored several of these schools, it refused to accept their graduates into the service. Under pressure from changing racial attitudes in America and concerted actions by advocates of racial equality, and influenced by political considerations, the air force established a pursuit squadron composed of 47 black officers and 429 black enlisted men at Tuskegee, Alabama, on July 23, 1941. The first class included 6 enlisted men, 1 officer, and 5 flying cadets. The officer was Benjamin O. Davis, who had graduated 35th in a class of 276 at West Point in 1936.[28]

Six hundred black pilots who graduated from Tuskegee fought in Africa, France, Italy, Romania, Poland, and Germany. The 99th Pursuit Squadron, made up of black pilots, flew approximately two hundred missions over Europe escorting U.S. bombers. They compiled an impressive war record, not losing to enemy fire any of the bombers they escorted.[29] Inspired by their success, supporters of racial equality provided lawyers to fight racial discrimination and continued to pressure the government to integrate the air force.

Prior to President Truman's executive order to integrate the military, General Idwal H. Edwards, air force deputy chief of staff for personnel, had argued that racial segregation caused waste and inefficiency in the air force; there were vacancies that could not be filled by qualified blacks because of segregationist policies, despite the lack of qualified white personnel. Obvious and pervasive inefficiency was clearly having an impact on the air force's budget. General Edwards persuaded the chief of staff that racial integration would not only solve problems created by the inefficient use of manpower but also diminish the possibility of reduced congressional appropriations. Truman's order to integrate the armed forces buttressed General Edwards's arguments. On May 11, 1949, the air force announced its new policy outlawing discrimination on the basis of race, color, religion, or national origin.[30]

Integrating the Army

As in previous wars, the army remained racially segregated as it fought against Germany's racist regime in World War II. The Army maintained segregation by creating all-black units that were essentially self-sufficient; these units were separated from white units to reduce contact between the two groups. Black units were, with few exceptions, commanded by white officers. Despite efforts to minimize contacts between black and white soldiers, it was impossible to keep them completely separate. When blacks and whites interacted, violence invariably ensued. Nevertheless, some blacks and whites managed to develop friendships and mutual respect.

The pressing demand for manpower as the war continued induced modifications in the Army's policy of racial segregation. Newly trained black volunteers were sent to fight alongside white troops in France, Belgium, and Germany. As the Battle of the Bulge, in which Americans were greatly outnumbered by Germans, intensified from December 1944 to January 1945, black platoons joined white platoons to strengthen the U.S. First and Seventh Armies.[31]

Black women also experienced segregation in the Women's Army Corps (WAC), the only auxiliary service to accept them in the early stages of America's involvement in the war. When the WAC established its first officer training center in Des Moines, Iowa, in 1942, 39 of the 440 women were black Americans. Like black men in the army, black women did menial jobs, ate at separate tables, stayed in separate living areas, and were segregated in virtually all recreational activities. When they completed their training, they were sent to work with the all-black army units.[32]

In addition to obvious inefficiency caused by racial segregation, other significant developments contributed to the eventual integration of the army. America had been changed by the war. Young men from isolated areas of the country suddenly found themselves in foreign countries and with other Americans who seemed also quite different from their neighbors and friends back home. Millions of women who left their homes to work in war industries were exposed to a different way of life and, more importantly, gained self-confidence as well as greater knowledge of race relations. Americans with African ancestry gained bargaining power as they obtained military-related jobs from which they had previously been excluded.

Perhaps the most crucial change was the rising level of education among blacks, especially those from northern cities. Compared to World War I, when 86 percent of blacks from the North and 97 percent of blacks from the South were limited to a grade school education or less, by World War II only 37 percent of blacks from the North and 67 percent of blacks from the South had such a low level of education. The proportion of black men from the North who had progressed beyond the eighth grade was as high or higher than that of southern whites.[33] Education's liberalizing effect was apparent to the entire society. As educated Americans became more aware of the fallacy of race and its magical nature, they were emboldened to resist racial discrimination.

Changes on the American mainland were accelerated by the army's experiences in racially diverse Hawaii during the war. In 1940, no ethnic group formed a dominant majority in Hawaii, where concepts of race were very different from those in mainland America. Because race is socially constructed, America's racial system was forced to confront Hawaii's. In this less racially conscious environment, which did not embrace America's bipolar racial view, blacks had a definite advantage. The army, preoccupied with winning the war, had to take local customs into consideration. Faced with the radically new circumstances of racial equality, black and white Americans were less securely anchored to their own perceptions of race.

This new environment provided an opportunity for blacks to reframe the concept of race. Although there was some segregation, blacks, whites, and Hawaiians generally worked together and used integrated facilities such as theaters, mess halls, and commissaries. As race lost its standing as an unchallenged indication of status, rank and occupation competed as sources of identity and power. The 369th Coast Artillery Regiment dealt with racism by reframing or recasting the meaning of race. Instead of stressing race, members of this regiment viewed themselves first and foremost as combat soldiers. By so doing, they were transforming the racial paradigm to one based on military protocol and rank. The military, because of societal conditions prevailing in Hawaii, became extremely conducive to a shift from racial identities to other identities.[34] Black and white soldiers alike now understood the power of rank.

Prominent Americans in California and elsewhere in the United States were also confronted with the war's implications for race relations. Following the Japanese bombing of Pearl Harbor on December 7, 1941, Americans prepared to defend the West Coast against a possible attack by Japan. Black soldiers from the 369th were ordered to participate in this coastal defense. Antiaircraft guns were mounted in the back yards of many of California's elites. Given the state of race relations at that time and widespread fears of blacks armed with guns, some white Californians resented being in close proximity to black soldiers. Others, such as the movie stars Humphrey Bogart and Rosalind Russell, welcomed the black soldiers who protected them. In a strong symbolic gesture of his support for racial equality, Bogart "told a group of the men they were welcome to use his house and gave them the keys to show he meant it."[35]

European Challenges to American Racial Segregation

Other challenges to racial segregation in the army came from allies in Europe, especially Great Britain and France. The army transported American racial attitudes and beliefs to Europe only to discover that most Europeans, with the notable exception of the Germans against whom the United States was fighting, did not subscribe to America's beliefs in racial segregation and discrimination. Given the relative lack of racial minorities in British society at that time, the British public embraced black soldiers, much to the chagrin of white Americans.

Whereas Americans were obsessed with race, the British were more inclined to focus on class and manners. Blacks were seen as polite, kind, and inoffensive by ordinary British people. Blacks had been given the most unglamorous work in the army and were perceived as assisting Britain at a time when it was gravely threatened. Furthermore, the relative economic deprivation of British citizens during the war helped forge a bond between them and Americans with African ancestry, the majority of whom had lived in poverty or at best in modest circumstances in the United States. Blacks did not complain about the lack of modern conveniences such as central heating, refrigerators, and cars, whereas many whites did.[36] Finally, as far as the British were concerned, America's treatment of its black soldiers directly contradicted its self-perception as a bastion of freedom and equality.

In sharp contrast to Americans, British citizens mixed socially with black soldiers. American WACs with African ancestry found the British polite and cordial. British people gravitated toward blacks and refused to allow white American servicemen to show disrespect for black WACs in their presence. Black women claimed that racial discrimination was not practiced in Britain.[37] Similar experiences are reported by black men.

Robert Dixon, for example, remembers the British as being objective and fair in their relations with black soldiers, despite the passing on of some American racial stereotypes to the British as the war progressed. Trained in an all-black unit at Fort Sill, Oklahoma, Dixon was a machine gun corporal who was stationed in England. The British regarded all the American troops as Yanks, believing that both black and white Yanks were fighting a common enemy on Britain's behalf. If blacks arrived in a British area first, they were treated more favorably than whites who came later, and vice versa. Dixon was adopted by an English family; attended the theater, dances, and other social events with English men and women; and had an altogether pleasant experience in England.[38]

British hospitality toward blacks and rejection of America's racial policies created friction between the United States and Great Britain. One solution was to restrict blacks to certain towns to avoid contact with white Americans while off-duty. General Dwight D. Eisenhower, supreme allied commander, reduced racial tensions by issuing an order to every officer in Great Britain stressing that the British people did not share Americans' racial attitudes. Official attempts to restrict social interaction between black Americans and the British were discouraged by General Eisenhower.[39] These developments helped challenge the army's racial policies.

By the end of World War II, the foundation was firmly in place for ending racial segregation and discrimination in the army. Like the other branches of the military, the army was affected by President Truman's order to promote equal opportunity in the armed forces. Individuals such as General Matthew B. Ridgway helped hasten the integration of the army. Believing that segregation was both un-American and unchristian, General Ridgway, who was put in charge of the Far East command in 1951, received permission from the Department of the Army to racially integrate the U.S. Army in Japan and elsewhere in the Far East.[40]

The Korean War: Fighting in an Integrated Army

America's involvement in the Korean War in 1950 marked the end of racial segregation in the army. Blacks accounted for 25 percent of the new recruits for the Korean War, and these large numbers made it difficult for black training units to absorb them all. Simultaneously, white units on the front lines in Korea were undersupplied. Military necessity led to ad hoc racial integration. On the battlefield as well as in research studies the general conclusion was that racial segregation limited the effectiveness of the army whereas integration had proven to be successful. Greater contact between black and white soldiers had resulted in improved race relations, as predicted by the theories advanced by Samuel A. Stouffer.[41]

Integration in Korea was followed by integration in Europe and elsewhere. Believing that the war in Korea was intended to divert attention away from Soviet expansion in Europe, the United States rapidly increased its military strength in West Germany. Although blacks had endured discrimination in the army, their opportunities were still greater there than in the civilian sector. Consequently, many of them remained in the military and more of them joined, thereby raising the number of black troops in West Germany from 9,000 to 27,000 in a brief period. By 1953, the proportion of blacks in the European command reached 16 percent of total troop strength. This sharp increase not only highlighted the inefficiencies emanating from racial discrimination and segregation but also made segregation unworkable. Bowing to realities both at home and abroad, the army disbanded the last all-black unit and officially ended segregation in 1953.[42] The military's accomplishments in improving race relations would not be matched by the civilian sector for almost two decades.

Ensuring Equal Opportunity

Compared to civilian society, where only feeble attempts have been made to put the issue of equal opportunity and treatment in the broader context of the common good, the military has finally anchored its equal opportunity programs within its general mission. The Department of the Army, in the *Commander's Equal Opportunity Handbook*, clearly articulates reasons for affirmative action policies. Among them are the need to create a more productive and team-oriented force; improve morale and strengthen unit cohesion and esprit de corps; and develop readiness. It is believed that "the

Army's advanced technology and modernization efforts would fail if leaders lost the sincere and dynamic commitment of the total well-being of the Army family."[43]

Discrimination and unfair treatment have harmful effects of which the military has been historically aware, as we have seen in the previous discussion. Prejudicial attitudes and discrimination are inimical to unit morale, which is the foundation of unit cohesion. High unit morale enhances the quality of interaction between soldiers and their leaders as well as among themselves. Discipline, which is essential to the accomplishment of the military's mission, is seriously impaired by racism. Soldiers who feel that they have been victims of unfair treatment will often perceive little discipline in a unit that condones or practices discrimination.

Military officials also realize that the environment beyond the military compound has a direct impact on the men and women who serve in the armed forces and, therefore, has serious consequences for the military itself. Racial equality in the military and equal opportunity and treatment in communities close to military compounds were seen by President John F. Kennedy's administration as being intertwined. In 1963, Secretary of Defense Robert McNamara ordered local commanders to extend equal treatment and opportunity for black servicemen and women to the civilian community. He endorsed the Gesell Committee report, which documented the link between racial equality off-base to morale and efficiency in the armed services.[44] Racial discrimination was now firmly established as a national security problem.

With the passage of the Civil Rights Act of 1964, which outlawed discrimination in public housing, the military took measures that directly affected civilian communities adjacent to military bases. It banned military personnel from attending schools that practiced racial discrimination, prohibited them from speaking to segregated audiences, and refused to advertise available housing that all races could not purchase or rent. Housing projects constructed wholly or in part with federal aid and all houses leased to the government had to be available to all military personnel and their families regardless of race.[45] In Virginia in the early 1970s, for example, the navy clashed with proponents of segregation who decided to close their schools rather than integrate them. But the navy's unrelenting support for racial equality, backed by its economic clout, finally forced Virginia to support equal opportunity and treatment.

Violent and nonviolent disorders in the late 1960s, coupled with a rapid increase in the proportion of Americans with African ancestry in the armed services, influenced the military to educate its personnel about race relations. Based on an interservice task force committee recommendation, the Defense Race Relations Institute (DRRI) was established in 1971 at Patrick Air Force Base in Florida; it offered a seven-week training program. Poor race relations were regarded as damaging to military efficiency, readiness, and effectiveness. The DRRI attempted to make students aware of the history of minority groups in the United States and their contributions to the armed forces. The institute also emphasized an understanding of minority groups' cultures and lifestyles. In addition to learning conflict resolution strategies and techniques, students were required to become aware of equal opportunity policies and their relationship to maintaining order and discipline.[46]

In 1979, the DRRI was upgraded into the Defense Equal Opportunity Management Institute (DEOMI) to reflect the focus on equal opportunity and gender issues. DEOMI provides training for military personnel who advise commanders and who are assigned equal opportunity responsibilities. It conducts research on equal opportunity and human relations issues and disseminates its findings to the military. The institute also provides input to the Defense Department's formulation and implementation of equal opportunity policy throughout the armed forces; it makes available its equal opportunity training and consultation services to various organizations in the department.

DEOMI developed the Military Equal Opportunity Survey, an instrument with which military commanders can assess the equal opportunity climate of their organizations. The survey tries to measure the perceptual climate, people's beliefs and judgments—the perceptions of unit members on issues such as sexual harassment and discrimination, overt racist and sexist behavior, and the overall equal opportunity climate. Information obtained from the survey is used to help commanders improve race relations and deal with problems of sexual discrimination and harassment. Training techniques developed by DEOMI are also used in the civilian sector. Mobile training teams conduct workshops for university employees, corporate personnel, law enforcement officers and administrators, and school board members. By 1995, approximately 16,000 civilians had been trained by DEOMI.[47]

Complying with the Defense Department's emphasis on promoting equal opportunity and treatment, Admiral Elmo Zumwalt, chief of naval operations, established the Navy Race Relations School in Millington, Tennessee, in 1972. The navy's own race relations program, which was implemented fleetwide, initially attempted to make navy personnel aware of racism by confronting individuals with personal and institutional examples of racism.

Race relations education specialists were trained in an intensive three-week program designed to familiarize them with a wide range of minority-majority personnel interaction issues.[48] This earlier emphasis on confrontation was later changed to focus more on consultation. Race relations education specialists, now called "equal opportunity program specialists," act as consultants to commanding officers who are responsible for enforcing equal opportunity requirements.

Affirmative action in the navy is narrowly construed—it is designed to ensure equal opportunity and treatment for each person in the service. All naval personnel, based on their talent, discipline, and effort, should rise to the highest level possible. To achieve this environment, the navy provides educational opportunities for individuals who desire to advance in their careers. At war colleges, postgraduate schools, and at the Senior Enlisted Academy, attempts are made to ensure that selections are equitable.

In 1994, the navy launched the Enhanced Opportunities of Minorities Initiative, which calls for the navy to examine all aspects of recruiting, promotion, retention, and augmentation. The primary intent of the initiative is to create a navy that reflects the demographics of American society across all ranks, rates, and designators. Based on Census Bureau population forecasts for the year 2005, the navy's goal is to be 12 percent black, 12 percent Hispanic, and 5 percent Asian American–Pacific islander. In 1994, the navy's officer corps was 5.12 percent black and 2.96 percent Hispanic; the service is clearly concerned about the small number of minorities in senior ranks. The demographics of the senior officer ranks are seen as fairly representative of the demographics of the officer ranks when these senior officers began their careers.[49] To rectify this imbalance, the navy makes education and training accessible to all personnel who qualify.

Despite sustained efforts to ensure equal opportunity and treatment, problems with minority representation remain. Blacks are underrepresented in technical areas and overrepresented in supply, administrative, and support areas. Whereas Hispanics, Asian Americans, Pacific islanders, and Native Americans are more equally distributed across most categories, they are much more underrepresented than blacks throughout the military. Minority officers are underrepresented in aviation, submarine warfare, special warfare, special operations, and the medical and dental communities; they are overrepresented in surface warfare, fleet support, the chaplain corps, the medical service corps, and the supply corps.[50] This imbalance in representation, however, does not blemish the widespread evidence of the navy's systematic efforts to implement equal opportunity and treatment policies.

Similar to the navy, the air force makes its personnel aware of the consequences of racial strife for its mission. Even though the air force had made significant progress toward racial equality, it has failed to establish equal opportunity offices at the various command levels to address legitimate minority grievances. Many black pilots, believing that they had not received equal treatment, incited a major riot at Travis Air Force Base in California in 1971. Widespread violence appears to have been the catalyst for the implementation of meaningful reforms in the air force that have contributed to a high degree of racial tolerance. Race relations courses became mandatory for all personnel, the equal opportunity office within the Directorate of Personnel Planning was upgraded in importance, and a Social Actions Directorate was established to monitor race relations and other social problems. It was in response to the riots at Travis that the Defense Race Relations Institute was formed.[51]

Mirroring society's racial and ethnic diversity, the army has led the services in efforts at racial integration, if such efforts are measured primarily on the basis of the number of military personnel involved. The army continues to attract many Americans with African ancestry. Comprising roughly 13 percent of America's population, blacks make up more than 30 percent of army enlistees. During the antiwar demonstrations in the 1960s, when predominantly white colleges forced the army to terminate its Reserve Officers Training Corps (ROTC) program on their campuses, many historically black colleges and universities allowed the ROTC not only to remain but to expand its activities. Both black patriotism and the relative lack of job opportunities in the civilian sector influenced many blacks to join the army.

Once the army decided to integrate racially, concerted efforts were made to improve race relations through up-to-date and challenging educational and training programs. Like the navy and the air force, the army trains sergeants and commissioned officers to conduct seminars on race, to investigate complaints about racial discrimination, and to advise commanders on the "race relations climate" in their units. The earlier confrontational approach to racial problems has been replaced with a more consultative environment and a commitment to ensure that race relations training takes place at the entry level and during all phases of leadership and professional development instruction.[52]

Intensive race relations training is accompanied by a strong commitment to equal opportunity and treatment for all soldiers. While maintaining high standards for advancement, the army provides training and educational opportunities to all soldiers who want to fulfill the required qualifications. Standards are the same for everyone, and blacks, whites, Latinos, and Asians who meet them know that they are equally qualified. Affirmative action in the army consists of setting goals to achieve racial diversity. Race and gender are taken into consideration when promotions are granted. However, the army does not set timetables for accomplishing goals. The general result is that race is not perceived as a major factor in professional advancement in the army.[53] This perception of fairness promotes and consolidates good race relations.

Reasons for the Military's Success in Race Relations

The recruitment of individuals from across the nation for a common purpose predisposes the military to success in integrating people from diverse backgrounds. The military is essentially an integrative organization. Consequently, once the military decided to end racial segregation, it became relatively easy to promote racial harmony, compared to the corresponding process in civilian society. Furthermore, the armed forces are generally perceived as the ultimate bastion of national loyalty and patriotism. Americans who voluntarily join the military are likely to be imbued with a strong sense of patriotism. Although such patriotism is sometimes tinged with negative racial attitudes, military officials have defined racism as being inconsistent with American values and the military's mission, and many recruits who hold racist beliefs are confronted with the choice of leaving the organization or trying to conform to it. Obviously, some individuals who are racially biased remain in the military and do not significantly reform their attitudes. But the military's focus on monitoring behavior makes it difficult for such individuals to overtly express racial prejudices.

Success in race relations also results from the unique nature of the military. It is, in effect, a separate culture with its own institutions. Members share common experiences and develop a common identity as they work in the same institutions in isolation from civilian society for long periods of time. Because maintaining a high level of discipline and order, obeying commands, and accepting training and indoctrination are essential aspects of military life, race relations issues are generally regarded as any other issues in the military. Orders must be obeyed without question. Those responsible for enforcing them are products of military culture.

As a hierarchical structure, the military is based on the concept of rank. Unlike civilian society, where race sometimes dominates virtually all aspects of a hierarchy, rank in the military is not dependent on skin color but, instead, on performance.[54] Each rank carries with it specific powers and privileges that are recognized as legitimate by military personnel. The president of the United States, as commander in chief of the armed forces, enjoys the highest rank. The president's orders on race relations or on any other matter are implemented throughout the military without overt challenge from military subordinates. Blacks and whites of the same rank are equals. With the proportion of blacks in the military increasing, more blacks now outrank whites, a reality that civilian society is not experiencing to the same extent.

Basic training, or "boot camp," an eight-week course that must be completed by all recruits, further contributes to diminishing the significance of race in the military. Boot camp marks a transition from youth to adulthood, from civilian status to military status. The course is designed to reduce all recruits to the same level, thereby rendering racial differences a secondary consideration. Friendship with people from different racial categories becomes essential to surviving the transition. All recruits face the same problems and are required to perform certain tasks in teams; they eat, sleep, and spend time in close proximity. Furthermore, basic training encourages a feeling of solidarity among the recruits in opposition to their instructors.[55] Race, under these circumstances, is less meaningful as a determinant of identity.

Cooperative activities, central to achieving military objectives, create strong bonds of friendship among people from different racial groups. War, the principal mission of the military, is an inherently unifying force, one that demands unfailing cooperation. The cooperative process helps alter soldiers' interpretations of each other and encourages them to bridge differences. As blacks and whites work together, they get to know each other as unique individuals; this process tends to have a positive influence on race relations. People from diverse racial and ethnic backgrounds begin to perceive themselves as a team as they cooperate to achieve common objectives.

Interpersonal bonds and friendship among peers is cultivated not for abstract reasons but for military efficiency and effectiveness. Training and personnel policies are designed to encourage the development of friendships. A ship's initial cruise tests the craft's mechanical aspects as well as the crew's interpersonal relations or esprit de corps. Air force and infantry units are not combat ready until their personnel have demonstrated an ability to effectively cooperate.[56]

The Military's Impact on Civilian Race Relations

Apart from influencing communities adjacent to its bases, the military has an impact on overall race relations through its insistence on connecting equal opportunity to national security and through the example set by military personnel who return to civilian life. Discipline, leadership skills, the ability to cooperate to achieve common goals, and experiences gained from contact with other cultures have an impact on civilian society. The self-confidence, self-respect, and respect for others that men and women acquire in the military contribute to the improvement of civilian race relations as former military personnel live and work with other Americans.

Many military values are practiced by ROTC students on college campuses. Former soldiers lead Boy Scout troops, work in libraries, and teach; they can be found in all professions and occupations in society, transferring military values and beliefs to civilian life. For example, a former soldier who is white recalls his experience with a group of black students in a university library, where he worked as the chief librarian. Whereas other white librarians seemed reluctant to ask the students to be quiet, this former soldier, accustomed to working with people from different racial backgrounds, walked over to the students and politely requested that they keep the noise down. Sensing his familiarity with black people and his respect for them, the students complied.

Many former military people interviewed believe that the military directly influenced their racial attitudes and behavior. A white man who was in the army for four years believes that the military was extremely enlightening. Like many recruits, he came from a small town and had not previously interacted with people from different racial backgrounds. In fact, the Ku Klux Klan is active in his hometown. Another former soldier states that serving in the military enhanced his tolerance of people from other races and cultures.[57] Many of these former servicemen and women have close friends from other racial groups. Some intermarried and have racially mixed children.

Experiences and values acquired in the military affect family members. Many people find themselves alone in a foreign country or an unfamiliar American town when their spouses leave for training exercises or for war. They develop close friendships with other military spouses regardless of skin color in order to cope with their own spouses' absence. These friendships are often maintained between entire families.

Children raised in the military seem very comfortable with people from different racial backgrounds when they return to civilian life. For example, Connie Horenkamp, who is white, grew up on an air force base in Puerto Rico and attended school with Puerto Ricans. Living in these circumstances facilitated interacting with people from many races and cultures. Now a nurse and partner with her husband in a dental practice, Horenkamp worked at Alton State Hospital in Illinois with people from all races. The influence of her experiences in the air force is evident in her children's lives as well. Her daughter works with racial minorities in a poor neighborhood in Los Angeles, and her son, who is studying race relations at a leading university, lived and studied in Brazil and worked as a volunteer in the Dominican Republic.[58] Horenkamp's case clearly demonstrates the broader positive effects of the military's racial policies on American society.

5

PROMOTING EQUAL OPPORTUNITY AND TREATMENT

In November 1996, Texaco, the giant oil company, agreed to pay $176.1 million to settle a lawsuit in which it was charged with systematically discriminating against Americans with African ancestry. The plaintiffs alleged that they had been denied promotions, subjected to racial slurs, and belittled by company executives. When an executive who had lost his job produced recordings of other executives making racist remarks and plotting to destroy documents the plaintiffs sought, Texaco decided not only to settle the lawsuit but also to commit the entire management team to the task of eliminating all traces of discrimination in the company. Jesse Jackson and others, using a strategy that helped dismantle apartheid in South Africa, urged stockholders to divest and consumers to boycott Texaco. As a result, Texaco promised to increase its business with minority-owned companies.[1]

Toward a Color-Blind Society

Texaco's settlement demonstrates that racial discrimination continues to be a problem in American society, despite significant progress toward enforcing equal opportunity policies. This case underscored the reality that America is not yet a color-blind society and that deliberate steps must continue to be taken to ensure equal opportunity and treatment for all Americans. Affirmative action, one of the most effective, albeit flawed, strategies available for addressing discrimination, has been systematically criticized as being not only unnecessary but counterproductive and discriminatory. However, as the U.S. armed services have found, when efforts to promote equality and racial harmony are relegated to the back burner, racial discrimination and tensions are likely to escalate. In the absence of a better alternative, affirmative action, defined as a strategy for ensuring equal opportunity and treatment, is still needed to reduce discrimination and help move the country beyond race. Convincing evidence does not exist to support the assumption that racial discrimination would diminish in the absence of equal opportunity programs.

Affirmative action has become so politicized by its supporters and opponents alike that it has become a liability. Unsuccessful applicants for employment or admission to universities use it as a crutch to explain their failure to achieve their objectives. Instead of being told that they faced competition from other well-qualified candidates, they are often informed that affirmative action policies necessitated the admission or hiring of a woman or racial minority. Further weakening support for affirmative action are generational changes and the rise of a strong black middle class. Extremism in the implementation of affirmative action programs and the ever-expanding categories of people who become beneficiaries of these programs have also strengthened opposition to them.

While younger, better-educated Americans discriminate less than older Americans, power in society is still held largely by men whose attitudes have been shaped by an earlier period characterized by the acceptance of racial inequality. The significant decline in racial prejudice has generated highly controversial views on affirmative action. A central argument in this book is that the more widely accepted traditional concept of equal opportunity and treatment should be favored over the overloaded and often baffling concept of affirmative action in relation to efforts to end discrimination.

Affirmative action policies were designed to eliminate or at least diminish the barriers dividing Americans and to bring Americans with African ancestry into the mainstream of American life. Rather than depriving Americans of opportunities, the purpose of affirmative action was to enlarge the pie, to give more Americans access to the American dream, and to put everyone at an advantage. In other words, the policy was viewed as a win-win proposition and not as a zero-sum game. Nevertheless, equal opportunity and treatment is bound to challenge racial beliefs. The idea that white Americans are naturally entitled to be always at the head of the line cannot endure in an open competitive society, a realization that is at the heart of the affirmative action controversy.

Despite their many obvious flaws, policies promoting equal opportunity and treatment have significantly contributed to achieving the goal of a color-blind society. But the term "color blindness" must be understood within the broader context of American history and contemporary society. So central is the social construction of race to how most Americans define themselves and others that attempts to create a color-blind society inevitably take race into account. Few white Americans are willing to trade places with black Americans, a reality that underscores the need to implement policies that are not entirely race-neutral. Totally ignoring race in a race-conscious society in the name of color blindness militates against efforts to get beyond race. But focusing too much on race can also be detrimental to progress toward greater racial equality. The delicate balance needed to get beyond race is destroyed by both those who advocate completely ignoring race and those who are preoccupied with race.

Equal opportunity has proven to be an effective strategy for bringing about greater racial equality and for building a more unified national culture and a stronger sense of inclusiveness and Americanness. By increasing the possibilities for members of different racial groups to come together as equals to discuss their differences and to observe their similarities, policies that promote equal opportunity and treatment gradually erode the rigidly constructed racial categories that form the bedrock of the social construction of racial reality. As blacks, whites, Latinos, Asians, and others work together, they build friendships, trust, and confidence in each other and in themselves. The economic gains that accompany equal opportunity and treatment contribute significantly to challenging racial stereotypes and group boundaries.

However, policies that stress racial categorization are likely to reinforce racial classification to the detriment of individualism. This suggests the need for a carefully balanced approach when implementing policies designed to achieve equal opportunity and treatment. Perhaps the military provides the best example of how this can be done, as discussed in Chapter 4. In many cases, instead of encouraging the development of friendships, cooperation, and informal interaction across racial boundaries, the emphasis on race in affirmative action programs has contributed to racial separatism and balkanization, thereby impeding efforts to get beyond race.

Often lost in the debate on affirmative action is an understanding and appreciation of the broader context of policies intended to promote equal opportunity and treatment. Compared to the military, where affirmative action programs are seen as serving an obviously compelling government interest in national security, the civilian sector has not consistently articulated the broader public interest in promoting equal opportunity. Detached from the incentive of a compelling government interest, affirmative action programs in the civilian sector have become extremely vulnerable to attack, in sharp contrast to the strength of similar programs in the armed forces.

Equal opportunity and treatment for all Americans reinforces fundamental American values and the universal virtues essential to America's self-definition. Affirmative action, defined as equal opportunity and treatment, strengthens the political system by fostering a widespread belief in its fairness and inclusiveness and by giving racial minorities a direct stake in its proper functioning and perpetuation. Broadening the social consensus is healthy for American democracy. Improved race relations, which are likely to result from programs promoting fairness, help build social capital and public goods from which society as a whole benefits. An inclusive society is generally more productive, stable, livable, and safe. America's commitment to racial equality has serious implications for its relations with other countries, especially in light of the country's leadership position in the world. Abandoning those policies that help ensure equal opportunity would clearly undermine America's efforts to encourage the promotion of democracy, human rights, and equality abroad.

More importantly, global economic competition and the growing racial diversity of American society exert great pressure on American society to eliminate barriers to the equal participation of racial minorities in all aspects of American life. The development of a multiethnic and multiracial workforce to engage in the increasingly competitive global economy has a direct bearing on America's global leadership position. Most American corporate executives realize that hiring and promoting more women and minorities is in their companies' interest. Sixty-five percent of corporate executives polled insist that even without affirmative action they would have to diversify their workforce and end discrimination in employment. This is because of changing market conditions; the shifting composition of the labor supply; the benefits resulting from racial, ethnic, and gender diversity; and other factors.[2] Yet, as the Texaco case shows, some company executives continue to resist implementing equal opportunity policies.

Definitions and Public Perceptions of Equal Opportunity

General Colin Powell, the most prominent black member of the Republican Party and one of America's most esteemed citizens, is a strong advocate of affirmative action. Powell observes that a history of discrimination as well as the continuing effects of the social construction of race make it necessary for society as a whole to provide a temporary means to help disadvantaged Americans catch up and compete on equal terms. Drawing on his experience in the army, he stresses that, as a matter of fairness, the military made sure that performance would be the only measure of advancement. But the army also realizes that when equal performance does not result in equal advancement, then something is wrong with the system and steps must be taken to rectify the problem. Stating that he was a beneficiary of equal opportunity and affirmative action in the army, Powell distinguishes between affirmative action and preferential treatment. From his perspective, affirmative action means programs that provide equal opportunity.[3]

Guaranteeing genuine equality of opportunity is what affirmative action is designed to do. Given the centrality of racial discrimination in American history, programs intended to effectively eliminate barriers to equal treatment inevitably take race into consideration. How could they not? A distinction commonly made between equal opportunity and affirmative action is that whereas the former merely requires that employers and institutions not discriminate on the basis of group membership, the latter mandates a consideration of race, ethnicity, and gender.[4] But this is a distinction without a difference, given the context and intent of equal opportunity policies. In a society where race arbitrarily determined access to opportunities, affirmative action, defined as a conscious effort to increase the representation of previously excluded groups in particular organizations, occupations, programs, and activities, is an integral component of efforts to provide equal opportunity and treatment. As I will discuss later in this chapter, President Franklin D. Roosevelt linked equal opportunity and "positive steps" in 1941.

Acknowledging the difficulties involved in bringing about change in race relations and the fact that harmful effects of racial stereotypes permeate American culture, advocates of equal opportunity and treatment stress the need to set general goals in relation to hiring racial minorities and women. The idea of establishing checks on public- and private-sector behavior is consistent with the American belief that unchecked power engenders unfairness. Some opponents of equal opportunity deliberately muddy the distinction between affirmative action and preferential treatment and quotas. By insisting on specific numbers and rigid group representation, some advocates of equal opportunity have facilitated efforts to equate affirmative action with racial and gender preferences.

Americans are generally conflicted and ambivalent about affirmative action because of how the concept is interpreted by groups with different political agendas. The public rejects affirmative action defined as quotas and preferential treatment. But most Americans accept affirmative action defined as equal opportunity and fair treatment. When pollster Louis Harris asked a sample of adults nationwide if they favored or opposed federal laws requiring affirmative action programs for women and minorities in employment and education, provided there were no rigid quotas, 75 percent were in favor and 22 percent opposed. When asked if they favored affirmative action programs in business for blacks and other minority groups, without specific reference being made to women and without ruling out the use of quotas, 57 percent approved and 33 percent were opposed. Whereas 61 percent of blacks supported quotas, 59 percent of whites opposed them.[5] Embracing quotas and preferences is inconsistent with public opinion and undermines attempts to ensure equal opportunity and treatment, an essential step toward getting beyond race.

Confusion about the meaning of affirmative action makes it difficult to neatly separate opponents and supporters of the policy. For example, among those surveyed who said they favored affirmative action, 56 percent opposed setting aside scholarships for minorities and women and 40 percent were against favoring a minority over an equally qualified white applicant. Among respondents who said they disagreed with affirmative action policies, 59 percent approved of companies making special efforts to recruit qualified minorities or women, 68 percent favored special job training programs, and 58 percent supported educational classes for minorities and women. A solid majority (73 percent) of Americans believe that companies should make vigorous efforts to recruit qualified minorities and women. About 82 percent of Americans approve of job training programs that enable minorities and women to obtain the necessary qualifications. Similarly, 75 percent of Americans support special education classes to help minorities and women overcome their disadvantages.[6] These findings suggest that affirmative action in the civilian sector should be more consistent with the basic premises of equal opportunity and treatment as they are implemented by the military.

As discussed in Chapter 4, the military provides educational and training opportunities for all personnel and monitors itself to ensure equal opportunity and treatment. While there are goals, there are no quotas or racial preferences in the military. Similar to the military, programs in the civilian sector that prepare minorities to compete receive strong public support. For example, 83 percent of Americans favor more Head Start programs to provide preschool education, 73 percent support spending more money to improve schools in black communities, and 72 percent agree that more federal funds should be allocated for job training programs.[7] These findings show that affirmative action that is narrowly defined and carefully tailored to provide equal opportunity and treatment is supported by most Americans.

Americans' commitment to egalitarianism and individualism facilitates the implementation of programs designed to promote equal opportunity and treatment.[8] A nation of immigrants, many of whom faced hardships, Americans believe that hard work, personal responsibility, and individual effort will virtually guarantee success. But there has been a fundamental contradiction between America's adherence to these ideals and its denial of equality to Americans with African ancestry. While the emphasis has been on achievement in general, the social construction of race incorporated ascription as one of its central components.

Testing, Merit, and Qualifications

At the heart of the controversy surrounding affirmative action programs are the issues of merit and qualifications. In sharp contrast to most European societies, which often stress the importance of family background and social class as criteria for various positions in society and government, Americans firmly believe that one's own individual accomplishments should decide one's success or failure. Merit is a cardinal virtue in American political thought. Testing is widely regarded as the best way to determine merit and qualifications. However, this belief did not apply until quite recently to Americans who were not of European ancestry.

Although there is general consensus that testing is essential in determining who will be admitted to college or selected for a job, questions abound about the usefulness of tests as measurements of future success. Howard Gardner, for example, has argued that current methods of assessing intellectual abilities are narrow and inadequate. They do not take into account many aspects of intelligence. From Gardner's viewpoint, the problem lies less in the technology of testing than in the ways in which we customarily think about the intellect and in our ingrained views of intelligence.[9] Similarly, Daniel Goleman believes that greater attention should be paid to what he calls "emotional intelligence," which includes self-control, zeal, persistence, the ability to handle relationships smoothly, and the ability to read another's innermost feelings.[10]

Standardized tests are limited in what they can accurately measure. They generally measure verbal and mathematical skills, but usually do not assess research skills, speaking abilities, the ability to exercise good judgment, or interpersonal skills. Qualities that are essential for success in American society, such as creativity and imagination, cooperativeness, decisiveness, and persistence, are not usually tested.[11] Furthermore, an outstanding test score is often a measure not so much of intellectual achievement but of the ability to take tests. The proliferation of special courses, coaching, and preparation books attest to the importance of practice in test taking for good performance on standardized tests.

In addition to test scores, academic grades are perceived as tangible evidence of merit and qualifications. Because of grade inflation at many high schools, there are generally more students with perfect grades than the number of seats available in some of the more prestigious colleges and universities. Consequently, with or without affirmative action, many students with high grade point averages (GPAs) would not be admitted. In 1996 at the University of California at Berkeley, for example, there were 3,500 places for which there were 25,000 applicants, 10,784 of whom had a 4.0 GPA, or a perfect high school record.

Just as students acquire test-taking skills through coaching, they also master strategies for getting high grades without necessarily accumulating corresponding knowledge. Some students have always shopped around for easy courses and accommodating teachers to obtain the highest grades. But test scores and grades were never the sole criteria for admission to colleges and universities. Intangible factors have always been weighed into the decisionmaking process; thus the importance of interviews, personal statements, and letters of recommendation.

Most Americans know someone who received high scores on intelligence tests but whose performance in life has been average at best. Students who excelled in high school sometimes become average students in college, and vice versa. The predictive power of tests appears to diminish over time.[12] Many students from disadvantaged backgrounds with less-impressive test scores and grades are often high achievers. Marilyn McGrath Lewis, director of admissions for Harvard and Radcliffe, believes that accepting students from modest backgrounds with high levels of ambition and energy, who are "hungry," is the best investment that Harvard and Radcliffe can make.[13]

Even though test scores and grades are important, most Americans measure success on the basis of performance. One's occupation, education, and income become the focus of attention. Few of us think about the test scores and grades of successful lawyers, doctors, plumbers, real estate agents, or businesspeople. In fact, studies of three classes of Harvard alumni over thirty years found a high correlation between success—defined by income, community involvement, and professional satisfaction—and low Scholastic Aptitude Test (SAT) scores and a blue-collar background.[14] Standardized test scores and grades are less reliable in America's growing service economy, in which interpersonal skills are extremely important. Virtues such as honesty and courage, which are essential for success in many occupations, are not assessed by written examinations.

Qualifications and merit, not easily definable, are often regarded as objective criteria for determining who should get what. Merit is closely linked to the purposes and objectives of organizations and is defined by broader societal and historical factors.[15] When Harvard, Princeton, Yale, and other universities were bastions of male privilege, women were excluded because of their gender and not because they lacked merit or qualifications. The concept of merit is broadened to reflect society's willingness to include members of groups previously regarded as outsiders. Legacies and merit have always been intertwined. The children of alumni of Harvard, Princeton, Yale, and the like have received special consideration because of their connections to these institutions, a practice not rejected by most successful applicants to these universities.

Public universities, supported by tax dollars and having a responsibility to educate citizens, may interpret merit in a way consistent with their broader purpose. Instead of concentrating solely on academic records and test scores to determine admission, should these institutions also consider the potential contribution of a student to the community, or the presence of a particular racial group in the community, in deciding whom to accept?

The issues of testing, merit, and qualifications in relation to affirmative action policies are complex.

Background of Affirmative Action

Like many aspects of American political theory and law, affirmative action has its origins in "the centuries-old English legal concept of equity, or the administration of justice according to what is fair in a particular situation, as opposed to rigidly following legal rules, which may have a harsh result."[16] Affirmative action in America was given national prominence in 1941, when President Roosevelt signed an executive order reaffirming the government's policy of encouraging the full participation of all Americans in the defense program. President Roosevelt stressed that discrimination in the employment of workers in the defense industries or government because of race, creed, color, or national origin was illegal. He also emphasized the need to enforce the policy. The Committee on Fair Employment Practice was established in the Office of Production Management to ensure that complaints of discrimination were investigated and that appropriate steps were taken to redress valid grievances.[17] Simply outlawing discrimination without taking affirmative actions to enforce the law, given the racial climate that necessitated the implementation of the executive order in the first place, would have been an exercise in futility. Thus the connection between affirmative action and ending discrimination was firmly established. This policy was continued by Presidents Truman and Eisenhower.

In Executive Order 10925, President John F. Kennedy explicitly used the phrase "affirmative action." Stating that discrimination because of race, creed, color, or national origin conflicts with the constitutional principles and policies of the United States, Kennedy created the President's Committee on Equal Employment Opportunity. All executive departments and agencies were directed to initiate studies of government employment practices. Based on their findings, the committee could recommend the implementation of positive measures for eliminating discrimination. Companies receiving government contracts were required to comply with the new guidelines that "the contractor will not discriminate against any employee or applicant for employment because of race, creed, color, or national origin. The contractor will take affirmative action to ensure that applicants are employed, and that employees are treated during employment without regard to their race, creed, color, or national origin."[18]

Instead of taking a passive approach to ending discrimination, which inevitably would have been ineffective, President Kennedy laid out specific actions. These included equal treatment in relation to rates of pay and other forms of compensation, selection for training and apprenticeships, promotion, demotion, and transfer. The executive order also required contractors to post job notices in conspicuous places and to state in all such notices that all qualified applicants would receive consideration for employment without regard to race, creed, color, or national origin.[19] This approach to ensuring equal employment opportunities is consistent with the concept of affirmative action as a proactive policy. Efforts to reach potential minority employees would include advertising job vacancies in minority communities instead of relying on word-of-mouth recruitment. Inherent in the push for equal employment opportunities was the goal of creating a more racially representative workforce.

Confronted with strong societal resistance to equal opportunity and treatment for Americans with African ancestry, greater emphasis was placed on ensuring compliance with antidiscrimination policies. In 1964, the courts were instructed by Title VII of the Civil Rights Act to order such affirmative action as may be appropriate in relation to employers found guilty of discrimination. Remedial efforts on the part of employers became central to the concept of equal opportunity and treatment. For example, employees terminated due to discrimination had to be reinstated, with or without back pay.[20]

Speaking at Howard University's commencement in June 1965, President Lyndon B. Johnson further strengthened the proactive approach to ensuring equal opportunity and treatment. Like Kennedy, Johnson believed that government employers and contractors had to recruit aggressively to include minorities in the applicant pool. Having been raised in Texas, Johnson was familiar with the formidable social barriers to racial equality. He told Howard graduates that "you do not take a person who, for years, has been hobbled by chains and liberate him, bring him to the starting line of a race and then say, you are free to compete with all the others, and still justly believe that you have been completely fair. We seek not just equality as a right and a theory but equality as a fact and equality as a result."[21] Violent opposition to black attempts to gain basic civil rights in the 1960s underscored the need for decisive government action to achieve equal opportunity and treatment.

Widespread domestic social unrest, combined with political expediency, influenced President Richard M. Nixon to require government contractors to ensure that racial minorities were employed and treated without discrimination. The Labor Department implemented the Philadelphia Plan in 1969 obliging contractors to increase minority representation in the construction trades, which had systematically excluded minority workers. But Nixon also saw affirmative action as a useful political strategy. Andrew Hacker believes that Nixon, determined to undermine the Democrats, gambled that white workers would direct their anger at those taking "their jobs" and overlook those who had put the plan in place.[22] Arguably, Nixon's landslide reelection victory in 1972 demonstrated the effectiveness of his racial strategy.

During the Nixon administration, the Labor Department issued regulations requiring federal contractors and subcontractors with fifty or more employees or a contract of at least $50,000 to identify underutilization of minorities and women in various job categories. To determine acceptable representation of excluded groups, federal contractors took into consideration factors such as the minority population in the area, the availability of qualified minorities and women, the existence of training institutions capable of training minorities and women in the requisite skills, and the extent to which the contractor trained minorities and women.[23] The basic intent of the regulations is to ensure that the makeup of the workforce reflect the racial composition of the surrounding community. This concern with group representation in different job categories, together with timetables for achieving employment goals, raised the issues of quotas and preferential treatment.

Amid significant progress toward racial equality in the 1970s and 1980s were developments that helped erode the view of affirmative action as an instrument of racial equality and integration. Members of racial minority groups became less enthusiastic about racial integration and more committed to racial separatism even as they were participating in the mainstream of American life in record numbers. This focus on race and racial categories and the growth of a black middle class helped engender a backlash against affirmative action as well as what many Americans perceived to be a retreat from the goal of a color-blind society. Many white liberals who had ardently supported the civil rights movement became disillusioned with the focus on race and racial groups instead of on individuals and a common Americanness. They found themselves in a strange alliance with conservatives, many of whom had vehemently opposed equal opportunity and treatment from the beginning.

Taking advantage of changing attitudes toward affirmative action, which was now widely believed to be synonymous with racial quotas and preferences, the administration of President Ronald Reagan proposed repealing affirmative action, ending many effective class-based remedies, and abandoning most racial discrimination cases except those filed on behalf of "identifiable" victims of discrimination. Aggressive governmental efforts to ensure equal opportunity and treatment were perceived to be not only ineffective but also an interference with the free market.[24] While critical of affirmative action, the Reagan administration did not present workable alternatives to address ongoing racial discrimination. Seeming almost oblivious to changing political and social realities, proponents of affirmative action essentially clung to the past and allowed affirmative action to become equated with promoting discrimination instead of with ending discrimination.

Influenced by his experiences with racial discrimination and pressured by political supporters, President Bill Clinton tried to rescue the country's embattled affirmative action policy by placing it in a broader context than that advocated by opponents of the policy. From Clinton's perspective, the challenge facing America was twofold: first, to restore the American dream of equal opportunity and the American value of responsibility; and second, to unite an increasingly racially and ethnically diverse country. After recalling his own experiences with racial discrimination, especially in the South, President Clinton attempted to put affirmative action back on its original track by confirming that its purpose is to provide a mechanism for addressing the systematic exclusion of talented individuals based on their gender and race from opportunities to develop, perform, and contribute.

Affirmative action, in Clinton's view, grew out of many years of trying to navigate between a passive approach on one hand and overzealous, draconian measures on the other to end discrimination. Affirmative action is designed to change "an inequitable status quo gradually, but firmly, by building the pool of qualified applicants for college, for contracts, for jobs, and giving more people the chance to learn, work, and earn."[25] This renewed definition of affirmative action did not differ significantly from the traditional and widely accepted concept of equal opportunity and treatment.

Arguments for Affirmative Action

A systematic and deliberate policy of excluding Americans with African ancestry from positions of power and influence in the United States followed more than two centuries of involuntary servitude. Treated as nonpersons, blacks had to fight for recognition of their humanness by American society. With the exception of Native Americans, no other group in American history has been subjected to such degradation and brutality. In a capitalist society that boasted of being the beacon of freedom for all mankind, slaves were not entitled to the fruits of their labor or their natural rights. Discussing affirmative action without considering the wider historical context will likely lead to shallow and misleading conclusions about how to achieve a color-blind society in the twenty-first century.

Supporters of affirmative action argue that the humiliation and suffering blacks endured as slaves and later as second-class citizens created a national obligation to redress past wrongs. In a society preoccupied with suing others for trivial errors and collecting millions of dollars in damages, the idea that blacks deserve recompense is viewed as being consistent with both law and tradition. Stanley Fish argues that the word "unfair" is hardly an adequate description of blacks' experiences. The belated gift of fairness in the form of a resolution to no longer discriminate against blacks legally is hardly an adequate remedy for the deep disadvantages that the prior discrimination has institutionalized.[26] Compensating a whole class of people for deprivations willfully inflicted by society is seen as an obligation of the government and the nation as a whole.

Thus, the argument that many individuals were not responsible for slavery and discrimination and should therefore not have to pay to redress past wrongs is rejected by many proponents of affirmative action. Affirmative action is viewed as therapy for a deadly cancer. The disease must be distinguished from the procedure used to eliminate it. As Stanley Fish puts it, "a cancer is an invasion of the body's equilibrium, and so is chemotherapy; but we do not decline to fight the disease because the medicine we employ is also disruptive of normal functioning."[27] This position is supported by John Rawls. In *A Theory of Justice,* Rawls contends that "an injustice is tolerable only when it is necessary to avoid an even greater injustice. Being first virtues of human activities, truth and justice are uncompromising."[28] A just society takes for granted the idea that all citizens should be treated equally.

Some proponents, as well as many opponents, of affirmative action call for ensuring equality of opportunity by providing a level playing field on which all Americans can compete. But those who argue for affirmative action tend to believe that positive and proactive steps must be taken to achieve this level playing field. They hold that the playing field has always been tilted in favor of those by whom and for whom it was constructed in the first place.[29] All the games are played at home, as it were, giving the home team a definite advantage. Put another way, those cutting the cake also get to distribute the slices, instead of following the widely accepted rule that one cuts and the other distributes in order to ensure fairness.

Just as advantages are usually passed on from one generation to another, often in the form of inherited wealth and access to power and knowledge, disadvantages also are often transferred to new generations. The current problems faced by many Americans with African ancestry are seen as being largely inseparable from historical realities. Consequently, the concept of fairness must be considered within the wider racial, cultural, and institutional history of the United States. The very concept of race divides people into relatively fixed categories. Rather than focusing on individuals, racial classifications draw attention to groups. To remedy the effects of past discrimination, most proponents of affirmative action point to the need to take group membership into consideration.[30]

Although acknowledging that significant progress has been made toward creating a more equal society, advocates of affirmative action contend that positive steps must continue to be taken to eliminate continuing discrimination. This belief is supported by numerous examples of unfair treatment by companies as well as by individuals. The federal government received more than 90,000 complaints of employment discrimination based on race, ethnicity, or gender in 1995. And there are numerous unreported instances of discrimination that many minorities face routinely. Chang-Lin Tien, chancellor of the University of California at Berkeley, recalls encountering the "ugly realities" of racial discrimination as a student in Louisville, Kentucky, in 1956. He worked as a teaching fellow for a professor who addressed him as "Chinaman." While agreeing that there have been significant advances in civil rights, Tien believes that the serious racial problems that persist in American society justify the continuation of affirmative action in higher education.[31]

Many white supporters of affirmative action, such as 1996 Republican vice presidential candidate Jack Kemp, former senator Bill Bradley, and President Clinton, witnessed discrimination as they interacted with their black teammates and friends in college. Most whites who have close personal relationships with members of minority groups are initially alarmed when their friends experience subtle and not-so-subtle discrimination. A white person is shocked to hear a white waitress ask her black friend, who has arrived for a dinner reservation, "How may I help you?" A black person who inquires about an apartment advertised in the local paper is told that it has been rented. A white friend who calls later is reassured that the apartment is still available and is invited to come see it.

In 1991, the television program *Prime Time Live* tracked two young men, one black and one white, with equal education, cultural sophistication, and apparent level of affluence as they engaged in a series of encounters with rental agents, landlords, taxicab drivers, employment agencies, and ordinary citizens. The black member of the pair was charged more for the same goods, was asked for a larger down payment for the same car, was addressed with contempt and irritation by clerks and administrators, and was generally treated unfairly.[32] For proponents of affirmative action, such real-life illustrations demonstrate that the task of ending discrimination is far from over and that affirmative action is still necessary to work out the lingering problems.

Lynn Martin, secretary of labor in the administration of President George Bush and an advisor to Mitsubishi Motor Manufacturing of America on equal opportunity and sexual harassment issues at the company's plant in Normal, Illinois, found that although more than 50 percent of the workforce is composed of women and racial minorities, their advancement is often hindered by artificial barriers, or "glass ceilings." Martin believes that the commitment and the actions that first helped women and minorities break through employment barriers must be maintained and enhanced if the goal of full and equal employment opportunity is to be realized.[33] Similarly, President Clinton drew attention to the persistence of the kind of bigotry that often influences in a subconscious way how we think about hiring, promoting, and making educational and business decisions. He specifically referred to the federal law enforcement officials who attended an event in Tennessee in 1995 known as the "good old boys roundup," an event "literally overflowing with racism—a sickening reminder of just how pervasive these kinds of attitudes still are."[34] Passive government approaches to these problems are deemed to be tantamount to indifference to racial discrimination.

As a representative democracy, the United States, it is argued, has a fundamental and compelling interest to embrace diversity. Given America's history of racial discrimination and the growing numbers of Americans classified as members of racial minorities, commensurate racial representation is a measure of America's commitment to inclusion. Affirmative action is perceived to be instrumental in holding a racially diverse country together. Racial segregation, which is most pronounced in relation to Americans with African ancestry, is regarded as inimical to national unity. Without affirmative action, segregation would become more pronounced and faith in the fairness of the system would undoubtedly diminish. This, in turn, would lead to greater demands by excluded racial minorities, particularly blacks, for what they regard as a fair share of wealth, power, and position.[35] In other words, affirmative action policies are a bargain compared to the alternatives.

By bringing Americans from different backgrounds together in workplaces, educational institutions, and informal settings, affirmative action is an integrative force. The free exchange of ideas generates new perspectives on social problems. Sharing different experiences often improves understanding among members of diverse racial groups and creates a greater awareness of both similarities and differences. Bringing people together is an essential step toward enabling them to learn to live together as Americans. Furthermore, affirmative action is seen as preparing students and others for work in a society that is undergoing significant demographic changes. The ability of a diverse workforce to cooperate and successfully interact with an equally diverse population of customers and clients is now regarded by many business executives, political leaders, and educators as critical to success in a fiercely competitive world economy.[36]

One of the strongest arguments in favor of affirmative action is that people tend to hire people like themselves because they feel most comfortable with like-minded colleagues. For example, many Americans who complain that affirmative action engenders reverse discrimination often seem oblivious to the obvious contradictions in both their views and their behavior. For example, David Missar of Iron Workers Local 401 in Philadelphia, while complaining about the effects of reverse discrimination, does not hesitate to bypass the union hall to recruit whites directly because they are the people he knows best.[37] Many companies, universities, and other organizations may subconsciously exclude minorities due to the narrow perceptions that often result from a racially homogeneous selection panel. The participation of minorities in the selection process can significantly broaden perceptions and affect hiring and promotion decisions.

"It is who you know and not what you know" is an important piece of advice with which virtually all Americans are familiar. Few question the fairness of using contacts to gain an advantage. In fact, both groups and individuals have always practiced networking. Many important first jobs are gained because relatives, friends, and acquaintances put in a word on behalf of the aspiring individual. One student who enjoyed the rare opportunity of spending a summer as an intern in the European Parliament pointed to the importance of contacts, not just academic achievements, in obtaining the position.

Qualifications are usually not as meaningful as having access to those who make decisions. One can hardly apply for a job one does not know about, no matter how qualified one might be. Lacking significant contacts with influential whites, many blacks tend to be excluded from crucial networks. Racial segregation makes it difficult for racially neutral procedures to be effective in achieving equal opportunity and treatment.[38] Fraternity brothers, sorority sisters, golfing buddies, and alumni of particular colleges and universities generally enjoy advantages that grow out of interpersonal contacts. In order to create equal opportunity, the aggressive recruitment of qualified women and minorities under affirmative action guidelines is regarded as the best available strategy to level the playing field.

Because few individuals or groups discard deeply held racial attitudes and beliefs without external pressure, affirmative action is viewed as essential in ensuring widespread compliance with laws designed to promote equal opportunity and treatment. Companies have been prodded by affirmative action to end the practice of hiring mostly white males and to remove barriers to equal opportunity for racial minorities and women. Richard D. McCormick, chairman and chief executive of US West, Inc., admitted that the impetus for affirmative action "came by virtue of a government kick we got in the fanny."[39] Affirmative action helps make companies honest, a transformation that many eventually find to be in their interest.

Studies made by the Office of the Federal Contract Compliance Program found substantial improvement in employment opportunities for women and minorities, especially when compared to corresponding opportunities at companies that do not have government contracts. This difference is explained by the fact that companies with government contracts are required by affirmative action regulations to make a conscientious effort to hire women and minorities. Compliance reviews, the principal instrument for ensuring compliance with these regulations, contribute to higher growth in the employment rates of women and minorities in companies with federal contracts.[40] As the army has discovered, compliance reviews are necessary to ensure that affirmative action policies are followed.

A final argument for affirmative action programs is that they contribute significantly to economic and social improvements for many women and minorities, thereby creating an environment conducive to getting beyond race. Enjoying a comparable economic status, blacks, white, Latinos,

Asians, and others are likely to have increasingly converging interests and more interpersonal contacts in cooperative settings. The growing number of economically successful minority citizens effectively challenges racial stereotypes, which are more easily justified when whites monopolize positions of power and wealth and minorities fall disproportionately below the poverty line.

As racial minorities gain employment in predominantly white organizations, they find opportunities to make friends and acquaintances with each other and with whites. Information networks become interracial. Cooperation engendered by the working environment helps erode racial boundaries. Job seekers from various races now have a better chance to learn about job opportunities and to benefit from informal contacts.[41] Racial minorities are likely to believe that organizations are not hostile if they are racially integrated. Minorities are therefore motivated to acquire the necessary skills to gain employment.

Successful minority individuals often become role models for young Americans. Although skin color does not determine a person's ability to be a role model, women, blacks, Latinos, Asians, and others are generally inspired when they see someone who belongs to their group in a leadership position. One of the harmful legacies of the social construction of race is the perception that skin color determines intellect, culture, and the ability to perform certain tasks. In light of these powerful stereotypes, which often have magical qualities, proponents of affirmative action believe that role models from various racial backgrounds are needed to demonstrate that race is no longer a barrier to equal opportunity and treatment in America. Max Frankel observes that when women, blacks, and Asians first joined white men as television news anchors, they ignited the ambitions of many youngsters who had never before imagined themselves eligible for such high-profile positions. So, too, with judges, generals, and editors.[42]

In the area of medicine, affirmative action has proven to be of great social significance. If one of the purposes of medical schools, especially those funded by taxpayers, is to train physicians and others who will help improve the health and well-being of all citizens, access to medical programs by individuals who are likely to practice in areas where Americans do not receive adequate medical care is consistent with promoting local, state, and national objectives. A study conducted by New York's United Hospital Fund and Stanford University found that 17 percent of white doctors treated blacks and 9 percent treated Latinos; 46 percent of black doctors treated blacks and 9 percent worked with Latinos; and 20 percent of Latino physicians served the black community and 31 percent worked with Latinos.[43]

Perhaps the famous Bakke case best demonstrates the need for affirmative action. Allan Bakke successfully challenged the University of California at Davis medical school's decision to reject him in favor of a minority applicant who had received lower test scores. Bakke, who finally was admitted to medical school at the University of California, is now an anesthesiologist in Rochester, Minnesota. He has no private practice and works on an interim basis rather than as a staff physician. Patrick Chavis, who initially took Bakke's place at the medical school, is an obstetrician-gynecologist with an enormous practice serving poor people on Medicaid in Compton, California.[44]

Arguments Against Affirmative Action

Opponents of affirmative action, some of whom originally supported the program, argue that it is corroding the nation's social climate without accomplishing anything. When asked what factors contribute to negative race relations, more than 80 percent of those interviewed mentioned affirmative action. Their responses are undoubtedly influenced by the widespread tendency among opponents of affirmative action to equate efforts to ensure equal opportunity and treatment with quotas, preferential treatment, and reverse discrimination. Minorities are assumed to be less qualified than whites, who are generally presumed to be qualified, a perception that often leads many whites to conclude that minorities enjoy an unfair advantage. But some employers and universities have lowered the standards for minorities. Glenn C. Loury, for example, argues that not holding minorities to the same standards required of whites can lower incentives for the acquisition of skills by minorities. This, in turn, can perpetuate the racial skill differential that made affirmative action policies necessary in the first place.[45]

Many minorities have come to rely too much on affirmative action. Instead of seeing the policy as giving them the benefit of the doubt in close cases, as a thumb on the scale in their favor, they see it as a heavy instrument that can be used to push them ahead of better-qualified white male applicants. Many whites, on the other hand, tend to reach hasty conclusions about minorities. For example, white students routinely assume that minorities at universities automatically receive financial assistance, despite the fact that many minority students are solidly in the middle class and, like many of their white counterparts, do not qualify for aid.

Compounding the negative perceptions of affirmative action are a selective view of history and the failure of many racial minorities and whites to cross racial boundaries to develop friendships. The selective view of history is that prior to the passage of the Civil Rights Act of 1964, racial discrimination was a serious problem in America. However, the period from 1964 to 1969 was characterized by less discrimination and greater racial harmony. The implementation of proactive policies after 1969 to end discrimination resulted in reverse discrimination and movement away from the ideal of a color-blind society. But as long as Americans define themselves racially, as members of socially constructed racial categories, a color-blind society will be impossible to achieve.

Racial stereotypes and ignorance are perpetuated by the failure of many individuals from different racial groups to make greater efforts to understand each other's basic concerns and perceptions of reality. Many whites seem afraid to join blacks for lunch on college and university campuses, and blacks too often are reluctant to sit at tables with whites. Opponents of affirmative action point to the low level of racial mixing as evidence of the failure of affirmative action to promote racial integration, which many of affirmative action's proponents claim has occurred. The balkanization of racial and ethnic groups in environments that provide opportunities for integration is regarded as inimical to achieving a color-blind society.

Another argument against affirmative action is that it inevitably leads to reverse discrimination and quotas because it gives racial minorities and white women preferential treatment. This view is based on the assumption of a fixed pie and a zero-sum game in which one person wins at another person's expense. A system that promotes racial preferences distributes benefits on the basis of skin color, thereby heightening color consciousness. This, in turn, encourages stereotyping and invites people to view others as carriers of racial characteristics, not as unique individuals.[46]

Preoccupied with the numbers of minorities in various positions in different organizations, some proponents of affirmative action adopt an adversarial "us-versus-them" approach in relation to white males in positions of power and influence. White males, regardless of their own unique struggles, are often believed to be inheritors of privileges that are beyond the reach of all but a very few minority group members.[47] Skin color alone is often deemed to be the determining qualification for preferential treatment. Yet complaints of reverse discrimination received by the federal government in 1995 comprised less than 3 percent of the more than ninety thousand complaints of employment discrimination based on race, ethnicity, or gender.[48]

Preferential treatment is seen as an integral part of a misguided policy that tries to rectify past injustice with a new form of injustice. In the process of implementing affirmative action, the federal government is believed to have gained excessive power and is determined, like a steamroller, to flatten everything in its path. It is argued that government activism has led to increased demands not for equal opportunity but for equal outcomes, proportional representation, racial balance, and gender equality as ends in themselves.[49]

Opponents of affirmative action argue that preferential treatment burdens all white women and minorities, whether qualified or not, with a stigma. Minorities and women are perceived, almost automatically, to be less qualified than white males. While proponents of affirmative action argue that fewer women and minorities would be employed or admitted to professional programs if race and gender were not considered, those who oppose affirmative action argue that racial preferences reinforce the stereotype that the beneficiaries are not bright enough to successfully compete with white males. The stigma of winning contracts through minority-preference mandates is sometimes seen by beneficiaries as cheapening all their other accomplishments.[50] Instead of breaking down racial barriers, affirmative action consolidates them. It devalues those minorities who work hard to succeed in a competitive environment.

But many opponents of affirmative action seem to overlook how the social construction of race closely links skin color with intelligence and white entitlement to various positions and privileges in society. Stigmatizing and self-doubt can result from the placement of less-qualified women and minorities in certain positions. But even well-qualified women and minorities are often made to feel inferior by white males threatened by those who challenge racial stereotypes. With or without affirmative action, minorities would still face the effects of the long-standing cultural belief in the inherent intellectual superiority of white males. Andrew Hacker observes that feelings of unworthiness seldom plague white Americans who profit from traditional forms of preferment. There is little evidence that those who have been aided by affirmative action feel many doubts or misgivings.[51] Few opponents of affirmative action strongly protest the not-too-infrequent practice of tailoring job requirements for a specific white male and then engaging in perfunctory advertising and job interviews to fill the position.

Another argument against affirmative action is that it helps the most skillful and well-situated opportunists. In other words, those who need help the least appear to benefit the most from the programs. Middle- and upper-class minority group members who are already advantaged are believed to be the primary beneficiaries of affirmative action. Furthermore, it is argued that the rapid progress enjoyed by blacks in particular is not the result of affirmative action. Their progress is seen as due mainly to the invalidation of southern segregation and to the promulgation of a federal standard by which Americans are expected to abide, rather than to federal government intervention.[52] These views, however, are contradicted by studies showing that minorities from modest economic backgrounds have benefited from affirmative action. Many of the gains have been in occupations such as law enforcement, fire fighting, and construction, vocations that are not very attractive to minorities from economically advantaged backgrounds.[53]

Americans who oppose affirmative action, and some who support it, find the ever-expanding list of beneficiaries confusing, unfair, and contrary to fundamental American values. As immigrants constitute a larger percentage of the American population and as members of different racial groups intermarry, the idea that individuals who have suffered little or no discrimination in the United States are entitled to affirmative action programs designed primarily for Americans with African ancestry weakens the argument for continuing affirmative action.

New arrivals are entitled to benefits simply because of their group membership. In 1977, for example, Pakistanis, Indians, and Sri Lankans were reclassified from white to Asian, thus allowing them to benefit from programs originally designed for victims of racial discrimination.[54] In an exceptional case, Richard Naing, an American born and raised in Burma, took full advantage of the system, demonstrating the serious weaknesses of affirmative action. Forced into bankruptcy court by creditors, Naing, who is believed to have assets totaling $30 million, enrolled in a minority set-aside program and arranged to buy a minority-owned firm that already had a backlog of government set-aside contracts. The company Naing acquired had 196 employees and $17.5 million in annual revenue.[55]

Simply having a Spanish surname or being an immigrant from Latin America usually entitles one to affirmative action benefits. Non-Hispanic white women married to Hispanics are also classified as ethnic minorities, but Latino women who marry men who do not have Hispanic surnames, assuming they give up their own surnames, are not automatically considered to be minorities. No matter how wealthy an immigrant from Latin America may be, that person is regarded as a member of a disadvantaged group. A young woman of Hispanic origin whose parents divorced when she was four years old was raised by her mother and her new husband, a wealthy white lawyer. The young woman had never interacted to any great degree with Latinos. However, she was accepted by the University of California at Berkeley as a Latina and given scholarships and other benefits that members of disadvantaged minority groups often receive. So common are these instances of misplaced assistance that opponents of affirmative action are able to build a strong case against the program.

Possible Solutions

The issue of affirmative action, like the problems of racial discrimination that gave rise to it, is complex. Responses to affirmative action are often emotional, visceral, and devoid of logic. The white male who complains that he was denied a job for which a hundred other Americans applied because of affirmative action might also have been beaten in the competition by another white male. Logically, regardless of skin color or ethnicity, ninety-nine applicants would be rejected. The general perception that racial minorities are the principal beneficiaries of affirmative action is also wrong. White women are the primary winners under affirmative action, and white women are related to white men. Contrary to the view that white men suffer because of affirmative action, the reality is that whereas some white men lose, many profit because their wives, mothers, sisters, daughters, and cousins benefit from what is regarded as preferential treatment. An important first step toward addressing the problems connected with affirmative action is to closely examine the myths that are assumed to be facts.

One of the most destructive myths embraced by affirmative action opponents is that white males are inherently more intelligent than racial minorities and white women and that white males are automatically qualified for the positions they hold. Such beliefs underscore the persistence of attitudes that perpetuate racial discrimination and thus underscore the need for some form of affirmative action to counter it. By making broad generalizations about minority group members and by glibly opposing attempts to ensure equal opportunity without offering adequate alternatives to current public policies, many opponents of affirmative action weaken their credibility as genuine champions of racial integration and equal opportunity. A strong position debunking the link between skin color and intelligence would enhance their credibility as opponents of racial discrimination.

Many proponents of affirmative action also inadvertently perpetuate racial stereotypes and discrimination by assuming that minorities are inherently disadvantaged and in need of special treatment. Preferences for minorities are not justified simply because there are preferences for athletes, children of alumni and major financial donors, and others. Both opponents and supporters of affirmative action should strive to eliminate all preferences, despite the difficulties involved in stripping away the many traditional advantages enjoyed by individuals with access to those in positions of power.

Although education alone has never been a sufficient deterrent to racial discrimination, affirmative action policies that focus on providing education and training opportunities to all Americans qualifying them for jobs are likely to be supported by most Americans. Affirmative action in the military, as we have seen, is not a controversial issue because the emphasis is on preparing individuals from all racial backgrounds to meet required qualifications. A focus on excellence would eliminate many complaints about affirmative action. But qualifications are not limited to test scores and grades. Attributes such as courage, interpersonal skills, determination, and creativity are also crucial in hiring and promotion decisions.

Private organizations, especially if they are supported by proponents and opponents of affirmative action alike, can play an important role in diminishing the problems generated by current affirmative action policies. Private organizations that focus on education help to expand opportunities for racial minorities and can gradually discourage the practice of preferential treatment. Furthermore, increasing minority contacts with influential people would give minority group members some of the advantages now taken for granted by most white Americans. The Ford Foundation, for example, allocates significant resources to educating and training minorities for leading positions in the academic world. Similarly, the National Action Council for Minorities in Engineering, a nonprofit organization based in New York, is dedicated to bringing more racial minority members into the engineering profession. Tangible efforts such as these indicate a commitment to ensuring equal opportunity and treatment.

One of the most effective ways to reduce the controversy over affirmative action is for both its supporters and opponents to focus on the illegality of discrimination and to support the vigorous and relentless prosecution of organizations and individuals engaged in it. Because discrimination against minorities is the justification for affirmative action, conscientiously enforcing antidiscrimination laws is likely to lessen the need for some aspects of affirmative action that many Americans oppose. Sixty-four percent of Americans favor the passage of tougher federal laws with stiffer penalties for companies that discriminate in hiring and promotion.[56] Like the military, civilian society should embrace a policy of "zero tolerance" of discrimination.

Companies such as Denny's, Texaco, and Shoney's became ardent opponents of discrimination after settling large discrimination suits. Shoney's, for example, under Raymond Danner's leadership, blatantly discriminated against Americans with African ancestry. White managers were instructed by Danner to dismiss blacks if they constituted a large share of the employees in outlets in predominantly white neighborhoods. Managers who refused to comply risked losing their own jobs. Applications from blacks were coded and many of them discarded, and Danner himself resorted to racial slurs. Like many companies, Shoney's was headed by older-generation board members. Even though significant progress has been made in race relations, many older Americans continue to be strongly influenced by a culture that is hostile to equal opportunity and treatment, a fact often overlooked by younger Americans who have grown up in a much more racially tolerant society. After settling a racial discrimination suit for $134.5 million, Shoney's realized that its racial policies had to be radically transformed and that a program of affirmative action was required to rectify the damage caused by its earlier policies of systematic racial discrimination. Shoney's not only terminated its unfair practices, it also increased business contracts with minority-owned firms, hired two black vice presidents, increased the number of black-owned Shoney's franchises, and appointed the first black to the company's nine-member board.[57]

Adopting a win-win approach and encouraging members of different racial groups to work together toward mutually agreeable solutions and to "expand the pie" are likely to lead to racial and ethnic reconciliation. An affirmative action strategy that creates adversarial relationships instead of cooperative ones is ultimately counterproductive and self-defeating. Having experienced much confrontation over affirmative action issues for thirteen years, the city of Birmingham, Alabama, decided that expanded opportunities for blacks and fair treatment of white contractors could both be achieved by establishing the Birmingham Construction Industry Authority. Jointly funded by the city and white contractors, this agency helps black-owned firms compete for both private- and public-sector projects without the threat of government mandates, set-asides, or quotas.

Realizing how expensive, both financially and socially, continued confrontation would be, blacks and whites in Birmingham decided to focus on their mutual interests and help each other. The Birmingham Construction Industry Authority serves as a conduit for bringing black and white contractors together and encouraging joint ventures. White contractors agreed to notify the agency of private construction jobs so that black firms can put in competitive bids. Equally significant, instead of just pointing out that blacks lack various skills, many white contractors mentor blacks and help them acquire essential managerial and marketing skills.[58]

One of the most divisive aspects of affirmative action is its association in the minds of supporters and opponents alike with identity politics. Race is increasingly viewed as the dominant, if not exclusive, determinant of identity. In order to shift the focus to a common humanity and a common American identity, affirmative action policies must concentrate less on race-conscious strategies and more on the inclusion of all disadvantaged Americans. Resentment is bound to increase as whites from economically impoverished backgrounds lose out to members of racial minority groups from economically advantaged backgrounds who can consolidate their privileged status by taking advantage of the opportunities offered by affirmative action programs.

Class-based affirmative action, as a component of a comprehensive approach to fighting discrimination, is likely to decrease racial tensions, provide an environment conducive to the achievement of a color-blind society, and motivate individuals to take the responsibility to work hard and be competitive.[59] As the country becomes even more racially diverse, the original purposes of affirmative action are weakened by the inclusion of groups designated as victims simply on the basis of skin color, surname, or national origin. Class-based affirmative action has the potential to promote cooperative behavior across racial groups and to help the country move closer toward the goal of getting beyond race.

6

IMMIGRATION AND TRAVELING ABROAD

Undermining the Concept of Race

As an immigrant nation, America has always been shaped by the arrival of large numbers of people from throughout the world. For most of its history, however, the United States strongly encouraged immigrants from northern and western European countries to settle the vast country, while barring large-scale nonwhite immigration. Europeans brought with them values and beliefs that influenced the very definition of America and the identity of the American. As shown in Chapter 2, "American" became synonymous with "European" and with whiteness in the social construction of race. The concept of whiteness was instrumental in uniting Europeans who had previously thought of themselves principally in nationalistic terms.

Immigrants from Latin America, Asia, the Caribbean, Africa, and the Middle East, allowed entry in greater numbers because of revisions in U.S. immigration policies in 1965, are not only changing the racial composition of America but are also altering some aspects of American culture. This influx of non-Europeans has been accompanied by increased anti-immigrant sentiments as well as by efforts to include immigrants into the mainstream of American society. For some Americans, immigrants from non-European regions have created anxiety and insecurity about who is an American in general and doubts regarding their own self-definition in particular. These new arrivals challenge the concept of race, which is seen primarily as black and white. In so doing, they strengthen the forces of change that are already present in the United States.

Race in America has been so powerful an organizing force for such a long time partly because Americans categorized as "white" are usually easily distinguishable from Americans categorized as "black." Furthermore, both whites and blacks generally accept these racial classifications as an integral component of the country's social construction of race. Newer immigrants, coming from diverse cultural backgrounds, do not necessarily share most Americans' views on the concept of race. Because of their different worldviews, they might look at society in terms of ethnic and class differences instead. Racial categorization is further weakened by the growing rate of interracial marriages, many of them occurring between immigrants and white Americans.

Immigration also contributes to undermining the concept of race by strengthening the power of American minority groups. In many important metropolitan areas, racial minorities are fast becoming majorities. The rapid growth of non-European immigrants creates the potential for intraminority conflicts; it also underlines the need for Americans of all racial backgrounds to establish interracial coalitions to secure shared interests. Another important way in which immigrants are helping to move the country beyond race is by challenging racial stereotypes through their economic success and their ability to build bridges across black-white boundaries. As more immigrants achieve positions of power, they are likely to make society more sensitive to racial problems.

Like immigration, travel abroad has an impact on race relations. Americans who visit or live in foreign countries are usually exposed to different ways of perceiving themselves. They are also made more aware of how others see them and what it feels like to be a minority, an outsider. What becomes obvious from traveling abroad is that America's concerns with race and its one-drop rule defining blacks are not universally accepted. Furthermore, many Americans of different races become more aware of their shared cultural characteristics as they operate outside their familiar social environments. As I will discuss later, Malcolm X and others dramatically altered their racial attitudes and behavior due to interpersonal contacts with people from different racial backgrounds during their travels abroad. Finally, American students studying in foreign countries and foreign students studying in the United States, in more modest ways, help erode racial barriers.

Demographic and Cultural Change

For most of its history, the United States favored unfettered immigration from western Europe to support its unprecedented economic growth and rapid territorial expansion. At the same time, racial realities and government policies essentially restricted non-Europeans from entering the country in significant numbers. Americans with African ancestry, who outnumbered Americans of European ancestry in some southern states, initially arrived in the United States under conditions of involuntary servitude and as property. Native Americans, largely perceived as part of the untamed wilderness, were killed or removed from areas desired by European settlers.

American attitudes and practices made it abundantly clear that non-whites were to be excluded, and attempts were made to establish the United States as a "white man's" country. President Thomas Jefferson and the American Colonization Society, for example, supported sending blacks to Africa and elsewhere, partly because it was believed that blacks and whites could not live together. But white dependence on black labor and the fact that blacks were already an integral part of American society rendered such schemes unrealizable.

Nevertheless, U.S. immigration policies continued to give preference to immigrants from northern and western Europe until the early 1900s. As the percentage of immigrants from these regions declined, immigrants from southern and eastern Europe increased. The enactment of a quota system favored immigrants from countries that already had large numbers of their former citizens living in the United States. There was an absolute limit of two thousand immigrants per year from the Asia-Pacific region. Confronted with opposition from domestic groups and foreign governments to what they regarded as blatant inconsistencies between America's democratic and egalitarian principles on one hand and its discriminatory practices on the other, the United States abolished the national-origin quota in 1965.[1]

Prior to 1965, substantial numbers of West Indians had immigrated to the United States under the quota system, which strongly favored British immigrants. Unlike the United States, which only reluctantly counted blacks as citizens, Great Britain, at least in theory, acknowledged the former slaves in its colonies as British subjects who were entitled to the same rights granted to other British subjects. Due largely to Britain's policy, between 1891 and 1910 more than 230,000 immigrants, most of whom were of African ancestry, arrived in the United States from the British West Indies. By the 1920s, British West Indians constituted approximately one-fourth of Harlem's population and exercised significant influence in New York politics.[2]

Whereas economic prosperity in Europe discouraged high levels of emigration after 1965, rapid population growth and continuing economic problems combined to push people from Asia, Latin America, the Caribbean, and Africa to the United States. By the 1970s, people from the Third World accounted for almost three-quarters of the four million immigrants who settled in the United States since 1965. In 1969, three immigrants arrived from Europe for every two from Asia. This pattern was reversed by 1976, when Asian immigrants outnumbered European immigrants two to one. Blacks and racially mixed people came in record numbers from the Dominican Republic, Haiti, Cuba, Puerto Rico, Guyana, Jamaica, and other Caribbean nations and territories. By 1980, the Dominican Republic had become the seventh-largest source of immigrants to the United States, ahead of Britain, Canada, and Portugal. Europeans have made up less than 20 percent of the number of immigrants arriving in the United States in the 1980s and 1990s.[3]

Between 1980 and 1990, due partly to immigration, the black population in the United States grew by 13.2 percent, whites by 6.0 percent, Asians by 107.8 percent, Latinos by 53.0 percent, Native Americans by 37.9 percent, and "others" by 45.1 percent. The increase in the number of Native Americans stems from the willingness of more whites to classify themselves as Native Americans, based on their mixed racial heritage. The Asian population is expected to double its current size by 2009, triple by 2024, and quadruple by 2038. It is predicted that by the middle of the twenty-first century, there will be five times as many Asian Americans as there are at the end of the twentieth century, or about 41 million. Latinos, who currently compose 10.1 percent of America's population, will constitute almost 20 percent by the year 2040. Blacks, who now make up 12.6 percent, will increase to 15.5 percent by 2040. Whites will decline from 82.8 percent of the population now to 73.8 percent in 2040. If whites of Hispanic origin are excluded, the percentage of the American population that will be white in 2040 will drop to 56.4 percent. And by 2050, whites who are not of Hispanic origin are expected to make up only 52.7 percent of the total population. Immigration is an important component of this overall shift in America's racial distribution.[4]

Such a dramatic alteration of the racial composition of the United States is bound to have a significant impact on race relations. Waves of immigration from Latin America, together with high birth rates among Latinos, will downgrade the status of blacks as the nation's largest racial minority. Latinos already outnumber blacks in Los Angeles, Houston, Phoenix, and San Antonio, and they are likely to soon overtake blacks in New York. While these developments have already engendered conflicts between blacks and Latinos, the need for interracial cooperation remains strong. Blacks, in order to avoid being further marginalized, will increasingly be forced to move beyond race to form coalitions based on interests. But these racial groups are not monolithic, and conflicts within groups are as likely to occur as conflicts among them, making race a less prominent factor.

Unlike the early European immigrants, who were separated from their countries of origin by the vast Atlantic Ocean, the new immigrants are arriving at the height of a technological revolution that facilitates travel and communication among people who are separated by great distances. To a much greater extent than the previous waves of immigrants, Asians, Africans, Latin Americans, Middle Easterners, and the people of the Caribbean maintain strong ties with the relatives and friends they left behind. The new immigrants are essentially transmigrants in the sense that they maintain multiple and constant connections across international borders.[5] In the process, they forge links between their societies of origin and the places where they settle. Furthermore, they have multiple identities, of which race might be relatively insignificant.

Latinos and Caribbean peoples, because of their home countries' geographic proximity to the United States, have the most thorough and wide-ranging contacts with their countries of origin. But fax machines, e-mail connections, televisions, telephones, and rapid transportation enable immigrants from more distant lands to also remain in contact with their families and cultures. It is much cheaper and often less complicated for immigrants living in New York to fly to San Juan, Puerto Rico, than it is for an American to travel from Chicago to Montana. Many immigrants from Mexico often cross a very porous border.

Instead of simply being assimilated into American culture, the new arrivals are changing American culture to a greater extent than earlier immigrants. Dominican and Puerto Rican newspapers are on sale in Manhattan the day of publication, and Mexican newspapers arrive in Los Angeles just as quickly.[6] Radio and television stations broadcast foreign-language programs throughout the United States, and Spanish in Miami and Los Angeles is often more prevalent than English. This ability to function in two or more cultures simultaneously reduces the incentive to fully assimilate into America's culture. The sense of separateness also allows new immigrants to more carefully evaluate America's racial assumptions. Constant contact with their old cultures reminds them that race is not always the dominant consideration.

Many immigrants from the Middle East bring with them the view that religion is the dominant factor in human relations and that race is not as significant. Islam, fast becoming a major force in American society, boasts of an ability to bring people of all races together. The number of Muslims in the United States is rapidly increasing, due primarily to immigration and conversions among Americans with African ancestry.[7] As Islam becomes more prominent in American society, its central tenet of racial harmony has the potential to contribute to efforts to get beyond race.

Immigration is a significant agent of demographic and social change in large cities as well as small towns throughout the United States. As nonwhite immigrants move into cities like New York, Chicago, Los Angeles, Houston, and Boston, some whites leave. In New York City, for example, the population increased by roughly 3.5 percent between 1980 and 1990,

but the white population declined by about 10.9 percent during that period. San Diego was the only major metropolitan area that attracted more
whites than it was losing. Unlike traditional "white flight" from cities to
suburbs, the new trend is characterized by whites abandoning entire metropolitan areas for destinations that are less attractive to immigrants.[8] But es-
caping demographic changes is becoming increasingly difficult.

Small towns, such as Worthington, Minnesota, with a population of approximately ten thousand, are experiencing an influx of immigrants from
remote corners of the world. Almost all-white a decade ago, Worthington
acquired a cosmopolitan veneer as immigrants from Mexico, Laos, Vietnam, Sudan, and Ethiopia came to work at ConAgra, a large pork-process-
ing plant.[9] Racial issues arise as old and new residents struggle to adjust to
each other, and community leaders and others must try to improve communication and understanding among the different racial groups.

These demographic changes often cause Americans to wrestle with what it
means to be white or black. It also forces them to think about what it means
to be an American. Ironically, Peter Brimelow, himself an immigrant from
Britain, worries about the implications of the new racial and ethnic balance
in America. He believes that the mass immigration of non-Europeans after
1965 risks making America an "alien nation," clearly implying that Americanness is equated with whiteness. In his view, "America will become a freak
among the world's nations because of the unprecedented demographic muta-
tion it is inflicting upon itself."[10]

Although Brimelow's concerns about threats to America's shared common culture are understandable, he clearly overlooks the reality of America
as a country that has been ethnically and racially diverse for a long time.
For the past few centuries, American culture has been flexible enough to incorporate people from throughout the world. The United States, in a very
real sense, has a universal culture. However, immigration, by dramatically
altering demographic realities, helps shape future race relations in the
United States.

Challenging the American Concept of Race

An outgrowth of slavery and segregation, the American concept of race is
based on the unusually sharp and rigidly fixed division between black and
white, which is designed to keep the two groups separate and unequal. The
established consensus has been that skin color is the predominant determinant of membership in these polarized and unbridgeable racial categories.
One drop of black blood automatically made someone of predominantly
European ancestry black, but not vice versa. This one-drop rule remains the
de facto determinant of race in America, but only in relation to blacks. The
consensus on this definition of black and white, initially obtained through

systematic coercion, has been generally accepted by both blacks and whites as social reality. The perpetuation of the concept of race and racism depends on widespread public acceptance of the binary or dichotomous black-white view of race.

Immigration, by further complicating an already racially diverse society, erodes the dichotomous approach that virtually guarantees the continuation of the significance of race in American society. The vast majority of new immigrants are neither black nor white. Many of them are mixtures of several racial groups who do not perceive themselves as belonging to any of America's narrowly defined racial categories. Their refusal to accept the American concept of race, combined with other important cultural changes, helps undermine the consensus on which the social construction of race depends. Who is white or who is black becomes more difficult to determine because of the increasing range of skin colors and intimate bonds among Americans of all colors. Under these circumstances, the meanings of and benefits that flow from conventional perceptions of race diminish.

Many immigrants not only refuse to subscribe to America's concept of race, they also challenge it on many levels. Several individuals who came to America in the 1960s or earlier recall their first reactions to race relations. A Russian Jew who came to the United States in the 1950s still harks back to his experiences with intelligence tests, on which he did poorly. He became a prominent chemistry professor but always remembers that Jews faced discrimination. These experiences have strengthened his relations with blacks and other minority groups. Chang-Lin Tien's experiences with discrimination were discussed earlier in Chapter 5. Tien further remembers his initial reactions to segregated seating on public buses. He says, "I didn't know where I belonged, so for a long time I stood near the driver. Finally he told me to sit in front, and I did. I didn't take another bus ride for a whole year. I would walk an hour to avoid that."[11] Tien strongly supports affirmative action.

Immigrants also challenge conventional ideas on race by devising alternative ways of categorizing individuals and by focusing on nonracial sources of identity. Immigrants augment the resurgence of ethnicity and culture as alternatives to race as primary determinants of identity. Distinctions among immigrants from the Caribbean and Latin America, for example, are largely based on nationality and class. Puerto Ricans, Haitians, Dominicans, Jamaicans, Cubans, and Mexicans are likely to emphasize ethnicity, partly because racial mixing in these regions has rendered attempts to neatly categorize people based on skin color virtually futile. These realities are increasingly becoming part of America's social fabric. Sharp black-white distinctions are weakened and the system of racial classification is made more difficult to maintain by the injection of immigrant values and attitudes into society.

Sally Katzen, administrator of the Office of Information and Regulatory Affairs in the Office of Management and Budget, which is responsible for the country's racial classifications, believes that the current standards of racial definition will become less useful as America grows more ethnically and racially diverse.[12] The census has difficulty counting Hispanics because many write in their nationality or check "other" when asked to classify themselves racially. In the 1990 census, for example, about 10 million Americans did not categorize themselves within the four racial groups (white, black, Asian–Pacific islander, and American Indian–Alaskan native), preferring instead to define themselves as "other." Between 1980 and 1990, the number of people in California who classified themselves as "other" rose from 2.36 million to 3.94 million, or an increase of 66.7 percent. In Los Angeles, the residents who selected the "other" category increased 102.3 percent during the same period.[13] This sharp rise was due largely to the influx of immigrants from Latin America.

Racially categorizing people from throughout the world is fast becoming almost impossible. For example, immigrants from the vast region between Morocco and Afghanistan encompassing the Middle East, North Africa, and Turkey are listed as "white, non-European." In other words, Egyptians, Sudanese, Saudi Arabians, and Libyans are "white," despite the fact that many of them are Africans with much darker complexions than most Americans with African ancestry, who find themselves in the "black" category. The illogic of this system is obvious and painful to many younger Americans.

Public schools struggle with trying to fit multiracial children into official racial categories. Some administrators, like census personnel, arbitrarily classify children. Others allow parents to provide their own label. However, as I point out in Chapter 7, interracial marriages also frustrate attempts to neatly categorize people in racial terms. In late 1997 the Census Bureau decided to allow Americans to check more than one racial category to reflect their racial mixture. Furthermore, many Americans seem confused about the difference between race and ethnicity. For some of them, "multiracial" means having parents or grandparents from different national backgrounds. The challenge posed by immigration to America's racial definitions is made clearer by examining various immigrant groups' views of race.

The fastest growing minority group in the United States, people of Hispanic background, do not generally subscribe to the American concept of race. As Dominick La Capra puts it: "The notion of race is particularly elusive with reference to Hispanics; no color definition actually applies."[14] Immigrants from Latin America and the Caribbean try to make sense of U.S. racial categories through the prism of their own experiences with and definitions of race. Puerto Ricans, for example, are predominantly a mixture of Europeans, Africans, and Caribbean Indians. Although they, like other Latinos, have developed their own racial categories, their definition of race is flexible and intertwined with economic considerations. Many Puerto Ricans who are regarded as white in the Caribbean are often categorized as black in the United States. Focusing principally on culture and national identity, most Hispanics attempt to downplay the significance of race in their communities. Unlike most Americans, they usually reject the one-drop rule.[15]

Historical, religious, and cultural influences originating in Europe help explain how Latinos perceive race. Unlike the British, who were relatively isolated from non-Europeans, the Spanish and Portuguese experienced greater exposure to the peoples of the Mediterranean world. The Mediterranean Sea facilitated contacts among the Spanish, Portuguese, Italians, North Africans, and Middle Easterners. Spain's geographic proximity to Morocco encouraged navigation, migration, and trade, as well as conflict. From 711 to 1609 the Moors made major contributions to the cultures and economies of Spain, Portugal, and other parts of western Europe. Several areas of Spain and Portugal had been ruled from the eighth century until the fifteenth century by the Moors, who were both darker skinned and better educated than the native Spanish and Portuguese. Consequently, the Spanish, many of whom were racially mixed themselves, did not automatically equate dark skin with political or cultural inferiority. Iberian racism tended to be milder and less pervasive than that found in northern Europe and later in the United States.[16]

Instead of concentrating on racial characteristics, the Spanish tended to merge race and culture and to elevate their cultural achievements above considerations of racial purity. Like the French, the Spanish tried to Hispanicize the people they encountered through language, culture, and religion. Mastery of the Spanish language theoretically, and often in practice, allowed anyone, regardless of skin color, to become a Spaniard. An important reason for this liberal approach to race was undoubtedly the strong influence of the Catholic Church in almost all aspects of national life.

Determined to convert "heathens" to Catholicism, the Church emphasized saving souls rather than constructing a rigid racial hierarchy. Arnold J. Toynbee discusses the relative ease with which an Inca in Peru could pass from the village to modern society: "The Indian can end up as President of the Republic and as the husband of the daughter of one of the traditional oligarchs. Every opportunity is open to him, once inside, and the terms of entry are not exacting. On these terms, every citizen of the United States who has African blood in his veins would have 'passed' long ago."[17]

Spanish experience with racial classification is indicative of future race relations in the United States. In Mexico and elsewhere in Latin America, the Spanish readily married or took as mistresses Native Americans as well as Africans. Interracial marriage was never prohibited in Mexico or the other Spanish colonies. In an attempt to take all aspects of a person's racial background into account, the Spanish devised a complex taxonomy of racial phenotypes. Pierre L. van den Berghe believes that the minutiae with which shades of color were distinguished and the complexity of the terminology that reserved a special term for every possible crossing of Indian, European, and African at least three generations back greatly lowered the reliability and validity of the classification.[18] Eventually, the system of racial categorization was rendered useless by its own complexity. Mexico, Brazil, and other Latin American countries now extol the virtues of racial mixing and racial democracy, despite continuing problems with race in those countries.

Similar to Latin America, the Caribbean has a flexible definition of race and generally does not focus exclusively on racial characteristics when making social distinctions. Although many of the islands were (and some still are) under British control, their demographic composition closely resembles that of Latin America. The small white population, which was primarily made up of men, not only produced racially mixed children but also often recognized and educated them. Racially mixed people become an intermediate group between blacks and whites, thereby helping to bridge racial divisions. These mixed-race offspring inherited property and competed with whites for position and power. Haiti is an example of a society where the *gens de couleur* fully embraced European culture. Many mixed-race Haitians were educated in France and inherited property, including slaves.

Instead of a rigid distinction between black and white, Caribbean societies emphasize many gradations of skin color. This approach encourages people to claim all their relatives. Colin Powell, whose parents are from Jamaica, notes that he is a combination of African, English, Irish, Scottish, Arawak Indian, and Jewish.[19] Recognizing one's own complex racial background militates against acceptance of America's binary view of race. It makes one more willing to accept others.

Widespread racial mixing, facilitated by the small size of the Caribbean islands, diminishes the significance of race but highlights the importance of class, ethnicity, and national identity. West Indians are keenly aware of ethnic identification as a unifying force. They are also convinced that ethnicity plays a pivotal role in the success that many of them achieve in the United States. It is quite common throughout the Caribbean for parents to point to successful West Indians like Colin Powell, Shirley Chisolm, and Sidney Poitier as role models for their children.

Apart from the fact that black West Indians are leaders in their own societies and cooperate closely with other West Indians of a wide range of skin colors, the islands' dependence on tourism is a strong motivation for people to work together to remove racial barriers. Many immigrants from the Caribbean to the United States are likely to have had positive relations with whites, reinforcing their belief that race is not always important. Their self-confidence and their reluctance to perceive the world primarily through a racial prism make it easier for whites to interact with them, and vice versa.

Many immigrants from the Middle East embrace views similar to those of Hispanics. Like Spain, the Middle Eastern countries stress religion as a unifying force as well as a divider between Muslims and non-Muslims. Religious beliefs matter much more than skin color. Racial mixing in the Middle East has made racial distinctions virtually meaningless. Although East Africans were slaves in southern Iraq's sugar plantations and salt marshes and elsewhere in the region, most Africans in the Middle East were domestic servants and concubines in the cities. African women often became part of the families of those who enslaved them, and close relationships developed between slaves and slaveholders. According to Muslim law, the Shari'a, slaves were to be treated kindly; freeing them was viewed positively.[20]

In sharp contrast to the United States, where slavery was equated with race, Middle Eastern countries enslaved non-Muslims of all races. Military slaves were taken primarily from central Asia and the Caucasus. Europeans were also enslaved. But slavery was a comparatively flexible institution. Slaves fought for various countries and supported and founded dynasties. Slaveholders recognized the children they had with slave women, and many slaves converted to Islam and were freed. Once freed, a slave could marry his master's daughter or conduct his business for him.[21] As was the case in Latin America, slaves were fully assimilated into Middle Eastern societies. Although Middle Eastern immigrants to the United States are not without racial prejudices, they are more inclined to elevate religion above race in their social categorization of individuals.

Emigrants from Asia come from cultures that generally stress social hierarchy and their own superiority over other racial groups, including Europeans. A visitor to China is not only struck by that country's long history but also by the Chinese confidence in their cultural superiority. Many Japanese hold similar perceptions. Moreover, Asians are more inclined to concentrate on national identity and social class than on race to distinguish themselves from each other. Consequently, many regard the concept of an "Asian American" as a myth. They know that there are significant ethnic and regional differences among Asians. The Japanese and Chinese hardly think of each other as belonging to the same racial category.

Cooperation and Conflict Among Racial Minorities

Anti-immigration sentiment has often led to conflict between the new arrivals, who often inspire tension, and established Americans who feel threatened by perceived competition and social change. However, because many immigrants experience racism in the United States, they tend to cooperate with America's racial minorities. These alliances are based on a perception of common interests and the need to work together to achieve them. Americans with African ancestry and West Indians, for example, have a long history of cooperation. However, conflicts among racial minorities are as frequent as conflicts between blacks and whites. Although immigration heightens racial tensions, it also vividly demonstrates that races are not monolithic, that race is not always the pivotal factor shaping relations between individuals. Immigration complicates the neatness of black-white conflict, thereby weakening the premise underlying the socially constructed concept of race.

Yet the strength of racial categorization in the United States often prompts new immigrants to adopt negative images of blacks. The development of antiblack attitudes and behavior is believed to be an essential component of the Americanization process. Negative behavior toward blacks is also adopted as a strategy for reducing the prejudice that newcomers are likely to face from established residents. Indeed, the global influence of American culture makes it difficult for most immigrants to wholeheartedly embrace positive attitudes toward Americans with African ancestry.[22] But the experiences of many immigrants in the United States push them toward rejecting some of their negative stereotypes of blacks.

The experiences of West Indians provide an example of the complex relations between immigrants and American racial minorities. As early as the 1920s, West Indians played a major role in building black self-confidence. The most obvious example is Marcus Garvey's "Back to Africa" movement. In the 1960s, another West Indian, Stokely Carmichael, articulated the "Black is Beautiful" philosophy to encourage blacks to accept themselves as equal human beings. Recently, Colin Powell and Louis Farrakhan, two Americans of West Indian ancestry with very different perspectives and approaches, have become leaders of the black community. West Indians in America and the Caribbean strongly identified with the civil rights movement and continue to support many of the issues embraced by Americans with African ancestry.

Nevertheless, West Indians also perceive themselves to be a separate cultural group and attempt to maintain their identity by withdrawing into West Indian enclaves and by building strong, successful families. Many black Americans perceive West Indians to be aloof and clannish. The relative success of West Indians reinforces negative feelings between the two groups. Like other immigrants in general, West Indians are ambitious, self-confident, and energetic. Many of them have technical skills and highly value education as the principal instrument of upward mobility. Partly in response to what they regard as West Indian arrogance, many black Americans have developed their own stereotypes of West Indians.[23]

Latinos and blacks both clash and cooperate on issues such as affirmative action, multiculturalism, and immigration. Native-born black Americans view the arrival of large numbers of Hispanic immigrants as a threat to their status as America's largest and most politically and socially significant racial minority; they also view them as competitors for the benefits that accompany that status. Many blacks resent the ability of Latinos, many of whom regard themselves as white, to qualify for affirmative action programs regardless of their economic status or length of residence in the United States. But the two groups also cooperate on issues of mutual interest.

Some of the most dramatic conflicts between minority groups in recent American history occurred in Los Angeles during the riots that were sparked by the acquittal of white police officers accused of using excessive force against Rodney King in 1992. Many Korean stores were looted and burned by blacks and Latinos. Blacks in particular believe that Korean immigrants hold negative stereotypes of them, exploit them, fail to employ them, and make few attempts to understand the communities in which they operate businesses. The lack of close interaction between blacks and Koreans stifles the emergence of trust.[24] In an effort to rectify some of the problems, Korean merchants have taken classes designed to help them adjust to American culture. Some of them have also employed community residents in addition to family members. But most are still reluctant to invest in black communities.

Despite Islam's teachings advocating tolerance and nondiscrimination, relations between immigrants from the Middle East, most of whom are Muslims, and blacks are characterized by both conflict and cooperation. Black Americans who have converted to Islam and who worship in mainstream mosques often discover that the egalitarianism they expect from Muslims can be elusive. However, both groups are making greater efforts to extend their fellowship and to embrace each other.[25] This relationship clearly demonstrates that an immigrant's cultural or racial background does not necessarily remain unaffected by the socially constructed reality of race in America.

Challenging Racial Stereotypes: West Indian Americans

In sharp contrast to earlier generations of immigrants, newcomers in the late twentieth century tend to be well educated and prepared to immediately enter the upper echelons of the American middle class. Their professional and technical skills bring them into contact with both whites and blacks across the United States. Medical doctors and nurses, for example, usually settle in large urban centers and practice in inner-city hospitals that serve poor Americans. A large number of them obtain additional training when they arrive in the United States, usually in hospitals frequented by racial minorities. Howard University in Washington, D.C., for example, attracts medical professionals from around the world who later practice in the Washington area.

Physicians from Asia, Latin America, Africa, and elsewhere often migrate to small towns and rural areas that do not attract American doctors, many of whom practice in the more lucrative urban centers.

Numerous personal contacts between whites and immigrant medical professionals from different racial and ethnic backgrounds help diminish racial stereotypes. The respected status of these immigrants shifts the focus away from skin color to their professional abilities. Furthermore, their close cooperation with white patients creates trust and a sense of a common humanity. Both these professional immigrants and the established residents whom they service are likely to make a conscientious effort to move beyond race in order to engender an environment conducive to the attainment of their mutual interests and the strengthening of their interdependent relationships.

Nonwhite immigrants directly challenge racial stereotypes by behaving in a manner inconsistent with the expectations many Americans still have of racial minorities. The immigrants' economic and professional success undermines many fundamental assumptions that undergird the social construction of race. As discussed in Chapter 1, successful minorities are most effective in challenging the notion that skin color determines intelligence and success. The magical qualities of race, which erect almost insurmountable psychological obstacles to minority progress, have little or no impact when applied to immigrants who have not been enculturated and coerced to believe them.

Because the social construction of race in America is based principally on a black-white dichotomy, successful black immigrants help cast doubt on the idea that skin color is equivalent to destiny. But more often than not, success by West Indians and Asians is often used not to challenge racial stereotypes but to reinforce them in relation to Americans with African ancestry. The conclusion frequently drawn is that West Indian success proves that American blacks themselves, and not white discrimination and racial attitudes, are responsible for their own continuing problems.[26] However, those making this argument inadvertently undermine the concept of race by supporting the view that culture and personal characteristics, not skin color, determine personal success or failure. In other words, the failure of many blacks cannot be entirely divorced from certain aspects of American culture.

Although Asians and Latinos also challenge racial stereotypes by their success in business and education, the example of West Indians is most telling in this regard because they are racially indistinguishable from Americans with African ancestry. Moreover, they share a common history of slavery. Because race in America is still largely thought of in terms of black versus white, West Indians vividly demonstrate the fallacy of the social construction of race and the stereotypes that emanate from it.

Comparisons between black Americans and West Indians must take into consideration the selective nature of immigration. West Indians who leave their societies are usually among the best educated and most highly trained on their respective islands. Many earlier West Indian immigrants had come from urban areas with a degree of sophistication that was lacking in many parts of the rural American South, the main source of blacks who migrated to urban areas in the North. Consequently, West Indians were better able to mix with whites in New York and elsewhere. As will be shown, Caribbean history differs remarkably from that of the United States, a circumstance that gives rise to major differences between West Indians and black Americans.

Colin Powell notes in his book *My American Journey* that history has played a pivotal role in the impressive record of accomplishments by West Indians.[27] Although the ancestors of both black Americans and West Indians arrived in the New World as slaves, slavery in the American South and in the West Indies differed greatly. Americans with African ancestry remained in slavery for more than a generation longer than West Indians, and after emancipation black Americans faced circumstances that in many cases bordered on involuntary servitude. Whereas black Americans struggled for basic human and civil rights for more than a century after they had been freed, West Indian blacks were immediately made British subjects with all the rights of any British citizen. Education was made mandatory, and West Indians assumed responsibility for running their own societies. Colin Powell believes that an important difference between black Americans and West Indians is largely psychological: West Indians did not have to endure the disparagement of their dignity for three hundred years, the fate of so many black American slaves and their descendants.[28]

Conditions during slavery laid the foundation for many of the differences between the two groups. By all accounts, slavery was harsher in the West Indies than in the American South. The plantations in the West Indies were much larger than those in the United States and the work was considerably harder. The tropical climate allowed agricultural production to continue throughout the year. The death rate among West Indians slaves was higher, due mainly to these harsh conditions. Approximately two million slaves were imported into the British West Indies alone before the slave trade was abolished in 1808, a figure five times larger than the number imported into the United States.[29] This harshness, paradoxically, promoted greater self-reliance among West Indians.

Compared to slaves in America, who were deliberately made dependent on slaveholders and their families, enslaved Africans in the West Indies were required to take care of themselves in addition to being forced to work on sugar plantations. West Indian slaves were given incentives to take the initiative. Slaveholders made it possible for slaves to own and cultivate land and to market the produce. They developed much experience in buying, selling, and managing their own affairs. This measure of independence gained during slavery was consolidated following emancipation. Their lives were difficult, but West Indian blacks escaped the crippling paternalism endured by American slaves.

Another major difference between slavery in the West Indies and in the United States is demographic. Blacks have always been the majority in the West Indies, with resident whites making up a small but powerful minority. Whites in the Caribbean generally viewed their tenure there as temporary. Their self-esteem and self-definition were securely anchored to their European homelands. Furthermore, they were generally managing the properties of European aristocrats and merchants who were considered their superiors. Consequently, whites had little vested interest in developing a racist ideology to justify their behavior and secure their social position. In sharp contrast, whites in the American South perceived their self-definition to be intertwined with maintaining a system of racial superiority. Unlike whites in the West Indies who had their homes in Europe, white Americans' homes were right where slavery existed. Independent and strong blacks were a direct challenge to whites' self-identity.

Given their history of self-reliance and entrepreneurship, West Indians in the United States are more likely to take advantage of opportunities than many black Americans. Many West Indians hold down several jobs to provide for family members, both nuclear and extended. A culture that encourages entrepreneurship influences West Indians to own their homes instead of renting apartments. To obtain their economic goals, they pool their resources, like many other immigrant groups. Jamaican women in New York, for example, often form mutual-aid societies called *chetas* or rotating credit and savings associations. Each member donates money on a weekly basis. Different members of the association borrow from the "pot" for business expenses, housing, college tuition bills, and other investments. These associations are often regarded as model financial support mechanisms for lower-income groups in America.[30]

At the heart of West Indian success in America is an almost religious embrace of education as an instrument of upward mobility, a conviction reinforced by strong family and friendship ties. Unlike most black Americans, who were denied economic opportunities even if they had earned advanced degrees from universities such as Harvard, West Indians assumed responsibility for the functioning of their societies and governments. Therefore, they regarded education as an asset. They were strongly encouraged by the British, by their own governments, and by each other to obtain an education. Consequently, they take full advantage of what they regard as unprecedented, abundant opportunities to acquire an education in America. Parents place the responsibility of achievement on their children and regard teachers as allies who should demand the highest-quality work from students. From the perspective of many West Indians, a person's ability to achieve is not limited by skin color but by lack of education.[31] These cultural values facilitate the ability of many West Indians to compete effectively with whites and to meet race-neutral qualifications for employment and promotion.

Immigrants as Bridge Builders: Black West Indians

Growing up in societies where race was not the dominant source of identity, many immigrants downplay the importance of race in the process of navigating the maze of complex relationships between blacks and whites in the United States. Their ability to avoid becoming immobilized by race is a result of how they perceive problems. When most West Indians, Latinos, and Asians encounter racial discrimination, they tend to reframe the problems in light of comparable experiences in their countries of origin. They are less likely to take discrimination personally.

Americans with African ancestry, on the other hand, are usually convinced that racism lies behind almost every aspect of their lives. Their experiences with pervasive discrimination in a society dominated by the white majority often lead many of them to conclude that no matter how hard they try, they will not be adequately rewarded for their efforts. Whereas most black Americans generally externalize failure, blaming the racist system, West Indians are inclined to believe that they are responsible for their own problems—that they didn't try hard enough or that they made serious errors. This is due in part to their own experiences in predominantly black societies in which skin color is not a primary determinant of success or failure.[32]

Partly because most West Indians do not perceive race as a major problem in their own societies, they do not relate to whites or blacks in the United States primarily on the basis of race. Class is more important to them than race. Many West Indians are discriminated against by members of the same race who enjoy a higher social status. Indeed, their experiences with whites who visit or live in the Caribbean are mostly positive. This further diminishes the significance of race for them. West Indians are therefore less apprehensive of and less hostile toward whites; they regard them as equals. White Americans generally do not expect race to dominate their interactions with West Indians, and vice versa. Positive relations between West Indians and whites are manifested by the preference many whites have for hiring West Indians instead of native-born black Americans. Mary C. Waters believes that when whites say they don't see race in relation to most West Indians with whom they work, they are actually saying that in West Indians they see immigrants or children of immigrants who do not carry the weight of American race relations with them. In general, whites do not perceive most West Indians to be angry at them personally.[33]

But the ease with which West Indians interact with whites strengthens the negative feelings that some black Americans have toward both groups.

However, given the many shared interests and positive interactions between black Americans and West Indians, the latter often help to serve as a bridge between black and white Americans. The role of J. Raymond Jones in bringing blacks and whites together supports this view.

Born in 1899 in St. Thomas, then a Danish colony, Jones came to the United States during World War I. Influenced by his experiences in the West Indies as well as by the realities of American society and politics, Jones attempted to promote equality for blacks through integrated party politics. His overriding objective was the achievement of an integrated society purged of bigotry.[34] Jones brought prominent West Indians and Americans with African ancestry together to build a political machine that translated black votes into public appointments and contracts. The group included Percy Sutton, Constance Baker Motley, Charles Rangel, and David Dinkins, essentially establishment insiders who finessed the white world's rebuffs to find individual whites with whom they could deal.[35]

Jones and other West Indian politicians were cosmopolitan and friendly with both blacks and whites. Unlike recent migrants from the American South, they had not experienced the humiliations of Jim Crow laws. Furthermore, they had accumulated enough positive experiences in the Caribbean to enable them to develop the self-confidence to deal with whites in nonconfrontational ways. Jones's political skills and personality helped him emerge as the leader of the entire Democratic Tammany organization in Manhattan by 1960. At the 1960 Democratic National Convention, Jones obtained a promise from U.S. House Speaker Sam Rayburn to make Representative Adam Clayton Powell Jr. of Harlem the chairman of the House Education and Labor Committee in exchange for his organization's support of Lyndon B. Johnson's presidential bid. Even though Johnson lost to John F. Kennedy, Jones and Rayburn honored their agreement.[36]

Other immigrants from the West Indies and their children who were born in the United States adopted many of Jones's approaches to race relations. Coming from countries in which blacks exercised political power, the newcomers felt confident that they could represent all blacks. Politicians such as Shirley Chisolm, Bertram Barker, William Thompson, Thomas Russell Jones, and Ed Griffith were all Caribbean immigrants or their children.[37] Shirley Chisolm, for example, in 1968 became the first African-American female to be elected to the U.S. House of Representatives. In 1972, she became the first black American to launch a serious campaign for the U.S. presidency, an effort that brought many blacks and whites together in her support.

Other Americans of West Indian descent continue to build bridges between blacks and whites in particular and between other races in general. These include Colin Powell, Harry Belafonte, Sidney Poitier, Jamaica Kincaid, Franklin Thomas, and Earl Graves. Powell has clearly demonstrated the ability to transcend race and to bring blacks and whites together. Public opinion polls consistently show that both whites and blacks strongly support him as a public figure. Popular entertainers like Belafonte and Poitier are embraced by many Americans of various skin colors. Graves, the founder and publisher of *Black Enterprise* magazine, and Thomas, president of the Ford Foundation, are advocates of racial integration. Thomas, in particular, rejects the view that race is identity, a position that has angered some black Americans who work with him at the Ford Foundation.[38]

Traveling Abroad: New Perspectives on Race

As discussed in Chapter 4, Americans in Europe during World War II were confronted with contradictions between their country's stated beliefs and its application of those beliefs in relation to racial equality. Furthermore, many Europeans reminded both black and white Americans that skin color was not their preoccupation. It is the Second World War that marked a decisive change in American racial issues, partly because of the war's impact on Americans with African ancestry. In his book *The Fire Next Time,* James Baldwin shows why World War II was a turning point in blacks' relationship to America. He writes: "You must put yourself in the skin of a man who is wearing the uniform of his country, is a candidate for death in its defense, and who is called a 'nigger' by his comrades-in-arms and his officers; and who watches German prisoners of war being treated by Americans with more dignity than he has ever received at their hands. And who, at the same time, as a human being is far freer in a strange land than he has ever been at home."[39] Returning to America with different perceptions, which had grown out of their positive interactions with many Europeans, black Americans now engaged in activities to hasten the realization of equal opportunity and treatment.

Traveling abroad, living with foreign exchange students, having relatives in foreign countries, following news stories about other societies, and belonging to organizations that have an international focus contribute to the development of new perspectives and broader worldviews. It is clear that traveling overseas often influences Americans to reconsider their racial attitudes and behavior. One of the most important implications of traveling abroad is that it forces people to listen to themselves and to others. At the heart of the poor relations between blacks and whites in America is a failure to listen to each other. Sharon Stanford and Linaya Leaf both stress how listening to people from different countries helped them improve relations with people from another racial background. Sharon Stanford says:

> I belong to an international organization. Working with persons from vastly different cultures, thus vastly different working styles, made me sensitive to ignoring many of my first impressions and initial judgments. I had to learn how to listen more carefully. Even though English was used as the second language, listening was necessary because both of us came to the table expecting different things because of our different backgrounds.[40]

Similarly, Linaya Leaf, who taught creative drama and writing to elementary- and secondary-school teachers and principals on the island of Truk in Micronesia for Eastern Oregon State University, stated: "I had to immerse myself in the culture and find those assignments which would trigger interest from a perspective other than my own—for people for whom English was a second language."[41]

Teaching and studying abroad are generally regarded as essential to gaining a better understanding of other cultures. Equally important is the perception one gains of one's own society and oneself. In 1993 and 1994, 76,302 American students studied in foreign countries. The majority, 67.4 percent, went to Europe, while 13.4 percent went to Latin America, 6.5 percent to Asia, 2.8 percent to the Middle East, and 1.9 percent to Africa. The rest went to Canada and the Caribbean. Of these students, 63 percent were women and 37 percent were men; 84 percent were white, 5 percent Hispanic, 5 percent Asian, 3 percent black, and 3 percent multiracial.[42]

One of these students, Janelle Gordon, an American with African ancestry, went to France. During her first two months there, she spent much of her time defending the American values about which the French seemed to have serious reservations. She saw how different the mind-sets of Europeans are in relation to race. Being French or Italian had nothing to do with the color of your skin. The difference between France and America was made clear to her one evening. She relates: "I was walking with two white American females from my university. One of them turned to me and said: 'I hope this doesn't offend you, but do you feel uncomfortable and out of place being a black person in France?' I feel what she said is a portrayal of American society and how overly concerned we are with race." Gordon believes that her experience in France changed her perceptions of America as well as her views on race and culture.[43]

Both Linda Giles and Jane Lee found that race was not a major consideration in Africa or Hawaii. Giles lived for three years in various parts of the East African coast conducting cultural research. During much of the time she lived and worked in situations where she was often the only person of her racial, national, cultural, and linguistic background present. She said that she was treated extremely well and was indebted to a number of people who exhibited great patience, goodwill, and generosity. For most Africans, race is not a major issue in interpersonal relations. Giles believes that, "as a result, one feels that a debt is owed and one should reach out accordingly to other strangers and minorities in one's own society."[44] Lee, who lived in both Hawaii and Botswana, found her belief that race should not matter strengthened by her experiences. During her stay in Hawaii, she studied with Asian professors and interacted with people of all colors while raising her own family. The multiracial composition of Hawaii diminished the significance of race. Lee says, "I didn't think of race in Hawaii." Her circumstances in Botswana differed from Hawaii; here, she was a white minority in a black society, was more aware of being different, and reacted differently. Being a minority in Africa heightened her sensitivity to and understanding of racial minorities in the United States.[45]

Traveling and living in foreign countries have helped many Americans realize that people do not have to share the same culture or racial characteristics to get along. Arlene Winslow, a white American, came into close contact with people of different racial and ethnic origins when she lived in Puerto Rico. When her husband brought two black men from the Dominican Republic to her home, Arlene was concerned about what the neighbors might think of her association with them. She says: "I talked with a close friend about my feelings. She gave me some very good advice: you need to find one person of that race and background whom you can love and accept." She found that advice helpful.[46]

Similarly, Katie Sawyer relates:

> Growing up in a country other than the country of my birth has opened my eyes to the need for improved relations with those of other races. I was a very white child growing up amid black children in the Belgian Congo in the late 1940s and 1950s. When I would walk in the villages, there were always children and grown-ups who wanted to touch my hair and skin. I would bargain with them that they could touch my hair if I could touch theirs, and it got to be a game for us.[47]

Katie, who calls herself an African American, still has childhood friends who came to see her when she returned to the Congo in 1988. She has close friends from various racial backgrounds.

As more U.S. citizens visit foreign countries, many of them realize that American blacks and whites have more in common than is generally acknowledged while they are in the United States. It is clearly impossible for two separate cultures, one black and the other white, to coexist unaffected by each other for three hundred years. Yet many Americans fail to see the fallacy of the assumption that blacks and whites have different cultures. But when they are abroad it becomes obvious to many that black and white Americans are very much alike and very different from Europeans. James Baldwin observed that it became terribly clear in Europe that Americans knew more about each other than Europeans ever could. He writes: "My own experience proves to me that the connection between American whites and blacks is far deeper and more passionate than any of us would like to think."[48] The belief that blacks and whites do not share a common culture is essential to the perpetuation of the concept of race and the practice of racism. Traveling abroad contributes to undermining both.

When Americans are in Japan, for example, many realize that the insensitivities, discrimination, and snubs they endure are not primarily because of race. Their experiences in Japan largely result from their foreignness, or being *gaijin*. Anyone who is not Japanese is treated as an outsider. Whites become just as conscious as blacks of their skin color. When Elaine Graybill, the managing editor of a university magazine, went to Japan in 1995, she thought that she was prepared for the racism she expected. She was told that many Japanese think whites smell funny and that they consider white skin to be repulsive. So when Graybill lowered herself into a hot mineral pool in Japan, the Japanese woman already in the pool said nothing, got up, and left. Graybill soon learned that some Japanese, despite their exquisite politeness, objected to bathing with a *gaijin*. The next morning, when the bath was full, she sat on a small stool in a row of naked women all sitting on their own stools scrubbing themselves. She says:

> I experienced a new perception of myself. I was embarrassed about the whiteness of my skin and the largeness of my limbs next to the Japanese women, who were brown, and mostly very small. A list of unflattering adjectives that I imagined some of these women were thinking about me raced through my mind as I sat and scrubbed.[49]

Such encounters have enabled Graybill to better understand how racial minorities in America are sometimes made to feel.

Perhaps Malcolm X is the most obvious example of how going to another country can dramatically alter racial attitudes and behavior. On his way to Saudi Arabia, Malcolm X stopped in Frankfurt, Germany, and was impressed by the German hospitality and politeness. At the Frankfurt airport, he saw Muslims from a great variety of countries, all on the way to Mecca, hugging each other in camaraderie and goodwill. They were of all imaginable complexions, and their apparently unplanned encounter exuded warmth and friendliness. Malcolm X wrote: "The feeling hit me that there really wasn't any color problem here. The effect was as though I had just stepped out of prison."[50]

Having lived in a very hostile and segregated America, Malcolm X generally disliked whites and expected them to dislike him. Nothing in his past had prepared him for the kindness he received from whites who were also on the pilgrimage to Mecca. It became clear to him that religious beliefs mattered more than skin color. This realization marked the beginning of his new outlook on "white men." Noting that the pilgrims were of all colors, from blue-eyed blonds to black-skinned Africans, Malcolm X recalled: "We were all participating in the same ritual, displaying a spirit of unity and brotherhood that my experiences in America had led me to believe never could exist between the white and nonwhite."[51] Traveling abroad not only profoundly changed Malcolm X; it also positively affects all Americans, and thus has a favorable impact on race relations in America.

7

INTERRACIAL RELATIONSHIPS AND THE ONE-DROP RULE

THE SOCIAL CONSTRUCTION OF RACE AND RACISM is dependent on the general acceptance of rigid racial boundaries and racial classification systems. Proponents of racial segregation have always understood that interracial relationships and the children they produce eventually undermine racism by challenging the assumption of monolithic, fixed, and inherently incompatible races. The clear demarcation of races, which is an essential cornerstone of the social construction of race, is weakened by the existence and recognition of widespread racial mixing. Consequently, those who favor racial separatism and believe in the concept of race are most likely to strongly oppose interracial relationships.

On the other hand, the approval of interracial relationships and the development of language that recognizes the offspring of such relationships as part of two or more racial categories are clear indicators that American society has achieved a significant degree of social, racial, and economic equality. Public opinion polls show an increasing acceptance of interracial relationships, with the younger generation of Americans more supportive of them than older Americans. The wide disagreement between the old and young on the issue of racial mixing is evidence of the radical alteration of racial attitudes over the past few decades.

Whereas only 27 percent of Americans over 50 years of age approve of marriage between blacks and whites, 56 percent of those between 30 and

49 years of age approve. But the most important finding, which supports the thesis that America is moving beyond race, is that 64 percent of Americans between the ages of 18 and 29 approve of interracial marriages.[1] Generational replacement is clearly conducive to significant changes in racial attitudes and behavior.

Public approval of interracial marriages has steadily increased among both whites and blacks since 1968. Whereas only 17 percent of whites of all ages favored interracial relationships in 1968, by 1991 the number had grown to 44 percent. In the case of blacks, 48 percent approved of mixed relationships in 1968, compared to 70 percent in 1991. Education, interpersonal contacts, income, and region also influenced attitudes on this issue. For example, whereas 70 percent of college graduates approve of interracial marriage, only 26 percent of Americans who did not graduate from high school approve.

Similarly, whereas 65 percent of Americans who live in large cities are supportive of interracial marriages, only 32 percent of rural residents approve. Sixty-one percent of Americans with annual incomes over $50,000 favor racially mixed marriages, compared to 37 percent of those with incomes under $20,000. Whereas 60 percent of Americans living in the West approve of interracial marriages, only 33 percent of those living in the South support them.[2] Based on these and other findings, it is reasonable to conclude that higher levels of education, increased interpersonal contacts, growing urbanization, and generational change combine to weaken the consensus on which the social construction of race depends.

Eroding Racial Boundaries

Arguably, interracial marriage is the most significant challenge to the concept of race and the practice of racism. Such partnerships contradict racial assumptions, draw attention to similarities between individuals from different racial backgrounds, and create ties that cut across racial boundaries. They increase sensitivity to and awareness of racial problems; provide greater access to social, economic, and political opportunities; and challenge the concepts of racial superiority and inferiority. The children of such relationships complicate the categorization of individuals based on the assumption of innate biological and cultural distinctions. Stated another way, interracial marriages, because of their intimate and long-term nature, test racial boundaries and the willingness of individuals from different racial groups to accept each other in essentially long-lasting egalitarian relationships.[3]

Because the maintenance of racial boundaries depends on an acceptance of exclusive racial group membership, an "us-versus-them" viewpoint, and the ability to easily distinguish between insiders and outsiders, interracial relationships effectively erode racial boundaries by making it more difficult to determine who belongs to a particular racial circle and who does not. Interracial relationships are about the inclusion of individuals in what are generally seen as exclusive racial groups. Marriage brings the families, friends, and acquaintances of the marital partners into close interpersonal contact. Ultimately, race problems break down when individuals of different races share common family members.

So thoroughly have interethnic and interfaith marriages weakened ethnic and religious boundaries that it is no longer a remarkable event when an American of Polish ancestry marries an American of English ancestry, or when a Jew marries a Catholic. But older American couples recall how ethnic and religious hostilities were almost as bitter as racial hostilities still are in some parts of the country today in relation to intermarriage. Just as blacks are not monolithic, whites are not homogeneous. Creating harmony among white ethnic groups was a gradual process, at the heart of which was an increase in interethnic marriages. As such marriages were gradually accepted, they created greater momentum toward increased rates of intermarriage.

As more Americans became multiethnic, ethnicity diminished as a social force. Group membership became more flexible and the children of interethnic relationships helped bridge the divide between two or more ethnic groups. Because intermarriage often reduces the strength of affiliation people of mixed ancestry have for any one group, interethnic marriages directly threaten the traditional bases for ethnic groups.[4] Although the process is taking longer, the same logic applies to racial groups.

Interracial relationships challenge the widely accepted view that physical characteristics determine group membership and identity. Equally important, mixed relationships strengthen individualism and freedom of choice, which help erode a central component of the social construction of race—namely, externally imposed definitions of who belongs to which particular group. Interracial marriages weaken racial cohesion, complicate racial group membership, and facilitate movement across racial boundaries.

Strong crosscutting ties that emanate from interracial marriages undermine the assumption of the existence of sympathizers based on racial identification, which is crucial to maintaining racism. The white dermatologist who complains to his white patient about his daughter's relationship with a young man from another racial group risks confiding in someone whose experiences with interracial relationships might be very different from his. Physical characteristics alone are not enough to determine who belongs to or supports socially constructed racial categories when a significant number of people from various racial groups develop intimate relationships.

Children of interracial relationships have always been a major concern for supporters of racial segregation because their very existence demonstrates the erosion of racial boundaries. As their numbers grow and their self-confidence strengthens, these children question the logic that forms the foundation for a binary approach to race in relation to blacks and whites. In her book *Notes of a White Black Woman,* Judy Scales-Trent discusses the unique views that multiracial people have of America's racial categories. She writes: "My position does not allow me the luxury of thinking that the notion of race makes any sense."[5] As more children of racially mixed couples reject the system of racial classification and declare their membership in two or more racial groups, they shake the foundation of the concept of race by effectively challenging whiteness and blackness as pure categories. Golfer Tiger Woods, for instance, claims all of his ancestors by calling himself a "Cablinasian," which stands for Caucasian, Black, Indian, and Asian.

Family members and friends of racially mixed children and people involved in interracial relationships play a vital role in augmenting the movement toward greater racial harmony. Despite their initial opposition to interracial marriages, many Americans eventually confront their prejudices and often end up embracing the interracial couple and their children. The arrival of grandchildren significantly modifies the attitudes of most grandparents, who recognize that racially mixed grandchildren are blood relatives. This acknowledgment is facilitated by wider public approval of interracial marriage, a sharp decline in society's tolerance of racism, and greater societal respect for individualism and freedom of choice.

Another important factor is the small but growing trend toward greater awareness and acknowledgment of racial mixture by white Americans. As the taboo against interracial relationships weakens, the penalty for admitting one's own racial mixture also becomes less severe. In fact, as families wrestle with interracial relationships, deeply hidden family secrets about past mixed-race liaisons sometimes emerge. In one white family, the mother and her three children openly discuss their black features, especially their skin color and hair texture. One daughter married an American with African ancestry and another adopted four racially mixed children.[6]

Interracial relationships often have a ripple effect that goes beyond immediate family members. Parents, siblings, grandparents, and friends often become advocates of racial tolerance because of their personal experiences with a racially mixed relationship. For example, Bill McCartney, the founder of the Promise Keepers, who was discussed in Chapter 3, influenced his organization to adopt racial tolerance as one of their seven "promises," partly because his own grandchildren are racially mixed. Instead of seeing blacks and whites as monolithic groups, people with mixed-race friends or relatives are likely to judge members of racial groups as individuals. Angela Dreessen, who is white, says that her black boyfriend was reluctant to meet her parents because he believed they would be "fake or rude." The meeting went better than expected, and it made a world of difference in his perceptions of white people. Equally important was his belief that he had been judged and accepted by the Dreessens on the basis of his character and personality.[7]

Perhaps one of the greatest implications of interracial relationships is their tendency to heighten awareness of racism and unequal opportunity and treatment, especially among white Americans. Being involved with a person from a racial minority group was cited as one of the most important experiences in helping whites understand the problems that racial minorities face daily. The intimate nature of their interaction, especially when children are involved, often exposes white partners to the kind of unfair treatment that many blacks often expect to receive simply because of their skin color.

In a sense, whites who develop strong personal ties with blacks are often perceived by other whites as outsiders and are treated accordingly. Mary Leuus, who is white, became more sensitive to unequal treatment when her Chinese husband was turned down for membership in the Lions Club in the 1970s.[8] Similarly, Ruth Fisher says that her daughter, who is white, dated a black man while at Harvard Law School and became keenly aware that skin color had permeated their relationship. When her daughter moved to Arizona to practice law on an Indian reservation, she had to decide if she would take her boyfriend with her to purchase a car. She finally asked herself, "Who are they going to treat worse, a white woman or a black man?" She went to buy the car alone.[9] Both of these examples show that interracial relationships usually heighten white partners' awareness of whiteness as an inherent, ascribed advantage.

Many whites respond to their exposure to racism by becoming angry and defensive. Patricia Fowler, who is white, dated a U.S. marine with African ancestry. Although the people they interacted with in the military respected the marine, when the couple left base they often encountered rude behavior and derogatory comments. Patricia says: "I always became angry and shot those people a look to let them know that they disgusted me."[10] More subtle aspects of racism also upset some whites. When Ruth Fisher attempted to gain custody of her sons, her husband's lawyer emphasized Ruth's relationship with a black man and gave the judge a "knowing look." She says: "I thought the court had been magically transported to Johannesburg, and I was being tried for an infraction of Apartheid. I have never gotten over the anger I felt at my ex-husband's—my society's—tactics. They were right about me though—I would never have taught my sons the proper prejudices."[11]

The Myth of Racial Purity

Belief in racial purity rests on the fallacy of the existence of biologically distinguishable groups of people called "races." But, as I showed in Chapter 2, race was socially and scientifically invented and has been rejected as a vi-able concept by most scientists. Apart from the generally accepted scientific fact that all human beings share the same biological origins, continuous racial mixing throughout the world over an extended period of time has effectively made the existence of pure races virtually a myth. For thousands of years, human beings have experienced hybridization as a result of wars, conquests, settlement, migration, and peaceful transaction.[12]

Coastal areas have been particularly prone to racial mixing, as travel by sea was for centuries the primary means by which people from different racial groups came into contact with each other. The Arabs came into contact with Africans along the Red Sea coast as well as across the Sahara Desert. The Africans forced into slavery in the Arab world have by now been completely absorbed by the large Arab populations.

Racial mixing in Europe was clearly more thorough in the Mediterranean area. Southern Europeans and North Africans have interacted continuously throughout much of recorded history. Spain and Portugal in particular have undergone extensive racial mixing. The Phoenicians, Romans, Moors, sub-Saharan Africans, and others have complicated Spain's racial composition. Large numbers of Africans came to Spain and Portugal as slaves with the Moors. Many more were brought by the Spanish and Portuguese themselves after 1444 to work as domestic servants and as laborers on estates. By the time the Spanish discovered America, there was a considerable African population on the Iberian peninsula, and the system of black slavery was well established in both Spain and Portugal.[13] The Africans eventually disappeared into the larger populations of these countries, further augmenting the racial mixture that had begun centuries earlier.

Ireland, although not as racially mixed as Spain and Portugal, also experienced an infusion of Africans. Its religious kinship to Spain and the relative ease with which it could be reached by travelers despite being an island facilitated racial interaction. It is generally believed that Spanish Moors mixed with the Irish in the southern part of the island centuries ago. Jack D. Forbes discusses a medieval Irish Gaelic saga that states that Danish-Irish raiders attacked Spain and Mauritania in the 800s. From Mauritania, they "carried off a great host of them as captives to Erin, and these are the blue men of Erin."[14] Although the accuracy of this story is debatable, it is generally agreed that some racial mixing did occur in Ireland.

A certain white Englishman who had lived in many parts of the world, including Africa, commonly referred to himself as a racially mixed person. Given the history of racial mixing in Britain, such a self-description is probably valid. The Roman armies that occupied Britain included a small number of Ethiopians and North Africans. In 1555, a few Africans arrived in England to learn English in order to facilitate the growing trade between that country and Africa. The African slave trade and the development of British colonies in North America, including the West Indies, were accompanied by increasing numbers of Africans living in England. By 1768, it was estimated that 20,000 black servants, out of a total population of 676,000, lived in London.[15] Roughly one out of every thirty-four Londoners was African. Some blacks who had fought on the British side in the American Revolution also settled in England.

Africans were also found in many other parts of Britain, especially in Liverpool, Manchester, and other major commercial centers. As early as the sixteenth century, black entertainers performed in Scotland, and Queen Elizabeth, like her father before her, kept an African entertainer and a black page in her court.[16] The majority of these blacks lived with poor whites in some of the most unsanitary ghettos in urban Britain. Many married English people from the same socioeconomic class. Unlike in the United States, mixed-race marriages were not prohibited, and class generally took precedence over skin color in determining the appropriateness of intimate relations. Consequently, many Africans were absorbed into the English population. Gretchen Gerzina, who has written about racial conditions in Great Britain, concludes: "There must be many thousands of British families who, if they traced their roots back to the eighteenth century, would find among their ancestors an African or a person of African descent."[17]

The racial mixing that occurred in western Europe was compounded in the New World as Europeans, Africans, and Native Americans mixed with each other and produced offspring for more than four hundred years. It is precisely because of extensive racial mixing in America that stringent laws were developed to prevent its continuance. The social construction of race resulting from these laws is so effective that few white Americans dare to acknowledge the African ancestors of whom they are aware, thereby helping to perpetuate the myth that whites and blacks are unrelated biologically.

From the beginning of the colonial period in America, white men and black women produced racially mixed children. Social prohibitions against intermarriage did not prevent sexual relations from developing, especially in frontier areas where there were few white women. As the institution of slavery grew, many states gained large numbers of Africans, many of whom lived in close physical proximity to whites. C. Vann Woodward describes the typical dwelling of a slave-owning family as a walled compound shared by both master and slave families.[18] This level of intimacy and the virtual monopoly of power enjoyed by slaveholders over slaves facilitated racial mixing.

But close relationships between blacks and whites were not limited to plantations. Members of the two groups interacted in cities as well as in rural areas. Cities tended to have more white men than white women and fewer black men than black women, a situation that led to a considerable degree of cohabitation between white men and black women and a growing population of racially mixed children.[19] The existence of Americans with a wide range of skin colors is obvious evidence of interracial sexual relations. Madison Grant, one of the strongest opponents of race mixing, wrote in 1916 in his book *The Passing of the Great Race:* "There was plenty of mixture with Negroes as the light color of many Negroes abundantly testifies."[20]

Prior to the full development of the institution of slavery, white landowners had relied mostly on indentured servants from Europe to cultivate the land. Indentured servitude was a common practice in England and across Europe at that time. It is estimated that 80 percent of the English immigrants who came to America during the colonial period paid for their passage with an average of seven years of "faithful" labor for temporary owners.[21] Many of them worked with enslaved Africans and had children with them. Legislators in Virginia, Maryland, South Carolina, Delaware, Massachusetts, Pennsylvania, and elsewhere began to prohibit interracial sex and instituted harsh penalties for those involved, especially if they were black men and white women. But these restrictions did not prevent some whites, blacks, Native Americans, and persons of mixed race from continuing to participate in interracial relationships.

Preoccupied with the differences among socially constructed racial groups, many Americans downplayed or overlooked racial mixing between blacks and Native Americans. Many blacks in the 1960s, ironically adopting the myth of racial purity, de-emphasized their Native American heritage in their focus on "black pride." This emphasis on black identity was in part a response to the tendency of some blacks to stress their Native American ancestry in order to divert attention away from their African roots, instead of claiming both with equal pride. Another factor contributing to the tendency of blacks to downplay their Native American heritage was the forced relocation of Native Americans, many of whom were racially mixed, to reservations. Edward Byron Reuter states that some of the Native American groups today are more black than Indian in their ancestry and that many of them incorporate a large percentage of African blood.[22]

Sexual relations between blacks and Native Americans were generally ignored by European settlers. Like Africans, some Native Americans were enslaved, a development that brought the two groups into intimate contact. Intermarriage was quite common among them, and many of the Native American slaves were gradually absorbed into the larger black population. Many enslaved Africans who managed to escape to freedom often joined Native American groups, such as the Seminoles of Florida. Some blacks were killed by the Native Americans and others were enslaved, but many were integrated into Native American societies as family members.

Many famous individuals who are regarded solely as black Americans are mixtures of African, Native American, and European. Crispus Attucks, who became a hero in the American Revolution because he was the first to be killed in the Boston Massacre, was of African and Native American ancestry. Paul Cuffee, a wealthy merchant and shipowner in Massachusetts, was also of such mixed parentage. Cuffee identified primarily with blacks and was actively involved in efforts to encourage freed slaves to settle in Sierra Leone in West Africa.[23]

An example of racial mixing between Native Americans and blacks can be found in the town of Boley, Oklahoma. When the Creek Indians were forced to leave their land in Alabama and Georgia in the nineteenth century, they were able to acquire territory in Oklahoma. Many blacks first arrived in what was then "Indian Territory" as slaves of the resettled Indians. They became an integral part of the community and were allocated land by the federal government, like the other tribal members, in the years following Emancipation.[24] Although Boley is now considered an all-black town, it is an example of how the myth of racial purity has managed to obscure the historical realities of racial mixing in America.

The One-Drop Rule

Interracial relationships and the recognition that the resulting children belong to more than one racial group have serious implications for the one-drop rule, which is at the heart of the concept of race and the practice of racism. As mentioned in Chapter 1, the one-drop rule essentially designates as black anyone who has any trace of African ancestry, regardless of physical appearance. Thus, Americans with blue eyes and blond hair are black if they have any black ancestors at all. The United States is the only country in the world that has institutionalized such a rigid definition of who is black and who is white. Incidentally, the rule applies only to blacks; one drop of Japanese blood, for example, is not enough to transform a white into an Asian.

To maintain the system of slavery and the diminished status of Americans with African ancestry, the one-drop rule was developed and strictly enforced in many parts of the United States. A central concern of colonial lawmakers was how to clarify the status of interracial children without upsetting the unequal balance between whites and blacks. Recognition of these children as both black and white would have undermined concepts of whiteness and blackness and the privileges and disadvantages that accompanied designations of white and black, respectively. Consequently, to maintain white privilege and status, legislators conferred the status of the black parent, most frequently the mother, on these children. In addition to increasing the number of slaves, this departure from traditional English law, in which children inherited their father's status, nullified the social and economic effects of interracial relationships. A racially mixed person was, in most cases, effectively removed as a potential economic or social rival, and the social status of whites was reinforced in a loosely structured society.[25] The one-drop rule cemented racial-group membership and buttressed the fallacy of racial purity by denying the occurrence of racial mixture.

But prior to widespread adoption of the stringent one-drop rule around 1915, racial designations were more variable and complex than the simple dichotomous black-and-white approach. In South Carolina, for example, a combination of "light skin" and wealth could enable a racially mixed person to be legally defined as white.[26] Different states developed their own rules, and enforcement varied from place to place.

During the nineteenth century, despite the one-drop rule, the general practice was to designate a person with a black parent and a white parent as half black and half white. Racial designations were based on the assumption that people could be exact genetic fractions. But scientists began to encounter serious empirical problems with both the fractional concept of racial inheritance and the idea of pure races.[27] The recognition of racial mixing raised serious questions about the social construction of race.

Social and economic considerations facilitated a more liberal application of the one-drop rule by both whites and blacks. Until the early 1900s, racially mixed people had been widely regarded as a separate category and had behaved accordingly. They enjoyed significant social and economic benefits from their connections with whites. During slavery, many of the offspring of enslaved black women and white slaveholders were given certain privileges such as learning a trade, working in the house, or even learning to read. Many were granted freedom by their fathers. The abolition of slavery and migration to the North enabled many racially mixed people to develop business and social contacts with whites and to assume leadership positions in the black community. Competition from the growing number of white immigrants, a larger influx of blacks from the South into northern cities in search of work, and growing racial tensions weakened their status within the larger society. Furthermore, an emerging black elite of largely unmixed heritage was keenly aware of the superior status enjoyed by racially mixed people.[28]

As racial tensions increased and after more states adopted the one-drop rule to draw sharper divisions between groups socially defined as black and white, the many differences among Americans with African ancestry based on skin color were downplayed. Given that racially mixed people represented a possible bridge between blacks and whites, they were often targeted by racists who feared what they called miscegenation. Confronted by growing hostility from many whites, blacks responded by mobilizing all Americans with African ancestry as a unified force to protect themselves and their interests. In other words, in response to common oppression, many blacks adopted the one-drop rule to promote racial solidarity. Social and racial factors became virtually indistinguishable.[29]

Ironically, many Americans with African ancestry continue to be strong proponents of the one-drop rule. They believe that they have a vested interest in maintaining it, despite its centrality to racism. One important reason for continued black support of the one-drop rule is that skin color within the black community still determines, although to a diminishing extent, who benefits economically and socially. Any major departure from the one-drop rule is generally perceived as detrimental to the interest of most blacks. Many blacks thus oppose the adoption of a multiracial category by the government.

That racial categories are socially constructed and are arbitrary is demonstrated by the once common practice of "passing." Many racially mixed people were able to "pass" themselves off as white by moving to another part of the state or country where the one-drop rule was not applied as rigorously. Because passing inevitably demanded great secrecy, the precise number of Americans with African ancestry who passed as white can never be ascertained. Also, white Americans whose families have been in the United States for several generations often cannot know with certainty that they themselves do not have African ancestry.[30]

Despite efforts to prevent people from changing their racial identity from black to white, the geographic mobility characteristic of the United States made such attempts virtually futile. Officials were bribed to register newborn children as white, baptismal records were often destroyed, and in many cases, appearance instead of ancestry often determined who was white or black. Even within the same family, often some children were regarded as white and others as black depending on the lightness of their skin. Some states, such as South Carolina, never precisely defined who was white, a judgment that was often left to the local white community.[31]

There are many examples of Americans with African ancestry who passed as white. One of the most famous is Susie Guillory Phipps of Louisiana. As discussed in Chapter 2, Phipps lived as a white but had been designated as "colored" on her birth certificate by a midwife who knew that Phipps's great-great-great-great-grandmother had been a slave. Another example is Thyra Johnson, a blue-eyed American whose announcement in 1947 that she and her husband Albert, designated as white on his birth certificate, were actually black stunned a nation preoccupied with racial distinctions.

Both Thyra and Albert Johnson were accepted as whites. Albert graduated with honors from the University of Chicago Medical School and studied radiology at Harvard University. He practiced medicine in Gorham, New Hampshire; headed the school board; served as a selectman; was president of the county medical society; and became chairman of the local Republican Party. Thyra was a civic and social leader, whose home in the exclusive Prospect Hill neighborhood was the scene of the annual Christmas social of the Congregational Church.[32] Neither Thyra nor Albert intended to deceive anyone; they were simply living as Americans.

In the case of Gregory Williams and his family, a deliberate attempt was made to circumvent socially imposed racial categories. In his autobiography, *Life on the Color Line: The True Story of a White Boy Who Discovered He Was Black,* Williams tells how he attended whites-only schools and swam in whites-only pools in Virginia until he was ten years old. When his parents divorced, Williams left with his father and brother for Muncie, Indiana, while two younger siblings stayed with their mother. On the way to Indiana, the boys learned from their father that he had been passing for white and that they were actually black. They joined the black community in Muncie and lived as blacks. Their younger siblings, with whom contact was severed, grew up as whites.[33]

Although the one-drop rule remains a reality in American society, it is being challenged by the growth of interracial relationships and by greater public awareness that this cornerstone of the social construction of race is seriously flawed. The simple act of claiming one's relatives from different racial backgrounds, as Tiger Woods has publicly done, is an important departure from the one-drop rule. To a large extent, the survival of the one-drop rule depends on the willingness of Americans, especially those of racially mixed ancestry, to accept society's definition of them as belonging to racially pure categories. The increasing number of interracial relationships and society's growing racial tolerance combine to weaken the one-drop rule and thereby the concept of race as well.

The Growth of Interracial Relationships

The significant growth in the number of interracial relationships since 1967, when the Supreme Court prevented states from prohibiting racially mixed marriages, attests to the progress Americans have made in getting beyond race. Because taboos against blacks and whites marrying each other have been the most tenacious, getting to the heart of the issue of racial separation, the increasing rates of black-white marriages are particularly important. Overall, there were 1.3 million interracial married couples in the United States in 1994, compared to 964,000 in 1990, 651,000 in 1980, and 310,000 in 1970. In 1994, interracial married couples accounted for 2.4 percent of all married couples, compared to 1.8 percent in 1990, 1.2 percent in 1980, and 0.6 percent in 1970. The number of black-white marriages has also risen dramatically since 1970. In that year, there were only 65,000 black-white couples, compared to 121,000 in 1980, 211,000 in 1990, and 296,000 in 1994. These couples represented 0.1 percent of all married couples in 1970, 0.2 percent in 1980, 0.4 percent in 1990, and 0.5 percent in 1994.[34] Between 1970 and 1994, the number of black-white married couples grew by roughly 450 percent.

These official figures, although impressive, do not include approximately 500,000 interracial couples who live together but are not married. Furthermore, they do not reflect the rapidly growing trend toward interracial dating, especially among younger Americans. In sharp contrast to the early 1970s, when an interracial couple could expect not only rude stares but also verbal and even physical abuse, most Americans now accept such relationships as individual decisions and do not strongly react to them, at least not overtly. The growth of interracial relationships helps condition society to accept racial mixing as ordinary behavior.

Rapid increases in interracial marriages have resulted in a relatively large number of biracial and multiracial children, a development that will lead to even more dramatic growth of interracial marriages and children in the future. Given the arbitrary way in which individuals are racially classified, many children who fall into the "black" category are in fact racially mixed. Moreover, since the father's racial characteristics are not recorded for about 16 percent of U.S. births, the number of interracial births is probably understated. It is estimated that such births more than doubled between 1978 and 1992, rising from 63,700 to about 133,200. During the same period of time, total births increased from approximately 3.33 million to more than 4 million, or by 18 percent. The largest increase per year in interracial births was among black-white couples, which more than doubled, growing from 21,400 in 1978 to 55,000 in 1992.[35]

Several factors account for the rapid and inexorable rise in interracial families and couples. One of the most important is the change in social attitudes that contributed to ending the so-called antimiscegenation laws in many states following the Supreme Court's ruling upholding the right of interracial couples to marry in *Loving* v. *Virginia* in 1967. Another factor is the steady removal of barriers to economic opportunities. As many blacks have gained greater access to jobs and middle-class status, their interactions with whites have increased significantly. Interpersonal contacts between individuals of relatively equal economic and social status have helped erode taboos against interracial marriage. Finally, the relative availability of partners from within or outside the socially designated group influences the occurrence of interracial dating and marriage. Because Americans of European descent currently make up a large majority of the population, most interracial relationships involve a white partner. The sizes of the racial groups involved help determine the rate of interracial marriage among their members. These factors work together to create a social climate that is more conducive to racial mixing.[36]

Interpersonal contact is the most important factor determining whether or not interracial marriage takes place. Parents have always known how choices of playmates, schools, colleges and universities, churches, and social activities influence their children's eventual choice of a spouse. As more blacks and whites live in racially integrated neighborhoods, attend the same schools, and participate in the same community activities, they are more likely to perceive each other as individuals with common interests instead of as members of racial categories. These interpersonal contacts reduce the prejudice and weaken the taboos that often work against choosing certain marital partners.[37]

Demography is an integral component of interpersonal contact. When blacks live in areas of the country that do not have large numbers of Americans with African ancestry, they are likely to marry the people with whom they live, regardless of color. In these largely white areas, black children are likely to have friends from different racial backgrounds. Eventually they may regard nonblacks as potential marriage partners, especially in light of the absence of group pressure to maintain racial solidarity by marrying within their racial group.[38]

Once blacks and whites marry, it is generally much easier for their younger relatives to also cross racial boundaries in search of mates. A black woman from Chicago, who dates interracially, said that not only did she grow up and socialize with friends from different racial backgrounds, there also have been interracial marriages in her family for generations. She attended integrated schools and was encouraged by her family to reject stereotypes. These experiences facilitated her own decision to date across racial boundaries.[39] In another example, a white woman was influenced to date interracially by her sister's marriage to a black man. This close connection with someone from another racial group contributed to her ability to look beyond skin color in her own relationships and to fall in love with a black man herself.[40]

The elimination of many racial barriers and the emergence of a strong black middle class over the past thirty years have contributed to an unprecedented level of interaction between blacks and whites on an equal-status basis. People of both colors meet in offices, work on joint projects, relax together at office parties, and develop close friendships. Economic status, generally a consideration among individuals seeking marriage partners in virtually all societies in the world, is clearly a factor in interracial relationships. People tend to marry partners from similar social and economic backgrounds.

Education is also an important determinant of middle-class status. Education generally encourages critical thinking, which often leads to a rejection of irrational ideas such as race being a determinant of moral character or intelligence. The pursuit of education often involves a major transition from the security and certainty of a particular community to a world with new ways of thinking that is populated by people from diverse backgrounds. Values, beliefs, and attitudes that were prevalent at home are likely to be challenged by other values, beliefs, and attitudes on university campuses. The farther away students are from their hometowns and the more education they receive, the less likely they are to retain racial stereotypes. They become more likely to marry someone from another racial background. One can expect a progressive increase in the percentage of interracial marriages among more educated groups of individuals.[41]

Another reason for the growth of marriages between blacks and whites is the lack of availability of marriageable black men, from the viewpoint of many black women. As more black women than black men attend college, obtain professional degrees, and achieve financial security, their interests often diverge. Black women clearly outnumber black men in professional occupations, largely because they achieve greater educational success than men. Black men experience high rates of unemployment, violence, and imprisonment, all of which contribute to a reduction in the number of black men deemed to be marriageable by black women. Faced with these realities, black women are increasingly dating and marrying white men.

Finally, the media have influenced society to become more tolerant of individual choices in relation to interracial marriage. The media, reflecting dominant social values, traditionally respected racial taboos, the most important being the taboo against interracial sex. However, the media has also challenged predominant societal values by producing movies such as *Guess Who's Coming to Dinner,* in which Sidney Poitier and Katherine Hepburn played leading roles. Movies and television shows are barometers of society's acceptance or rejection of interracial relationships. Judging from the number of programs and films today with interracial sexual content, the "taboo" that represents a cornerstone of the social construction of race is steadily being weakened.

Fear and Rejection of Interracial Relationships

As discussed in Chapter 3, in early 1996 the leaders of Barnetts Creek Baptist Church in Thomasville, Georgia, asked the relatives of a racially mixed baby buried in an exclusively white graveyard to exhume the body and bury it in a graveyard designated for blacks.[42] Although the deacons who made the decision later apologized, partly in response to pressure from church members and the Southern Baptist Convention, this unusual case underscores deep residual fears about racial mixing. But it also demonstrates an erosion of consensus on one of America's oldest social taboos.

An essential component of constructing race as social reality is the invention and enforcement of taboos. Defined as a ban or prohibition, a taboo becomes an integral part of a larger social system and culture. Like many aspects of culture, taboos are generally accepted as natural and inherently logical by those belonging to that particular culture. Outsiders, however, often perceive such taboos as irrational. Whereas outsiders often see alternatives to taboos in a given society, that society's members are usually prevented by their embrace of taboos from being able to visualize reality differently. Visible differences, such as skin color, help reinforce taboos

because they make it easier to claim that prohibitions against certain behavior emanate from nature.[43]

Underlying the social construction of race is the view that racial categories are based on biological differences among human beings. For many
who subscribe to this view, racial mixing must be discouraged to maintain
the natural order. Violation of this taboo must be severely punished, and
support of the taboo must be reinforced by tangible as well as intangible
social and economic benefits.

Madison Grant, chairman of the New York Zoological Society, trustee of
the American Museum of Natural History, and councillor of the American
Geographic Society, articulated the view that racial mixing has had disas-
trous consequences for societies where it has been practiced. Using Mexico
as an example, Grant cited the mixing of Spanish, Indians, and Africans to
produce modern Mexicans and concluded that Mexico's incapacity for self-
government is attributable to this mixing. His basic assumption was that
"higher races" lose their superior abilities when they mix with "lower
races."[44] Similarly, whites who mix with other races, especially blacks, risk
losing their white identity and the privileges that accompany it. Perhaps
even more importantly, their children can never be white and, therefore,
will never be entitled to the privileges reserved for whites. The one-drop
rule was a natural outgrowth of this way of thinking. According to this
logic, as discussed earlier, racial mixing can transform white society without affecting black identity, largely because all offspring from unions between whites and blacks are black. It is obvious, then, that whites are likely
to be fearful of racial mixing because their punishment for violating the
taboo is extremely severe and largely irreversible. Such fears are diminishing as society's belief in the taboo is undermined by forces of social change.

Opposition to interracial marriages and relationships is deeply rooted in
the fear that whites will lose their superior status if blacks gain access to
white families, especially white women. Insecurities among many white men,
based on their misguided assumptions about black sexuality, continue to influence their attitudes toward racial mixing. Intermarriage is resisted because
it potentially gives blacks equal access to advantages enjoyed by many whites
and because it is the most potent symbol of racial and cultural equality.

Some black men also reject interracial relationships out of fear and a sense
of betrayal. Given the racial history of the United States and the widespread
acceptance that blacks are inherently inferior to whites, it is difficult for some
blacks to extricate themselves from the chains of racial thinking. When black
women date and marry white men, some black men react with great hostility.
This is partly explained by historical memories of the almost absolute power
white men held over blacks during slavery and of their frequent sexual relationships, both coerced and voluntary, with black women. Black men's reactions are also based on their perception of being rejected by black women.

Many black women, on the other hand, express anger and fear when black men date and marry interracially. They generally believe that these men have "abandoned their race." The increasing number of relationships between black men and white women has led some black women to conclude that black men have succumbed to the standards of beauty prevalent in America. Ironically, it is clear that many black women also subscribe to these standards of beauty. A more common complaint voiced by some black women is that, given the shortage of marriageable black men, interracial relationships deprive them of the possibility of marrying.

Some black men give in to social pressure to marry within "their race," even if they have been dating white women. Lucille Holcomb, who is black, recalls a white friend's experience of being rejected by a black man she dated for several years. Lucille and her friend Barbara met in Washington, D.C., in 1968 and became "as close as sisters." Barbara was hurt by the rejection because the man she dated married a black woman on the basis of race.[45] This example demonstrates that many black women and men, like the rest of society, essentially accept racial categories as determinants of social behavior. It also underscores a belief in racial solidarity and the view that skin color confers rights of ownership of another person. Both whites and blacks who oppose interracial marriage tend to ignore the individual's freedom of choice.

Because interracial marriages raise fundamental questions about who is white and who is black, rejecting such marriages is an important way of marking and maintaining racial boundaries. When whites cross the boundaries by marrying blacks, some families respond by banishing these "mavericks" from their own race-based societies. A common experience of many white women involved in interracial relationships is what could be called "social death." Many of their relatives treat them as though they did not exist. The impact on the individual is often traumatic. The act of disowning a family member grows out of a perception that blacks and whites are inherently and unalterably very different and must therefore remain separate. The white family member who disagrees with this view and marries a black person is therefore not only rejected but is also symbolically "unwhitened."[46]

A Multiracial Category?

Perhaps no other development better supports the view that America is moving beyond race than the initiative supporting the addition of a multiracial category to the existing four racial categories as defined by the Census Bureau. Rising rates of immigration from Latin America and elsewhere and an increasing rate of interracial marriages combine to effectively render the concept of race less powerful than it has ever been at any time in American history. The United States is clearly on a path toward eliminating all racial categories. Efforts to inaugurate the multiracial category mark the beginning of this process, one that will gain momentum with changing demographic realities.

Racial classifications are the cornerstones of any society in which race is a significant factor. Census data on race vary from one period to another, depending on the prevailing racial ideologies. Prior to the general acceptance of the one-drop rule, four categories applied to people with African ancestry: black, mulatto, quadroon, and octoroon. By 1900, the latter three categories had been eliminated. The 1930 census listed ten racial groups including Chinese, Japanese, Mexican, Filipino, Hindu, and Korean.[47] Although it is arguable that the steady increase of racially mixed people could simply result in adding more categories instead of eliminating the entire system, attitudinal changes, unprecedented interaction between people of different races, and other factors strongly support abolishing racial categories altogether. The mere physical presence of so many racially mixed people renders the fallacy of racial classification painfully obvious.

What makes the multiracial category an important catalyst of racial change is the growing refusal on the part of many multiracial people to disregard part of their ancestry in order to fit into existing categories. Just as ethnicity has ceased to be an insurmountable barrier between different white groups, primarily because most Americans of European ancestry embrace their multiple ethnic backgrounds, race is also becoming less of a barrier as more people claim their multiple racial heritages and identities. Across the country, racially mixed people are asserting their rights to full personhood by claiming all their relatives and, by extension, all of themselves.

Multiracial children and their parents increasingly refuse to check any of the offered categories on various forms to indicate their race. Many check "other," some write in "multiracial," and others leave the form blank, much to the frustration of government officials, school administrators, and others who insist on conformity with rigid notions of race. For example, when Teja Arboleda refused to indicate his ethnic or racial identity on the 1990 census form, a Census Bureau employee noted his name, olive-tone skin, and dark hair, and marked him down as Hispanic. But Arboleda's maternal grandparents are European. His father's mother is African American. His father's father is the son of Filipino and Chinese parents. To further complicate matters, Arboleda was born legally white.[48]

Partly in response to rejection by their white relatives, many racially mixed Americans have disassociated themselves from their white ancestry. This is particularly prevalent in the case of children of black-white marriages. Acquiescing to society's definition of who is black, many white parents attempt to encourage their racially mixed children to adopt a black identity. An underlying assumption is that by so doing, conflicts about racial group membership, experienced by many interracial people, can be resolved. But as external pressures to choose one parent over the other for purposes of racial identity diminish, more interracial persons are embracing both parents.

Ursula M. Brown found that there is a difference in how interracial children define themselves publicly and how they see themselves privately. About 66 percent of them, absent external pressures, identified themselves as interracial.[49] Furthermore, as the number of interracial couples increases, more parents of racially mixed children are rejecting society's definitions and insisting on public recognition of their own inclusive definitions of racial identity.

Partly motivated by their goal of convincing the Census Bureau to adopt a multiracial category by the 2000 census, many racially mixed people, their relatives, and supporters have formed more than thirty nationally coordinated organizations to achieve their objectives. The most prominent of these groups are Project RACE (Reclassify All Children Equally), based in Atlanta; Multiracial Americans of Southern California; The Biracial Family Network of Chicago; and San Francisco's I-Pride. These groups are linked by a site on the World Wide Web, "Interracial Voice" (http://www.web-com.com/intvoice/). Several organizations for multiracial people have been formed on college campuses, reflecting the intense discussions on race and identity that permeate college life. Books by and about multiracial people, and magazines such as *New People, Interrace, Black Child,* and *Child of Colors,* have proliferated.

Like other interest groups, the multiracial identity movement, which is composed of all racial blends, has lobbied state legislatures and members of Congress to include a multiracial category on various forms, including the census form. More than twelve states, such as Ohio, Georgia, Florida, and Illinois, have been persuaded to require the addition of the multiracial category on all state forms where racial identity is requested.[50]

But many Americans oppose the creation of a new racial category, partly because the categories already in existence seem to confuse them. Some Americans fail to distinguish between race and ethnicity, claiming to be multiracial if they are both Irish-American and Italian-American, for example. A more important reason for opposition to the multiracial category is the feeling that all racial categories give credence to the social construction of race and, therefore, the existence of a racial hierarchy. Even among individuals favoring greater social recognition of multiracial people as combinations of different races, the idea of a separate multiracial category raises serious concerns. It seems to contradict their view of racial inclusivity by promoting yet another form of racial exclusivity.

Furthermore, it is believed that emphasizing a multiracial category will reinforce problems that emanate from racial identity politics. Racial categories are perceived as essential to the prolongation of racism. One of the leading opponents of legislating racial identity is Candy Mills, formerly a strong advocate of the multiracial category and the publisher and founding editor of three magazines dealing with multiracial issues.[51] A *Newsweek* poll found that 36 percent of whites and 49 percent of blacks favored adding a multiracial category to the U.S. census; 51 percent of whites and 42 percent of blacks expressed their opposition to it. When asked if the Census Bureau should stop collecting information on race and ethnicity, 47 percent of whites and 48 percent of blacks said yes, while 44 percent of blacks and 41 percent of whites favored continuing the practice. In late 1997 the Census Bureau decided to allow Americans to mark more than one racial category instead of adding a multiracial category.[52]

Although many blacks support the inclusion of a multiracial category in the census and other forms, the strongest opposition to it comes from leaders in the black community. An uneasy alliance in relation to race has always existed among Americans with African ancestry, mainly because many of them continue to subscribe to a skin-color hierarchy similar to that endorsed by society as a whole. The one-drop rule consolidates Americans with any African ancestry. Acceptance of a multiracial category threatens black solidarity by undermining the one-drop rule. Many black leaders fear that a multiracial category will contribute to the "pigmentocracy" that exists in America; they believe that light-skinned blacks will want to minimize their African heritage and identify themselves as belonging to more socially acceptable multiracial categories. Instead of stressing racial heritage, many black leaders suggest that racial classification should reflect actual social standing.[53] But the black community has never been monolithic, and the experiences of Americans with African ancestry vary from region to region, from city to city, and from one individual to another. Nonetheless, most blacks do share some common experiences.

A more persuasive argument advanced by blacks and others against the multiracial category is that their interests would be adversely affected if significant numbers of blacks and others identify themselves as multiracial. Their political power would be greatly weakened, and efforts to fight racial discrimination would be impeded. Census Bureau data on race are widely utilized as evidence of discrimination, to protect the civil rights of minorities, and for drawing political boundaries. Organizations such as the National Association for the Advancement of Colored People (NAACP), the National Council of La Raza (a Hispanic advocacy group), the National Congress of American Indians, and the Equal Employment Advisory Council oppose adding the multiracial category because of its perceived impact on affirmative action programs. A general concern is that a multiracial category will make it difficult to follow federal antidiscrimination guidelines and to implement affirmative action programs. It is argued that members of the multiracial category, with no clear history of discrimination against them, would not benefit from affirmative action.[54] But the movement toward ending affirmative action or basing benefits on economic status and social background weakens these arguments.

Alliances based principally on racial identities in an increasingly multiracial society that is making significant progress toward equal treatment and opportunity are bound to struggle. Fundamental changes in the racial composition of America and the willingness of more Americans to assert their claims to a multiracial identity strongly suggest a Hawaiian approach to race relations.

In Hawaii, for example, miscegenation laws never existed, and people of all races have intermarried freely. The Hawaiian monarchy disavowed racial prejudices. Early black American residents on the islands, some of them escaped slaves who became sailors or whalers, married Hawaiians and were integrated into society. Increasing rates of interracial marriages, reaching 45.9 percent of all marriages in 1991, influenced various groups to negotiate their differences, to find common interests, and to stress cooperation.[55] Mainland America is gradually but inexorably moving toward the Hawaiian model.

8

TRANSRACIAL ADOPTION

Building Bridges
that Transcend Race

TRANSRACIAL ADOPTIONS, like interracial marriages, provide irrefutable evidence of profound changes in American racial attitudes and behavior. Transracial adoptions personalize racial issues, help erode racial boundaries, and challenge the "us-versus-them" mentality by bringing whites, blacks, Asians, and Latinos together as families. Racial issues become family issues, involving the immediate family as well as the extended family, friends, and acquaintances. One interracial family has an impact that reaches far beyond its members. Transracial adoptions provide tangible examples of different races living together in the most basic and important human institution: the family. They challenge racism and the tendency of society to view many of its problems through a racial prism. They reinforce society's efforts to get beyond race by building the most basic transracial alliance.

For Americans who embrace racial ideologies, transracial adoptions must be resisted, precisely because they challenge the fundamental assumptions on which race is constructed and on which it depends for its social power and perpetuation. Such adoptions force Americans to confront their beliefs about racial and cultural distinctions as well as their perceptions of who belongs to the American family. It is clear from interviews with transracial adoptive families that most individuals who adopt across racial lines are deeply committed to humanitarian beliefs. They recognize a common humanity that transcends race.

But opponents of transracial adoptions, often with good intentions, see this humanitarianism as a heavy burden that is borne primarily by black and interracial children. The National Association of Black Social Workers (NABSW), as will be discussed, has strongly opposed transracial adoptions. Many of its members argue that allowing white parents to raise black children is the equivalent of cultural genocide. Yet conditions within the black community put many black children at extreme risk. The benefits of transracial adoptions are often disregarded by opponents such as the NABSW because of ideology. The danger of racial ideologies, like ideologies in general, is that they encourage individuals to overlook the immediate suffering and humanity of others in their pursuit of a perfect world. Few pause to ask what would have happened to abandoned black children if they had not been adopted by white families.

Contesting Racial Boundaries: Matching and Placement

Attitudes and policies concerning transracial adoptions reflect the state of America's race relations. Matching and placement decisions indicate the degree to which individuals and society as a whole are willing to cross racial boundaries. Prior to the successes of the civil rights movement, few white families attempted to adopt black or racially mixed children, largely because such an act was considered to be deviant, unacceptable, and even punishable.

Mirroring society's racial beliefs and behavior, child welfare agencies believed that only white children should be adopted by white parents and that only black children should be placed with black parents. This approach to adoption was part of the larger policy of matching children and families who were as physically indistinguishable as possible from each other, making it more difficult to distinguish birth children from adopted children. Similar physical characteristics were seen to be essential to the children's ability to identify with their adopted parents. The concept of matching was based on the assumption that adoptions were more likely to be successful if adopted children and their parents literally matched on skin color, religion, and emotional and cultural characteristics.[1]

Transracial adoptions increased primarily because of social change. As a result of World War II, large numbers of children were orphaned. Some of the orphaned black children were adopted by white families. However, the dominant tendency was still the adoption of white children by white parents. Social changes allowing more readily available abortions, thus reducing the number of white children available for adoption, and a decline in the number of adoptable children from abroad combined to draw greater attention to black and racially mixed children in America who were spending their lives in foster homes.

At the same time, the civil rights movement and the general idealism of the youth of the 1960s placed great emphasis on the unity of humankind and the need for America to improve race relations. Intercountry adoptions had begun to pave the way for transracial adoptions within the United States. Changing racial attitudes made it easier to draw attention to the black and racially mixed children who were not being adopted by white families. These factors led to a departure from the traditional concept of racial matching and to a dramatic increase in transracial adoptions. Statistics compiled by the Boys and Girls Aid Society of Oregon, the only organization that gathered such information at the time, showed that nationally 733 black children were placed in white homes in 1968, 1,447 in 1969, 2,274 in 1970, and 2,574 in 1971. However, the majority of black children were still adopted by black families.[2]

This growth in transracial adoption not only challenged the practice of racial matching but also called into question the racial attitudes and assumptions supporting it. Because the racial composition of families has significant consequences for the maintenance of racial boundaries, many blacks and whites with traditional views of both race and family strongly opposed the trend toward greater societal tolerance of transracial adoption. The NABSW took a vehement stand against transracial adoptions during its convention in Nashville in 1972. Members were asked to encourage black families to make a greater effort to adopt black children. The rules and procedures regarded as barriers to blacks who wanted to adopt were also opposed by the NABSW. But the most violent reactions to transracial adoptions came from whites.

Clarence Evans, a black man, married Mary Gingrich, a white woman. In 1980, Evans indicated that he wanted to adopt his wife's six children from a previous marriage. The children's biological father, Donald Gingrich, strongly opposed the idea. Evans received threatening phone calls. The family was threatened that their home would be burned, the words "Kill Nigger, KKK" were painted on their door, and chunks of asphalt were thrown through their bedroom window. Sensing impending violence, Evans and his wife took out a fire insurance policy and transferred the children to their relatives' homes. Although Evans closely monitored his own house from a parked car, arsonists still managed to set the house on fire during one of Evans's periodic trips to visit his wife, who was working.[3] This violent response shows how threatening racially integrated families are to some Americans.

Because race continues to matter, the adoption laws of many states generally give preference to placing children with families who share their racial or ethnic identity. Even in states that have laws forbidding racial discrimination in adoptions, social workers and others often allow their own biases to dominate their decisionmaking processes, thereby effectively circumventing the law. Furthermore, pressure from the NABSW and other groups often deters adoption agencies from placing children transracially.

Although all states specifically require that the best interests of the child be taken into account when placing that child with adoptive parents, most states directly or indirectly allow race to be taken into consideration. Some states prescribe set periods of time in which agencies must attempt same-race matching and placement before transracial adoptions can occur. Many families who attempt to adopt children from a different racial or ethnic category are often discouraged from doing so by adoption agencies. States such as Texas, Kentucky, Maryland, New Jersey, Wisconsin, Connecticut, and Pennsylvania prohibit the use of race to deny an adoption or placement. These states do not allow race to be a determining factor in the adoption process.[4]

Concerned about the large number of black children who languish in foster care primarily because it is difficult to find black adoptive parents, Senator Howard M. Metzenbaum pushed through Congress the controversial Multiethnic Placement Act in late 1994. This legislation makes it illegal to delay potential transracial adoptions while social workers search for an adoptive family matching the child's race or ethnic background; to establish a list of criteria for placement based on race, culture, or ethnicity; and to require caseworkers to justify interracial adoptions. These laws apply to all agencies and entities that receive federal assistance.[5] The Multiethnic Placement Act is an extension of Title VI of the Civil Rights Act of 1964, which prohibits recipients of federal assistance from discriminating on the basis of race, color, or national origin in their programs and activities and from operating their programs in discriminatory ways.

Based on guidelines issued by the Department of Health and Human Services for implementing the Multiethnic Placement Act, adoption agencies may take race into account only when such a consideration would advance the best interests of a specific child. If a child has lived in a particular racial, ethnic, or cultural community for an extended period of time, an adoption agency may assess the child's ability to make the transition to another community. An agency may also consider the attitudes of prospective parents to determine their capacity to nurture a child from a different background. The prospective parents' racial beliefs, which might psychologically damage a child, are not overlooked in placement decisions.[6] Some critics of the Multiethnic Placement Act, such as Representative Charles B. Rangel of New York, argue that few blacks would be given preference over whites to adopt a "beautiful, blonde-haired, blue-eyed child." Representative Jim Bunning, a white Republican from Kentucky whose daughter adopted a black child, to counter Rangel pointed to the number of black children who await adoption.[7]

Although disagreements are likely to continue about hypothetical scenarios, the reality is that many black children are waiting to be adopted. There are approximately half a million children in America's foster care system, and more than half of them are racial minorities. Parental rights have been terminated for about twenty thousand of these children, which frees them to be legally adopted, a process that takes an average of two years and eight months. Forty-four percent of the adoptable children are white and 43 percent are black. Most of them are older children between the ages of six and twelve years. In 1990, 4 percent of all children awaiting adoption were under one year old, 36 percent were ages one to five, 43 percent were ages six to twelve, and 17 percent were twelve years and older.[8]

Among the hard-to-place children, 67 percent are black and 26 percent are white. Hard-to-place children are usually older, of African ancestry, or handicapped. It is generally agreed that it takes substantially longer to find homes for minority children. Although 67 percent of all American families waiting to adopt are white and 31 percent are black, despite the passage of the Multiethnic Placement Law, an emphasis on racial matching effectively excludes whites from adopting black children who are awaiting placement with a permanent family. Because many black families are inclined to adopt "light-skinned" black children, the outlook for darker-skinned black children is even more difficult than the statistics suggest. In many states where blacks make up a relatively small percentage of the population, the overwhelming majority of children awaiting adoption are black. In Massachusetts, for example, about 5 percent of the population is black, yet black children constitute nearly half of that state's children in need of foster care or adoptive homes.[9] Despite this obvious racial imbalance, matching still has many powerful proponents.

Arguments for Racial Matching

Beginning in the early 1970s, the NABSW and leaders of some black political organizations strongly endorsed racial matching and opposed transracial adoptions. The foundation of opposition to transracial adoptions was largely political. Just as society was becoming more accepting of racial integration, black nationalists and others endorsed a policy of separatism. Instead of focusing on what blacks and whites have in common, they emphasized the largely superficial differences between members of the two groups. They embraced the belief in a monolithic black culture and the view that black identity was determined by adherence to that culture. Since black culture is believed to be significantly different from white culture, black children who are adopted by white families would be deprived of their culture. Following this line of reasoning, the NABSW and leaders of Native American groups see transracial adoptions as a form of cultural genocide.

Apart from the fact that the number of black children adopted by white parents was relatively small, totaling fewer than three thousand in 1972 when the NABSW adopted its policy condemning transracial adoption, an objective analysis of the prospects of black children in foster care would lead one to conclude that transracial adoptions were having a minor impact on black culture. Furthermore, given the diversity among Americans with African ancestry, the belief that there is one identifiable black culture is fallacious.

The assumption that this so-called black culture is inherently beneficial for black children is contradicted by what is widely regarded as a pathology within the poorest parts of the black community from which much of black culture derives. The assumption overlooks the economic problems, the hopelessness and despair, the widespread acts of random violence, and the dysfunctional families typically found in the inner city. Given the high murder and imprisonment rates among young blacks, the view that transracial adoption is tantamount to genocide is disingenuous. In fact, black children are more likely to reach adulthood if they are adopted by middle-class white families who reside in safe neighborhoods than if they remain in the inner city.

Another argument advanced for matching is that it ultimately enhances black political power. This assumes that a black person who grows up in an interracial family will automatically identify with interests that are inimical to the black community. The weaknesses in this viewpoint are many and they are obvious. Although numbers are important in politics, political skills, access to people in positions of power, an understanding of the culture one is trying to influence, and the ability to effectively communicate with those in power are much more important. Furthermore, it is extremely difficult for a black person raised in America to completely avoid racial issues. Societal forces are likely to influence blacks who are adopted by white families to play a constructive role in improving race relations, which is essential for the enhancement of black political power.

One of the strongest arguments used to support racial matching is that transracial adoptions contribute to identity problems for black children. This issue is discussed in greater detail later in this chapter. The basic idea is that ethnic and racial identities are best preserved by racial matching. Separating black children from black families, it is argued, prevents them from developing as psychologically healthy black people. Many black children raised by white parents are believed to lack the necessary skills to deal with racism when they confront it. Furthermore, as Toni Oliver, leader of the NABSW, puts it, when people live by the maxim "love is all it takes," they often overlook the real impact that race has on our society. Somehow, when the issue is adoption, race suddenly does not matter anymore.[10]

Although race is certainly important, the broader context of transracial adoptions makes the racial issue less significant. As long as race is emphasized as the dominant source of identity, efforts to make society less race-conscious will continue to encounter resistance. In other words, the position adopted by the NABSW helps to reinforce the racial problems with which it is concerned. Racial rigidity by blacks, whites, Asians, or Latinos strengthens racial intolerance and promotes segregation.

Proponents of racial matching often point to the financial obstacles faced by black parents who wish to adopt black children. Expenses for adoptions generally range from $5,000 to $10,000, an amount that many black families who want to adopt cannot afford. Another barrier is cultural. Many Americans with African ancestry, due partly to historical memories of their ancestors being sold as slaves, have difficulty accepting the idea that one should pay for a child. Adoption within the black community has historically been an informal effort that families negotiate with each other. One solution to this problem is to use the church as a vehicle for placing black children with black families. Several organizations, including One Church, One Child, and the Institute for Black Parenting, are actively involved in efforts to match black children with black families.[11]

Faced with criticism from transracial adoption advocates and the reality of large numbers of black children languishing in foster homes, the NABSW has modified its position on racial matching. However, its primary emphasis remains finding black homes for black children. Transracial adoption is seen by the NABSW as the third option behind the preservation of biological black families and the placement of black children in black homes. The NABSW is now focusing on the reasons why black children are removed from their homes and is attempting to find solutions. If a child is abused, the NABSW advocates child-abuse counseling for the family. If living conditions are unsuitable, an attempt is made to find adequate housing. When financial difficulties are the main issue, agencies are urged to provide advice in financial management. In the aftermath of the October 1995 Million Man March on Washington, promoted by Louis Farrakhan, the NABSW launched an aggressive campaign to find homes for about 25,000 black children in need of adoption.[12] Despite these efforts, many black children are still waiting to be adopted.

Arguments Against Racial Matching

One of the strongest arguments against racial matching is the severe shortage of black homes for black children waiting to be adopted. Because the number of white parents looking for children to adopt exceeds the number of white children to be adopted, racial matching is unworkable. Whereas the NABSW believes that racial identity and pride are of paramount importance in deciding where to place children, many black children bear the costs by spending years in foster homes. Although proponents of racial matching may have the best intentions, the consequences of their policies for the children they purport to care about are extremely painful. Children who are deprived of a parent or of a caring extended family are victimized in a fundamental way, and their chances of ever being adopted dramatically plummet with each passing year. In effect, attempts at racial matching often result in depriving children of an opportunity to belong to society's most basic institution: the family.

Opponents of racial matching, many of whom favor racial integration, believe that matching perpetuates the racial problems that the NABSW and other organizations use to justify their policies promoting a monolithic black culture. Randall Kennedy, a professor of law at Harvard University and a strong advocate of transracial adoptions, argues that racial matching "buttresses the notion that people of different racial backgrounds really are different in some moral, unbridgeable, permanent sense. It affirms the notion that race should be a cage to which people are assigned at birth and from which people should not be allowed to wander."[13] Racial matching when applied to blacks is as racially biased as when applied to whites. In other words, using race as the determining criterion in placing a child reinforces negative racial attitudes and behavior, with the highest costs falling, once again, on the most vulnerable and disadvantaged members of society. Instead of judging individuals on the basis of their character and ability to undertake the daunting responsibility of raising a child properly, advocates of racial matching judge potential adoptive parents primarily on the basis of skin color.

Another argument advanced by opponents of racial matching is that assumptions about the inherent abilities of black adoptive parents to raise black children better than white parents are unsupported by evidence. But the idea that black adults are better equipped by their experiences with racism to raise a black child cannot be easily dismissed. Black children can learn from successful black parents how to overcome racial barriers. On the other hand, a preoccupation with racism and a tendency to view problems through a racial prism can also contribute to the development of a distorted and self-defeating view of the world. Furthermore, black children must eventually navigate an increasingly racially integrated world. Children raised in black families could be disadvantaged in many ways when they are forced by economic, social, and political realities to navigate the world beyond the black community.

Similarly, critics of racial matching point to the advantages enjoyed by black children adopted by white parents. Many of these parents are likely to be racially liberal, well educated, and middle class. Elizabeth Bartholet, a professor of law at Harvard University and a parent who has adopted interracially, makes a strong case against automatically assuming that white parents cannot help a black child. Whites often are in a better position than blacks to teach children how to maneuver in the white worlds of power and privilege. Bartholet believes that for black children growing up in a white-dominated world, there would be a range of material advantages associated with having white parents.[14] White parents often can give a black child immediate access to people of influence in the white community. An understanding of both whites and blacks could ultimately be a source of power that would prove helpful in improving race relations. Many of America's prominent black leaders, including Vernon Jordan and Colin Powell, had access to whites during their youth.

Finally, opponents of racial matching strongly disagree with the view advanced by proponents that matching is designed to prevent the child from feeling uncomfortable in a disapproving surrounding community. Opponents of racial matching point out that arguments once advanced to keep blacks segregated are similar to arguments now used by supporters of racial matching in adoptions. In both cases, the dominant argument is that segregation is meant to protect blacks. Moreover, advocates of racial matching are viewed as being oblivious to the existence of racially mixed people, who belong to more than one racial group.[15]

Perhaps the most important argument against racial matching in adoption is that the alternatives to transracial adoptions are generally detrimental to the children involved. Although the NABSW makes it appear that there is a choice between placing a black child with a black family or with a white family, the reality is that the black child often has the option of being placed with a white family or being deprived of a permanent family. If safeguarding the best interests of the children is the major concern, then it is clear that the adoption of these children by caring and responsible families, regardless of color, must outweigh ideological considerations. The humanity of an individual transcends race.

Broadening Racial and Cultural Identities

Because the belief in an exclusive racial identity is so central to the social construction and maintenance of race, transracial adoptions challenge racist beliefs by broadening the number of identities one may claim. Opposition to transracial adoptions stems not primarily from the fear that black children will lose their black identity, however defined, but that they will acquire competing identities that enhance their ability to cross racial lines. In a world of "us versus them," any appearance of weakness in group solidarity is not generally tolerated. Many white parents who adopt black children are also perceived as threatening by those who believe in racial solidarity. These parents, as well as their families, friends, and acquaintances, broaden their own cultural and racial identities as they help their adopted children learn about other subcultures. Because of their experiences with each other as well as with individuals from black, Asian, Latino, and white racial groups, interracial family members are likely to reject a rigid racial prism and to adopt the broader framework of human virtues.

As mentioned previously, opponents of transracial adoption argue that a white family is at a disadvantage in providing an environment conducive to the development of a child's black identity. Three reasons are given to support this assumption. First, the child cannot identify with the parent because they do not share the same racial heritage. Second, the black child is likely to be isolated from other black children. Third, because white parents are unlikely to personally experience racism and prejudice, they are ill equipped to prepare black children to face a world in which they will almost inevitably encounter racial prejudice.[16] These arguments have been forwarded by a few blacks who have been adopted by white families.

These assumptions are evidence of prejudice on the part of those who advocate them. One cannot be sure that white parents are not equally capable of preparing a black child to deal with racism. In fact, because most whites are ordinarily treated decently, their experience with the prejudice they face themselves as part of an interracial family is likely to motivate them to teach their children strategies to effectively counter racism. Whites and blacks have traditionally cooperated to end racial discrimination. Indeed, racists have always supported racial solidarity because they understand that racial boundaries inevitably erode when blacks and whites work together to weaken racial identities.

Preoccupation with developing a black identity grows out of the philosophy of black autonomy, which is based on the view that a strong black identity will help children develop self-confidence, positive self-images, and a sense of security. The interest in developing a positive black identity in children grows from the negative self-concepts and feelings of powerlessness that have traditionally plagued Americans with African ancestry. Advocates of black autonomy generally perceive the world in terms of two hostile camps that are neatly divided into black and white. They argue that transracially adopted children do not belong to either the black or white worlds: In effect, they are marginalized people who are not adequately prepared to function in either world.[17]

An underlying weakness of the black identity argument is its failure to clearly and logically define "blackness." The diversity within the black community makes it impossible to develop a set of criteria that definitively determines blackness. As discussed in Chapter 1, the differences between blacks and whites have been greatly exaggerated in order to justify and perpetuate unequal treatment based on skin color. Apart from the fact that blacks and whites have much in common, regional and class differences among blacks have always made efforts to place all blacks into a rigid and fixed category difficult to carry through.

Racial identity is largely in the eye of the beholder. Behaviors that are considered integral components of black identity are not necessarily conducive to the healthy development of black children or to their success in

American society. An identity based on the artificial construction of race is bound to be shallow and limiting. Furthermore, few black children in black families escape identity problems as they wrestle with the pressures of the larger society and the contradictions in relation to black identity that one finds within the black community.

Based on extensive research, Rita Simon, Howard Altstein, and Marygold S. Melli conclude that both during adolescence and later during adulthood, transracially adopted children are aware of and comfortable with their racial identity. Although black children adopted by white families realize that how they dress and speak and the music they listen to may differ from what is generally regarded as "black," they believe that the variations characteristic of the black experience in America allow them to be no less "black" than children from the inner cities.[18] The major difference between them is that transracially adopted children tend to de-emphasize racial identity and to regard cultural identity, based on their socioeconomic environment and family traditions, as being more important. Furthermore, adopted children tend to see race as only one of many sources of identity.

Embracing multiple identities enables many transracially adopted children to cope successfully with racial problems. Whereas advocates of racial identity believe that a strong black identity is essential for survival and success in a hostile racial environment, their preoccupation with race is often counterproductive. Apart from missing opportunities to move society toward greater equality, they are also more likely to exhaust themselves struggling against what they perceive as racism to protect their self-esteem. Although few blacks escape experiencing some form of racial discrimination, children who embrace multiple identities are not as negatively affected by prejudice as children who see race as the sole or dominant source of their identity. By recognizing the insignificance of race within the broader framework of human virtues, children with multiple identities are less vulnerable to racial attacks.[19] They are less susceptible to the magic inherent in racial categorization.

Closely related to the idea of black identity is the notion that race determines culture and that the two are synonymous. Proponents of racial identity strongly promote African culture as black culture, precisely at a time when many Africans are attempting to abandon those cultural practices that impede their efforts to join a world dominated by American culture. Just as there is no one dominant definition of black identity, there is no commonly accepted definition of black culture. Blacks in inner-city Washington are keenly aware that their culture differs significantly from that of blacks who live in wealthier neighborhoods elsewhere in the metropolitan area.

Most Americans with African ancestry realize that there are great variations in how families raise children. There is no evidence to support the assumption that there is a consensus on how to raise black children. Although most blacks share a sense of being separate from the larger society and of having similar historical experiences, they are not a monolithic cultural group. Some blacks believe that celebrating Kwanza or listening to rap music constitutes black culture, whereas others dislike rap music and prefer to celebrate Christmas. Clarence Thomas and Louis Farrakhan are unlikely to agree on a definition of black culture, but both men are black.

Transracially adopted children are likely to embrace the middle-class values common to most Americans, thereby broadening the concept of cultural identity. Whereas many advocates of black culture are ambivalent about fully supporting achievements they regard as belonging to white culture, such as academic excellence and economic success, blacks who are less constrained by perceptions of black culture are likely to strive for greater academic and financial success. Because most transracially adopted children understand from their experiences in interracial families that grades and test scores are essential for success in American society, their performance in school and beyond is likely to be better than that of children who view the dominant white culture as hostile and foreign. The success of black children, whether they are adopted by white families or raised in black families, is essential to the process of destroying racial stereotypes and the racism that emanates from them.

Transracial adoptions are instrumental in bringing different components of American culture together. Instead of depriving black children of what is regarded as black identity and culture, many white adoptive parents endeavor to broaden their children's cultural experiences by exposing them to both the black and white worlds. Although not all parents who adopt interracially are sensitive to the cultural needs of children, black or white, most interracial families are generally cognizant of the advantages of broadening their children's awareness and appreciation of many different cultures.

Sheila Welch, an author of children's books and mother of seven children, the last six of whom are of African ancestry, is an example of how transracial families enrich their children's lives by exposing them to a variety of cultural experiences. Sheila and her husband Eric, who are white, are conscious of the need to help their children understand their ethnic background. They fill their home with books, magazines, and other materials that feature people from racial minority groups. Sheila often seeks out books and other reading materials to help her learn black history and to gain insight into the thinking of contemporary black writers. She has taught her children about important contributions that Americans with African ancestry have made in all aspects of life in the United States. Her commitment to expanding her children's cultural awareness continues with her three grandchildren. Sheila purchases books for them "that will help them feel positive about their racial heritage."[20] Her children are clearly comfortable with their black and other identities.

Parents who adopt children from overseas also are sensitive to identity issues. Jane Liedtke, who is white, adopted a child from China after making several educational trips to that country. Jane says she is conscious of her daughter Emily's need to identify with Asians as role models and to be knowledgeable about Asian culture in general and her Han Chinese heritage in particular.[21] To accomplish this objective, Jane reads books about China to her daughter, in the process building an impressive library of books and other materials. Emily is also immersed in other cultures, which is a reflection of her mother's interest in racial and ethnic diversity.

Many adoptive parents create both a multiracial and a multicultural environment for their children to help them deal with identity issues. Mary Campbell and her husband, who are white, adopted a child whom the adoption agency believed was of mixed-race (black-white) parentage but who did not show any visible physical indications of black ancestry. Because the child tended to deny his probable racial background, due partly to societal preferences for whiteness, his parents exposed him to school programs, friends, and activities they hoped would nurture positive impressions of different races. They also taught him to accept and appreciate diversity by hosting exchange students from Australia, Hong Kong, and Japan, and they became foster parents to five young Vietnamese men who were refugees from the Vietnam War. However, their son continues to reject his own probable racial mixture. The Campbells also adopted two Korean children, who have not experienced the identity problems of their oldest son. The Koreans are accepting of Asian culture; they have developed an ethnically diverse group of peers in their school environment. As their mother puts it, "Birthday parties and sleepovers have always looked like a mini–United Nations group."[22]

Although most transracially adopted children are comfortable with multiple racial and cultural identities, some reject their parents and embark on a search for their cultural heritage. But their behavior, when placed in the larger context of adoptions in general, does not differ significantly from that of children adopted in families with whom they share the same racial characteristics. Furthermore, viewed in the broader context of American culture, the search for identity by black children who were adopted by white parents is similar to what many other adolescents experience. David Watts, a biracial social worker in New York who was raised by an adoptive white family in the Midwest, is an example of a person who is struggling with racial identity issues. Watts stands out because of his active campaign against transracial adoptions, based on his belief that it is a bad idea to put a black child in a white home. He also argues that it is impossible for someone from one culture to teach children about another culture.[23]

David was what adoption agencies call a "hard to place child." Included in this category are older children, children with African ancestry, and children who are handicapped. Given the predominantly white racial composition of central Illinois in the late 1960s, it was unlikely that David would have found a black adoptive home. He was eventually adopted by a white family; his father, Richard Watts, a minister who was deeply committed to the civil rights movement and fought for fair housing in the small town where they lived, agrees that David's alternatives to being adopted by a white family were not very encouraging. When the family moved to Cleveland, they attempted to expose David to different racial and cultural groups by enrolling him in a school with a diverse student body and a progressive curriculum. David had many friends in the white area of Cleveland where he lived and was more concerned about class differences than about race. Like many children of all races, David did not want to leave his friends to live in a more racially integrated part of Cleveland when his parents suggested moving.[24]

After David, at the age of twenty-one, left Cleveland to live in New York, he realized how isolated he had been from black culture. Although his parents had made an effort to expose him to black history and prominent leaders in the black community, David believes that he was not adequately prepared to cope as a black person, that he was never taught the differences between black culture and white culture, and that he did not have a black identity. His experiences in New York led him to conclude that he had missed out on not only the obvious aspects of black culture, such as food, dress, and music, but also on the more subtle aspects of the culture, such as "the jokes told, how loud you speak, how much you touch when you talk, and the relationships between mothers and sons."[25] The culture that David describes also equates blackness with an antiwhite mentality.

Many young black men and women in small towns and integrated suburban neighborhoods are often pressured by urban blacks into believing that behaviors associated with inner-city residents constitute black culture. There is a pervasive tendency to oversimplify black experiences and to either romanticize black culture or to demonize it. Instead of attempting to broaden his cultural identity by learning as much as possible about the complexity of the black community, David accepted a simplified view of what it means to be black, thus inadvertently reinforcing the negative stereotypes that many blacks regard as impediments to black success. Despite the obvious strains placed on David and his family by his decision to distance himself from his parents and to oppose transracial adoptions in the national media, David, according to his father, is now more accepting of his parents. Although hurt by their son's beliefs, David's parents continue to embrace him.[26] This and other examples clearly demonstrate that transracial adoptions play a vital role in broadening a family's racial and cultural identities.

Bridging the Racial Divide

Transracial adoptions are instrumental in bridging racial divisions, just as interethnic marriages have significantly reduced conflicts among various European groups in America. Transracial adoptions have significant consequences for the members of the interracial family as well as for their relatives, friends, and people they encounter. Both parents and children gain a greater understanding and appreciation of people from different racial categories. Many of them come to realize that blacks, whites, Asians, Latinos, and others have much in common, leading them to reject the irrationality of racial classification. Transracial adoptions, by personalizing racial issues, are a cornerstone of the bottom-up approach to improving race relations.

It is clear that those white parents who have adopted black, Asian, and Latino children were already strongly committed to racial integration and equality. Although they come from diverse backgrounds, these individuals share a common belief in the unity of humankind; are generally strongly religious; are committed to social justice; and are tolerant of racial, religious, and other differences. Richard Watts, Sheila and Eric Welch, and Mary Campbell, for example, share the view that people of all colors must come together, find common ground, and live and work in the same communities.[27] Several parents who have adopted children of another race are members of the Bahai'i faith, which emphasizes the unity of humanity and the oneness of the human race.

Whites involved in transracial adoptions are most likely to have been raised in families that stressed racial equality. Many grew up in all-white towns, but their families were generally positive toward other racial groups. Their families' values were usually reinforced by religious teachings, especially the belief all people are equal in God's sight. Some grew up with black neighbors or had parents who taught in predominantly black schools. Others experienced discrimination themselves because of their religious beliefs or because they had grown up "on the wrong side of the tracks," as they put it. Mary Campbell's experiences are typical of parents who adopt transracially. Mary says: "Our family was never, never allowed to say anything negative about anyone. We were never allowed to tell a joke which made fun of another ethnic or racial group. My father worked hard in his trades union to help people organize and get better wages and working conditions."[28] Mary and the other parents interviewed had very strong positive attitudes about race prior to adoption.

Despite their already strong commitment to racial equality, many parents involved in transracial adoptions perceived changes in their own racial attitudes and behavior. Most of them became more racially and socially sensitive. Because of their children, race had become a personal issue. Consequently, they came to believe even more strongly than before in equal treatment and in downplaying distinctions based on racial characteristics. A few parents believe that transracial adoption makes them more aware of their own prejudices. It also makes them more determined to change their behavior.[29]

By crossing racial boundaries, many white adoptive parents also experience prejudice. As in the case of interracial marriages, whites who form an interracial family are sometimes perceived by other whites as traitors "to their race" and are treated as if they were blacks. Eric Welch, who together with his wife Sheila adopted six racially mixed children as discussed above, said that when he and Sheila were looking for houses, agents would take them to different neighborhoods depending on whether their children were with them or not. Eric's experiences with prejudice are similar to those endured by many racial minorities. He says: "It is ironic that I almost was denied my current job because of our biracial children. The dean, who was the supervisor of the woman who hired me, said to her, 'You know, they have colored children.' Fortunately, that lady, a Southerner, replied, in essence, 'So what?' That was the end of that."[30] Eric is now the affirmative action director at his college.

Made more aware of racial problems and the need to bridge the racial divide, many adoptive parents search out and create opportunities to get to know people from diverse backgrounds and to help others do the same. Dick Rundall, for example, takes students to the Lac du Flambeau Indian Reservation in Wisconsin several times a year, brings Native Americans on field trips to Rockford, Illinois, and has created a nonprofit program that is based in one of the poorest neighborhoods in that city. He also serves as a mentor to a group of blacks between the ages of ten and fifteen.[31]

Many white parents who adopt interracially become more aware of racial discrimination and make an effort to end it. As Jane Liedtke puts it, "My antennae are up! I notice and hear more. I react when situations that are discriminatory arise—I always did, but now it is hitting closer to home."[32] Like any other parent, she reacts to defend her daughter, Emily. Other parents let their friends and colleagues know that racial jokes and remarks are not tolerated. A white newspaper reporter in central Illinois, for example, told his colleagues that their jokes about racial minorities insulted him because his son is a minority. Adoptive parents generally have the courage to speak up when they hear racist comments.

Although they face negative reactions from people opposed to interracial families, most transracial adoptive parents have a positive impact on the people around them. As an author of children's books, Sheila Welch influences others through her stories, which reflect her own acceptance of people from various backgrounds. Her most recent book is about two children, one black and the other white, who are introduced as neighbors and who become close friends. In real life, her neighbors in the small, white rural community where she lives have been positive about her interracial family. Several mothers have told Sheila that they are glad their own children have a chance to know and become friends with children from another racial group. Most families are very willing to invite Sheila's children over to visit and participate in their activities. Even when some white boys in high school express anger at the thought of black boys socializing with "their" white girls, Sheila believes that these students are nevertheless learning something about the similarities of all people when they rub shoulders with her sons day after day in school and in the community.[33]

Transracial adoptions also have an important impact on the families of adoptive parents. Following a transracial adoption by a family member, many parents, grandparents, and siblings who had negative attitudes toward racial minorities not only become more accepting of others but also attempt to change their friends' racial attitudes. Jane Liedtke, for example, has observed significant attitudinal and behavioral changes in her family. Instead of showing little or no interest in her daughter, Jane's relatives have responded positively. Although Jane's parents never expressed negative feelings during the adoption process, they did not get excited about the imminent addition to the family either. But, as Jane says, "The day they saw Emily, played with her, and took her into their arms, she was their granddaughter and her race was no longer a factor. Maybe it never was, but they changed. They are now proud grandparents with tons of photos to show their friends and other family members."[34]

Both the biological and adopted children in interracial families usually embody the concept of getting beyond race. These children generally embrace their parents' commitment to an integrated society in which people are judged on the content of their character and not on their skin color. They not only believe in a color-blind society, they practice it. In light of the positive impact of generational replacement on race relations, even a relatively small group of young men and women who are strongly committed to racial equality plays a crucial role in helping to move society beyond race.

Biological children in interracial families care about and protect their black, white, Latino, or Asian brothers and sisters. They tend to believe that racial distinctions are meaningless, and they develop a strong sense of social justice and equal treatment. Some of them are outspoken in support of improved race relations. They are comfortable with people from different races, which is an asset in a society that is becoming increasingly racially diverse. Most parents in these multiracial families believe that their adopted children have influenced their biological children in very positive ways. Perhaps most importantly, they see their biological children perpetuating their own values and behavior.

Most minority children who are adopted into white families are comfortable among whites in general. When their black, Latino, and Asian friends make antiwhite comments, these children have the benefit of a very different perspective from which to judge such comments. Their experiences growing up in an interracial family give them an advantage over most blacks and others in dealing with whites. Dick Rundall, for example, says that his children have close friends from different backgrounds and are able to be themselves in racially diverse groups. They treat people as people.[35] Their familiarity with whites helps facilitate their success in what many regard as the white world. Being adopted by a white family has given them immediate access to middle-class values and a middle-class life.

Transracial adoption clearly challenges the idea of race and the view that members of different racial categories cannot live together as a family. It is precisely because transracial adoptions erode racial boundaries that individuals who believe in racial separatism are strongly opposed to them. Parents who adopt transracially are integrationists who believe in the unity of all humanity. Their children, both biological and adopted, strengthen their commitment to creating a color-blind society.

CONCLUSION

Getting Beyond Race

ALTHOUGH RACE CONTINUES TO MATTER IN AMERICA, significant progress in race relations over the past thirty years offers hope for eventually getting beyond race. While it is easy to find examples of how racial problems continue to plague American society, this book focuses on positive developments in race relations. It suggests that building on success will generate greater momentum toward the achievement of a color-blind society than dwelling on failure. An emphasis on what is wrong often tends to reinforce feelings of despair, hopelessness, and cynicism, which ultimately militate against progress in race relations. Highlighting success helps encourage, motivate, and inspire Americans to continue striving for an improved understanding of each other and to search for common ground.

At the end of the twentieth century, major changes that have recently occurred in American society offer hope for the realization of better race relations in the twenty-first century. These include the dynamic force of generational replacement, the shifting of the demographic landscape, the growth of a strong black middle class, the enlistment of large numbers of racial minorities in the U.S. military, and the gradual erosion of racial boundaries resulting from increasing rates of interracial marriages and transracial adoptions. These changes make it difficult to maintain the status quo in relation to race.

Generational replacement and demographic changes weaken the foundations on which race is socially constructed. As discussed in Chapter 3, each successive generation of Americans becomes more tolerant and supportive of racial integration and equality. Greater access to education, increased interaction among individuals from different racial backgrounds, and society's growing intolerance of racist attitudes and behaviors consolidate this trend. The influx of immigrants also helps weaken racial boundaries by complicating the concept of race and racial categorization.

When analyzed within the broader context of American history, relations between blacks and whites have clearly undergone tremendous change. The U.S. military provides the strongest evidence to support this view. Mirroring the society that produced it, the military at first practiced racial segregation. However, domestic pressures for change, combined with pragmatism, eventually influenced the military to integrate its forces. The military now stands as a model of success in race relations.

Getting beyond race is a gradual but relentless process in which the emphasis on racial identity and racial categories declines and in which equal treatment regardless of skin color becomes a reality. Although progress in race relations stems from both top-down and bottom-up approaches to dealing with problems, the removal of legal barriers to full participation in American life makes a shift toward the bottom-up approach necessary in order to address more subtle aspects of discrimination.

Adopting a Bottom-Up Approach

A bottom-up approach to improving race relations places greater responsibility on individuals to do what they can to get beyond race. General concern about how races interact must be supported by specific actions on the part of ordinary Americans toward each other, not as monolithic groups but as unique individuals. Ultimately, race relations are about individuals getting along with each other. The bottom-up approach endorses the view that the best way to foster understanding between members of different racial categories is to get to know someone of another race as a friend. Inviting coworkers of a different race to one's home or to go on a family outing is one way of learning to see people as individuals rather than as members of a particular group. Eating meals with someone from a different racial background, living in a racially integrated neighborhood, attending plays and musical events that feature performers from diverse racial backgrounds, and sharing public spaces with individuals from another racial group can help improve race relations. Whenever racist comments are made, one should clearly state one's disagreement if at all possible. Silence often implies agreement and nurtures suspicions that encourage division between members of various racial groups. Each individual must feel personally responsible for helping move society beyond race.

Reframing the Issue

In order to improve race relations, it is essential to reframe the issue, or change the way one looks at it. Race is a difficult matter to confront directly because it remains a major part of most Americans' self-definition. Race symbolizes difference. What begins as a dialogue on race often degenerates into accusations, blame, and emotionally loaded charges of racism. A racial frame encourages one to view ordinary human problems in racial terms. Reframing allows individuals to perceive the world within the broader context of human behavior. This book suggests that reframing problems in terms of human virtues instead of race facilitates dialogue between members of various racial groups to resolve conflicts that may otherwise be left unsettled.

Beyond Racial Identity: Focusing on Interests

The growing complexity of American society diminishes the importance of racial identity. As more blacks, Latinos, and Asians enter the middle class and as racial discrimination declines, the need for these minorities to strongly identify with members of their own groups diminishes. For example, like many whites before them, the black middle class has distanced itself both physically and psychologically from disadvantaged blacks by moving from the cities to the suburbs. While many blacks leave the inner city to gain access to better schools, affordable housing, and open spaces, they also leave because of the violence, negativism, and incivility that are pervasive in most inner cities.[1] Increasing numbers of blacks share with many whites a fear of the violent crime committed by some blacks.

Blacks who live in exclusive neighborhoods continue to have strong ties to family members in urban areas. However, they often do not have many interests in common with inner-city blacks. These new realities suggest a need to focus on interests instead of race. Members of different racial groups with the same socioeconomic characteristics are likely to have more in common with each other than with members of their own racial group with different socioeconomic characteristics.

Focusing on interests can be instrumental in bringing blacks, whites, Asians, and Latinos together to form interracial coalitions. The interests of the poor often diverge from those of the middle class, regardless of skin color. Working together to achieve common objectives facilitates the development of close interpersonal relations and a sense of belonging to a particular group. Concentrating on interests reduces the significance of race by helping members of different racial groups realize that they share a common destiny. An emphasis on interests also strengthens other sources of identity, thereby lessening the tendency to regard race as the dominant determinant of identity.

Simply American

More than most Americans, blacks have a deeply rooted history in the United States. From the American Revolution to current U.S. military deployments in Bosnia and elsewhere, Americans with African ancestry have attempted to gain recognition of their humanity and Americanness by demonstrating willingness to shed blood for their country. As discussed in Chapter 4, blacks' claims to full citizenship were inextricably linked to their military service. Consequently, in an effort to maintain the racial status quo in American society, the country's leaders limited black participation in the military for as long as possible, until forced by realities on the battlefield to fully include them. The resentment shown by many whites toward uniformed black soldiers returning from Europe after both world wars underscores the resistance that had to be overcome to achieve such integration and fully recognize the Americanness of blacks.

Despite continuing problems in race relations, many Americans with African ancestry have always realized that by embracing the American creed and the basic values upon which the American dream is based they would eventually move into the mainstream of American life. A central theme of this book is that the perpetuation of racism depends to a large extent on emphasizing the differences between those regarded as insiders and others viewed as outsiders. The genius of the civil rights movement was its appeal to fundamental American values and beliefs. It inspired many blacks to strongly identify themselves principally as Americans who are entitled to inclusion.

During the late 1960s, many blacks, cognizant of the power of naming, wrestled with what they should be called. They decided to reject the terms "Negro" and "colored" and to endorse the terms "black" and "Afro-American." Relabeling was instrumental in strengthening group loyalty by renewing a sense of difference from and grievance toward the larger American society.[2] This strategy has contributed to the realization of major social, economic, and political gains for Americans with African ancestry. However, as more blacks become affluent and occupy positions of power and influence in virtually all aspects of American life, stressing racial differences becomes more of a liability than an asset. To secure their own stake in their country and to help shift the focus away from racial identity and toward national identity, blacks must become more willing to be referred to simply as "Americans."

Eliminating Self-Imposed Barriers

Any attempt to get beyond race begins with individual self-examination. Self-awareness is essential to understanding others and to diminishing the tendency to believe that one's fears are caused by another's ill intentions. While much of the effort to improve race relations concentrates on changing other people's behavior, a more productive approach involves an attempt to begin with ourselves. It is much easier to change our own behavior than it is to convince others to alter their behavior. Taking responsibility for oneself is essential to self-empowerment and to developing the courage to effectuate change. By paying closer attention to self-imposed barriers to improved race relations, one is better able to reduce the occurrence of negative racial experience.

Pervasive violence in black communities and other self-destructive behaviors are the most obvious examples of barriers that blacks impose on themselves. Although factors that are beyond one's control often influence one's behavior, the individual must ultimately assume a measure of responsibility for refraining from destructive behavior. When blacks engage in violence against each other as well as against whites, negative racial stereotypes are reinforced and racial boundaries are more clearly delineated and strengthened.

Despite the strong record of black success in education and the social and economic equality that emanates from it, too often many blacks must wrestle with the notion that achievement is tantamount to betraying one's black identity. Given the pivotal role that education plays in self-improvement as well as in promoting interracial understanding, the view that proficiency in standard English and a strong record of scholarly achievement are aspects of white culture is one of the most dangerous and unnecessary barriers many blacks continue to impose against themselves. The irony of rejecting academic success becomes more obvious when one considers that throughout much of America's history, preventing blacks from learning to read and write and denying them access to equal education were instrumental in maintaining black subordination.

Consistent with the bottom-up approach, individuals need to be more aware of the walls they construct to exclude others who might otherwise wish to be included. Racial segregation on college campuses is an example of how walls are created between members of different racial groups. Instead of taking the risk of getting to know someone from another race, many students from different racial groups bury their courage and embrace the safety of racial solidarity. By so doing, they forego opportunities to improve race relations and to potentially resolve personal problems concerning identity and allegiance.

Broadening the Concept of Community

A cornerstone of the social construction of race is the belief that humanity is neatly divided into fixed racial groups. Flowing from this premise is the view that skin color determines human bonds. People who physically resemble each other are automatically assumed to belong to a particular community. Each racial community is circumscribed by carefully drawn social, economic, and political boundaries. Rewards and punishments are distributed in ways that help maintain the separateness of people who are assigned to these different racial categories. These inducements come from sources both within and outside the racial communities. In time, internal forces may become much stronger enforcers of the racial status quo. Prominent members of each community, who often benefit most from separateness, usually convince those who are disadvantaged that reinforcing the already impregnable walls is in their best interest.

But for many individuals from various racial, social, and economic backgrounds, broadening the concept of community is a win-win proposition. Instead of seeing community strictly in racial and class terms, people can broaden their conception of community by lowering the artificial barriers that separate them from each other. Consistent with the bottom-up approach, the first step toward such a broadening would occur within one's own neighborhood. The security generated by a sense of order, mutual respect, and mutual concern would enable ordinary citizens to establish connections across racial community boundaries. Working together promotes civility, builds social capital and trust, and ultimately strengthens American democracy.[3]

Demographic changes demand a rethinking of the conventional racial beliefs that impede the formation of interracial linkages and alliances. Strategies that proved effective during segregation and the intense struggle for civil rights are no longer as useful in a society that has experienced significant racial change. Unlike in the 1960s, when Americans with African ancestry stood out as the country's largest and most disadvantaged minority, the rapid growth of Latino and Asian populations is changing the racial landscape. It is projected that Latinos will become America's largest racial minority early in the twenty-first century. Furthermore, progress toward ending racial discrimination and the growing complexity of American society are making old approaches to racial issues obsolete. Coalition politics and strategies that enhance interracial cooperation are likely to be more effective in the twenty-first century than they have been in the past.

Broadening the concept of community also facilitates interracial networking. One of the major arguments in favor of the controversial affirmative action policies is that employers tend to hire people they know. As long as communities develop primarily along racial lines, efforts to provide equal treatment and opportunity for all Americans are likely to be frustrated. Networking across racial boundaries has the potential of bringing more minorities into the mainstream of American life. It is also likely to consolidate the many economic and political gains that racial minorities have made since the 1970s. Networking helps eliminate many subtle as well as overt forms of racial discrimination.

Looking for Opportunities to Change Perceptions

Racial problems emanate, in part, from misperceptions and stereotypes about others who are regarded as different. The greater the physical and social distance between groups of individuals, the stronger these misperceptions and stereotypes tend to be. Getting to know people on an individual basis is the most effective way of overcoming stereotypes. Understanding another person's background, family, interests, and concerns facilitates revising stereotypical beliefs and behavior. Knowing the history, culture, and concerns of a particular individual can also be helpful in correcting misperceptions.

Behavior that confirms information upon which a stereotype or misperception is based will serve to reinforce that stereotype and strengthen barriers to getting beyond race. One of the best ways to change a person's racial perception is to send that person a message that is obviously different from what is expected.[4] Refuting information usually influences individuals to reassess their perceptions. When whites, for example, interact with blacks on an individual level, the stereotypes that these groups hold about each other are usually adjusted if their behaviors consistently contradict those stereotypes. Colin Powell is an excellent example of how one person's behavior can change stereotypes. His interaction with people from many different backgrounds throughout his life enables him to see how others are likely to see him. He is able to empathize with the other side and is knowledgeable about how they are likely to respond to certain behaviors. As discussed in Chapter 1, whites respond positively to Colin Powell because his character refutes negative racial stereotypes.

Despite the controversy surrounding the Million Man March on Washington in October 1995, the march sent a message that was inconsistent with society's general perceptions of how black men behave. In so doing, it was a significant step toward changing negative racial attitudes. The marchers who gathered on the Mall in Washington disproved many long-held stereotypes about black men. Contrary to the view that most blacks are members of the so-called underclass, a poll conducted at the Million Man March by Howard University researchers found that 38 percent of those surveyed had completed four or more years of college; 77 percent of the men earned $25,000 or more in annual salary, while 41 percent of them reported incomes of more than $50,000. In sharp contrast to the stereotype of blacks as dangerous and dysfunctional, the men on the Mall embraced family values and lawful behavior. There was no evidence of drug dealing, drive-by shootings, or gang activity. Police made one arrest for disorderly conduct.[5] By emphasizing the positive and focusing on success within the black community, the Million Man March helped change blacks' self-perceptions as well as others' perceptions of them.

Focusing on the Future

Although an understanding and appreciation of history is essential to getting beyond race, preoccupation with the past instead of an emphasis on the future is usually counterproductive and self-defeating. In South Africa, for example, the recent past has been far more brutal and dehumanizing than what Americans with African ancestry have experienced since the 1960s. Yet many black South Africans realize that, despite their overwhelming majority status, dwelling on the past is not conducive to making progress on solving the problems that continue to plague the new South Africa. Knowing history is not enough to effectuate change. A pragmatic approach to improving race relations and moving toward a color-blind society requires looking forward with a purpose. Although few of us can change the past, we have an opportunity to fashion the future.

Contemporary approaches to race relations dwell too much on the past. We spend too much time looking back over our shoulders instead of thinking about where we want to go and directing our actions toward that objective. The forward-looking approach presented in this book embraces the virtue of forgiveness. Understanding the past should not imprison us in the past, and it should not prevent us from realizing that we have to deal with current realities. Focusing on the future demands courage and taking responsibility for oneself. It requires us to risk rejection as we reach out to others from different racial backgrounds. Although concentrating on the past is safe and self-gratifying, it does little to solve current problems; in fact, it often reinforces the walls between people. Focusing on the future opens the possibilities for learning from each other, for forming interracial alliances to achieve common goals, and for getting beyond race.

NOTES

Chapter One

1. James G. Martin and Clyde W. Franklin, *Minority Group Relations* (Columbus, Ohio: Charles E. Merrill, 1973), 60.

2. Judith Goldstein, *Ideas, Interests, and American Trade Policy* (Ithaca: Cornell University Press, 1993), 3.

3. Ronald J. Fisher, *The Social Psychology of Intergroup and International Conflict* (New York: Springer-Verlag, 1990), 6.

4. *The Gallup Poll Monthly,* February 1993, 35.

5. F. James Davis, *Who Is Black? One Nation's Definition* (University Park: The Pennsylvania State University Press, 1991), 23–25.

6. Joel Kovel, *White Racism: A Psychohistory* (New York: Columbia University Press, 1984), xxxvii.

7. Bob Blauner, "White Radicals, White Liberals, and White People," in *Racism and Anti-Racism in World Perspective,* ed. Benjamin P. Bowser (Thousand Oaks, Calif.: Sage, 1995), 128.

8. Jennifer L. Hochschild, *Facing Up to the American Dream* (Princeton: Princeton University Press, 1995), 73.

9. Richard Morin, "Across the Racial Divide," *Washington Post National Weekly Edition,* October 16–22, 1995, 6.

10. Andrew Hacker, *Two Nations: Black and White, Separate, Hostile, Unequal* (New York: Charles Scribner's Sons, 1992).

11. *The Gallup Poll Monthly,* October 1993, 8.

12. *New York Times*/CBS News Poll, May 6–8, 1992; and Peter Applebome, "Racial Divisions Persist 25 Years After King Killing," *New York Times,* April 4, 1993, A12.

13. Roger Fisher and Scott Brown, *Getting Together: Building a Relationship That Gets to Yes* (Boston: Houghton Mifflin, 1988), 5.

14. Virginia R. Dominguez, *White By Definition: Social Classification in Creole Louisiana* (New Brunswick, N.J.: Rutgers University Press, 1986), 266.

15. Charles Taylor et al., *Sources of the Self: The Making of Modern Identity* (Cambridge: Harvard University Press, 1989), 27.

16. John P. Hewitt, *Self and Society: A Symbolic Interactionist Social Psychology* (Boston: Allyn and Bacon, 1991), 128; and Michael A. Hogg and Dominic Abrams, *Social Identifications: A Social Psychology of Intergroup Relations and Group Processes* (New York: Routledge, 1988), 7.

17. Dominguez, *White By Definition*, 262; and Thomas K. Fitzgerald, *Metaphors of Identity: A Culture-Communication Dialogue* (Albany: State University of New York Press, 1993), 34.

18. Harold R. Isaacs, *Idols of the Tribe: Group Identity and Political Change* (New York: Harper and Row, 1975), 206.

19. Dorinne K. Kondo, *Crafting Selves: Power, Gender, and Discourses of Identity in a Japanese Workplace* (Chicago: The University of Chicago Press, 1990), 48.

20. Lewis A. Coser, *The Functions of Social Conflict* (Glencoe, Ill.: The Free Press, 1956), 38.

21. Lise Noel, *Intolerance: A General Survey*, trans. Arnold Bennett (Montreal: McGill–Queen's University Press, 1994), 207.

22. John C. Turner and Penelope J. Oakes, "Self-Categorization Theory and Social Influence," in *Psychology of Group Influence*, ed. Paul B. Paulus (Hillsdale, N.J.: Lawrence Erlbaum, 1989), 246.

23. Kenneth J. Gergen, "The Significance of Skin Color in Human Relations," in *Color and Race*, ed. John Hope Franklin (Boston: Houghton Mifflin, 1968), 123; and David A. Wilder, "Some Determinants of the Persuasive Power of In-Groups," *Journal of Personality and Social Psychology* 59, no. 6 (1990):1204.

24. Hacker, *Two Nations*, 31.

25. Ibid., 60.

26. Marc Howard Ross, *The Management of Conflict* (New Haven: Yale University Press, 1993), 27.

27. Richard L. Allen, Michael C. Dawson, and Ronald E. Brown, "A Schema-Based Approach to Modeling an African-American Racial Belief System," *American Political Science Review* 83, no. 2 (June 1989):435.

28. William Ryan, *Blaming the Victim* (New York: Pantheon Books, 1971), xv.

29. Noel, *Intolerance*, 188.

30. Robert Hughes, *Culture of Complaint: The Fraying of America* (New York: Oxford University Press, 1993), 9.

31. Gerhard Schutte, *What Racists Believe: Race Relations in South Africa and the United States* (London: Sage Publications, 1995), 350; and bell hooks, *Black Looks: Race and Representation* (Boston: South End Press, 1992), 19.

32. Glenn C. Loury, *One By One from the Inside Out* (New York: The Free Press, 1995), 30–31.

33. Denise Beurskens, interview by author, 1995.

34. Glenn C. Loury, "Free at Last? A Personal Perspective on Race and Identity in America," in *Lure and Loathing*, ed. Gerald Early (New York: Penguin, 1993), 9.

35. Joe Klein, "Can Colin Powell Save America?" *Newsweek*, October 10, 1994, 26.

36. Donald McHenry, interview by author, 1995.

37. Marian Wright Edelman, *The Measure of Our Success: A Letter to My Children and Yours* (Boston: Beacon Press, 1992), 7.

38. *Time*/CNN Poll, April 10, 1992.

39. Samuel L. Popkin, *The Reasoning Voter: Communication and Persuasion in Presidential Campaigns* (Chicago: The University of Chicago Press, 1991), 81.

40. Shanto Iyengar, *Is Anyone Responsible? How Television Frames Political Issues* (Chicago: The University of Chicago Press, 1994), 11.

41. Victor Turner, *Dramas, Fields, and Metaphors: Symbolic Action in Human Society* (Ithaca: Cornell University Press, 1974), 67.

42. Audrey Smedly, *Race in North America: Origin and Evolution of a Worldview* (Boulder: Westview Press, 1993), 7.

43. Mary R. Jackman, *The Velvet Glove: Paternalism and Conflict in Gender, Class, and Race Relations* (Berkeley: University of California Press, 1994), 9.

44. Elinor Lenz and Barbara Myerhoff, *The Feminization of America* (Los Angeles: Jeremy P. Tarcher, 1985), 20; and Joyce O. Hertzler, *A Sociology of Language* (New York: Random House, 1965), 44.

45. Cornel West, *Race Matters* (Boston: Beacon Press, 1993), 4.

46. Beth Bailey and David Farber, "The Double-V Campaign in WWII Hawaii: African-Americans, Racial Ideology, and Federal Power," *Journal of Social History* (Summer 1993):886.

47. David Molpus, "Mississippi Highway Patrol Changes Greatly in 25 Years," *All Things Considered,* National Public Radio, May 14, 1995, 13.

48. Ruth Fisher, interview by author, 1995.

49. Renford Bambrough, *The Philosophy of Aristotle* (New York: Mentor, 1963), 302.

50. Fisher and Brown, *Getting Together,* 5.

51. Christopher Lasch, *The Revolt of the Elites and the Betrayal of Democracy* (New York: W. W. Norton, 1995), 136.

52. Anne Wortham, interview by author, 1996.

53. Edelman, *Measure of Our Success,* 38.

54. James D. Wallace, *Virtues and Vices* (Ithaca: Cornell University Press, 1978), 15; and William J. Bennett, ed., *The Book of Virtues: A Treasury of Great Moral Stories* (New York: Simon and Schuster, 1993), 599.

55. John Rawls, *A Theory of Justice* (Cambridge: Harvard University Press, Belknap Press, 1971), 4.

56. Judith Martin, "The Oldest Virtue," in *Seedbeds of Virtue,* ed. Mary Ann Glendon and David Blankenhorn (New York: Madison Books, 1995), 53.

57. Mark Kingwell, *A Civil Tongue: Justice, Dialogue, and the Politics of Pluralism* (University Park: The Pennsylvania State University Press, 1995), 230.

58. Wallace, *Virtues and Vices,* 15.

59. *New York Times*/CBS Poll, February 15–17, 1994.

60. Bennett, *Book of Virtues,* 107.

61. Donald W. Shriver Jr., *An Ethic for Enemies: Forgiveness in Politics* (New York: Oxford University Press, 1995), 7.

62. Fisher and Brown, *Getting Together,* 34.

63. Rick Bragg, "Emotional March Gains a Repentant Wallace," *New York Times,* March 11, 1995, A1.

64. Robert Dahl, *A Preface to Economic Democracy* (Berkeley: University of California Press, 1985), 162.

65. C. Eric Lincoln, *Coming Through the Fire: Surviving Race and Place in America* (Durham, N.C.: Duke University Press, 1996), 126.

66. Everett Carl Ladd, *The American Ideology* (Storrs, Conn.: The Roper Center for Public Opinion Research, 1994), 5.

67. Robert N. Bellah et al., *The Good Society* (New York: Alfred A. Knopf, 1991), 227.

68. Hochschild, *Facing Up*, 56.

69. John Stuart Mill, *On Liberty* (New York: W. W. Norton, 1975), 44; and Stephen K. White, *Political Theory and Postmodernism* (Cambridge: Cambridge University Press, 1991), 128.

70. Al Gore, "The Revolutionary Forces of Sympathy and Compassion," *Harvard University Gazette,* June 17, 1994, 8.

71. Audrey Edwards and Craig K. Polite, *Children of the Dream: The Psychology of Black Success* (New York: Doubleday, 1992), 249.

72. Claudette E. Brown, *The Black Population in the United States: March 1994 and 1993,* Bureau of the Census, *Current Population Reports,* 9 (Washington, D.C.: U.S. Government Printing Office, 1995), 20–480; and "Study: Education Gap Is Narrowing," *Chicago Tribune,* September 6, 1996, sec. 1, A3.

73. Martha L. Hollins et al., *Enrollment in Higher Education: Fall 1986 Through Fall 1994,* NCES 96–851 (Washington, D.C.: U.S. Department of Education, 1996), 111.

74. Denise K. Magner, "More Black Ph.D.'s," *The Chronicle of Higher Education,* June 14, 1996, A25.

75. "A Benchmark in Black Education," *Chicago Tribune,* September 16, 1996, sec. 1, 12.

76. Claudette Brown, *Black Population,* 23.

77. Sam Roberts, "The Greening of America's Black Middle Class," *New York Times,* June 18, 1995, sec. 4, 4.

78. Claudette Brown, *Black Population,* 22; see also James P. Smith and Finis R. Welch, *Closing the Gap: Forty Years of Economic Progress for Blacks* (Santa Monica, Calif.: Rand, 1986), viii-ix.

79. Udayan Gupta, "Black-Owned Businesses Rose By 46%," *Wall Street Journal,* December 12, 1995, B2.

80. John R. Wilke, "Mortgage Lending to Minorities Shows a Sharp 1994 Increase," *Wall Street Journal,* February 13, 1996, A1.

81. "Oprah Tops Forbes Money List," *The Pantagraph,* September 10, 1996, D4; and Randall Lane and Josh McHugh, "A Very Green 1995," *Forbes,* December 18, 1995, 212–215.

82. Reginald F. Lewis and Blair S. Walker, *Why Should White Guys Have All the Fun?* (New York: John Wiley and Sons, 1995), xv; and Jeff Gerth, "Being Intimate with Power, Vernon Jordan Can Wield It," *New York Times,* July 14, 1996, A1.

83. Anonymous, interview by author, 1995.

84. Sissela Bok, *A Strategy for Peace: Human Values and the Threat of War* (New York: Pantheon Books, 1989), 151.

85. Jan Crawford Greenberg, "Rising Hopes, Lingering Concern," *Chicago Tribune,* September 22, 1996, sec. 1, 1.

86. Victoria Pierce, "Mississippi Building," *The Pantagraph,* September 22, 1996, A1.

87. Lucia Mouat, "Mending New York's Mosaic," *Christian Science Monitor,* December 19, 1990, 8; and "Food, Drink, and Frank Talk on Race," *Chicago Tribune,* June 7, 1996, sec. 1, 10.

88. Bob Aaron, "Scholarship Mentoring Program for Inner-City Youth," *Illinois Wesleyan University News Service,* February 14, 1996.

89. *The Gallup Poll Monthly,* October 1993.

90. Martin Luther King Jr., *A Testament of Hope* (San Francisco: Harper and Row, 1986), 117.

91. Barbara Hinckley, *Coalition Politics* (New York: Harcourt Brace Jovanovich, 1981), 5.

92. Herbert Aptheker, "Anti-Racism in the United States," in *Racism and Anti-Racism in World Perspective,* ed. Benjamin P. Bowser (Thousand Oaks, Calif.: Sage, 1995), 70.

93. Michael Reich, *Racial Inequality* (Princeton: Princeton University Press, 1981), 233.

94. Elizabeth Jacoway, "An Introduction," in *Southern Businessmen and Desegregation,* eds. Elizabeth Jacoway and David R. Colburn (Baton Rouge: Louisiana State University Press, 1982), 8.

95. Veronica Byrd, "Black Bankers Seek Broader Market," *New York Times,* September 6, 1993, Y17.

96. Sam Howe, "Dallas, in a Historic Vote, Elects a Black to Be Mayor," *New York Times,* May 8, 1995, A8.

97. Roger Fisher, "Dealing with Conflict Among Individuals and Nations," *Psychoanalytic Inquiry* 6, no. 2 (1986):143.

98. Morton Deutsch, *The Resolution of Conflict: Constructive and Destructive Processes* (New Haven: Yale University Press, 1973), 370.

99. Ibid., 363–364.

100. Henry Louis Gates Jr., "Powell and the Black Elite," *The New Yorker,* September 25, 1995, 70.

101. Roger Fisher, William Ury, and Bruce Patton, *Getting to Yes* (New York: Penguin, 1981), 25; and Angela Dreessen, interview, by author, 1995.

102. Beurskens, interview.

103. Martin Luther King Jr., *I've Been to the Mountaintop* (New York: Harper San Francisco, 1963), 34.

104. C. Daniel Batson et al., "Information Function of Empathic Emotion," *Journal of Personality and Social Psychology* 68, no. 2 (1995):300; and David Woodruff Smith, *The Circle of Acquaintance: Perception, Consciousness, and Empathy* (Dordrecht, Netherlands: Kluwer Academic Publishers, 1989), 117.

105. Nancy Lind, interview by author, 1996.

106. Donna Richter, interview by author, 1996.

107. Roger Fisher, "Negotiating Power: Getting and Using Influence," *American Behavioral Scientist* 27, no. 2 (November-December 1983):155.

108. Francis Fukuyama, *Trust: The Social Virtues and the Creation of Prosperity* (New York: The Free Press, 1995), 26.

109. Jeffrey Z. Rubin and George Levinger, "Levels of Analysis," in *Conflict, Cooperation, and Justice,* ed. Barbara Benedict Bunker and Jeffrey Z. Rubin (San Francisco: Jossey-Bass Publishers, 1995), 29.

110. James S. Coleman, *Foundations of Social Theory* (Cambridge: Harvard University Press, 1990), 96.

111. Niklas Luhmann, *Trust and Power* (New York: John Wiley and Sons, 1979), 72.

112. Bernard Barber, *The Logic and Limits of Trust* (New Brunswick, N.J.: Rutgers University Press, 1983), 21.

113. Coleman, *Foundations,* 302.

114. Robert D. Putnam, *Making Democracy Work: Civic Traditions in Modern Italy* (Princeton: Princeton University Press, 1993), 169.

Chapter Two

1. William J. Cromie, "Geneticists Find the Ancestors of All Men," *Harvard University Gazette,* May 25, 1995, 1.

2. L. Luca Cavalli-Sforza, Paolo Menozzi, and Alberto Piazza, *The History and Geography of Human Genes* (Princeton: Princeton University Press, 1994), 19.

3. Ibid.

4. Sharon Begley, "Surprising New Lessons from the Controversial Science of Race," *Newsweek,* February 13, 1995, 67–68.

5. Michael Omi and Howard Winant, *Racial Formation in the United States* (New York: Routledge, 1989), 61.

6. John R. Searle, *The Construction of Social Reality* (New York: The Free Press, 1995), 2.

7. Omi and Winant, *Racial Formation,* 67.

8. Roger Sanjek, "Enduring Inequalities of Race," in *Race,* ed. Steven Gregory and Roger Sanjek (New Brunswick, N.J.: Rutgers University Press, 1994), 3.

9. Frank M. Snowden, "Europe's Oldest Chapter in the History of Black-White Relations," in *Racism and Anti-Racism in World Perspective,* ed. Benjamin P. Bowser (Thousand Oaks, Calif.: Sage, 1995), 21.

10. Oliver Cox, *Caste, Class, and Race* (New York: Doubleday, 1948), 328.

11. Jacques Barzun, *The French Race: Theories of its Origins and Their Social and Political Implications* (Port Washington, N.Y.: Kennikat Press, 1966), 11–12.

12. Liston Pope, *The Kingdom Beyond Caste* (New York: Friendship Press, 1957), 24.

13. Gary B. Nash, "Red, White, and Black: The Origins of Racism in Colonial America," in *The Great Fear: Race in the Mind of America,* ed. Gary B. Nash and Richard Weise (New York: Holt, Rinehart and Winston, 1970), 11; and George M. Fredrickson, *The Arrogance of Race* (Middletown, Conn.: Wesleyan University Press, 1988), 191.

14. Reginald Horsman, *Race and Manifest Destiny: The Origins of American Racial Anglo-Saxonism* (Cambridge: Harvard University Press, 1981), 3.

15. Noel Ignatiev, *How the Irish Became White* (New York: Routledge, 1995), 96.

16. Theodore W. Allen, *The Invention of the White Race,* vol. 1 (London: Verso, 1994), 14.

17. Ruth Frankenberg, *White Women, Race Matters: The Social Construction of Whiteness* (Minneapolis: University of Minnesota Press, 1993), 203.

18. David R. Roediger, *The Wages of Whiteness: Race and the Making of the American Working Class* (London: Verso, 1991), 133.

19. Ignatiev, *How the Irish,* 41.

20. Ibid., 3.

21. Frankenberg, *White Women,* 6.

22. Peggy McIntosh, "White Privilege and Male Privilege," in *Race, Class, and Gender,* ed. Margaret L. Andersen and Patricia Hill Collins (Belmont, Mass.: Wadsworth Publishing Company, 1995), 76; and Marilyn Frye, "White Woman Feminist," in *Overcoming Racism and Sexism,* ed. Linda A. Bell and David Blumen-feld (Lanham, Md.: Rowman and Littlefield, 1995), 115–116.

23. Thomas F. Gossett, *Race: The History of an Idea in America* (Dallas: Southern Methodist University Press, 1963), 7.

24. Sanjek, "Enduring Inequalities," 4.

25. Suzanne Preston Blier, *African Vodun: Art, Psychology, and Power* (Chicago: The University of Chicago Press, 1995), 23.

26. Gossett, *Race,* 30.

27. Thomas Sowell, *Race and Economics* (New York: David McKay Company, 1975), 20.

28. Fredrickson, *Arrogance,* 203.

29. Frank Tannenbaum, *Slave and Citizen: The Negro in the Americas* (New York: Alfred A. Knopf, 1947), 107.

30. David Brion Davis, *The Problem of Slavery in Western Culture* (Ithaca: Cornell University Press, 1966), 263.

31. Tannenbaum, *Slave and Citizen,* 46; and Louis Hartz, *The Founding of New Societies* (New York: Harcourt, Brace, and World, 1964), 52.

32. Tannenbaum, *Slave and Citizen,* 64; and Stanley M. Elkins, *Slavery: A Problem in American Institutional and Intellectual Life* (Chicago: The University of Chicago Press, 1976), 233.

33. Tannenbaum, *Slave and Citizen,* 58.

34. Elkins, *Slavery: A Problem,* 236.

35. Calvin Trillin, "American Chronicles: Black or White," *The New Yorker,* April 14, 1986, 62–78.

36. Audrey Smedly, *Race in North America: Origin and Evolution of a World-view* (Boulder: Westview Press, 1993), 9.

37. Edward Byron Reuter, *The American Race Problem: A Study of the Negro* (New York: Thomas Y. Crowell, 1938), 108.

38. Ignatiev, *How the Irish,* 1.

39. Anthony W. Marx, "Race-Making and the Nation-State," *World Politics* 48, no. 2 (January 1996):187.

40. Jack D. Forbes, "The Manipulation of Race, Caste, and Identity: Classifying Afroamericans, Native Americans, and Red-Black People," *The Journal of Ethnic Studies* 17, no. 4 (1990):34.

41. Stephen Jay Gould, *The Mismeasure of Man* (New York: W. W. Norton, 1981), 22.

42. Thomas S. Kuhn, *The Structure of Scientific Revolutions* (Chicago: The University of Chicago Press, 1970), 4.

43. R. C. Lewontin, *Biology as Ideology: The Doctrine of DNA* (New York: HarperCollins, 1992), 7.

44. Richard J. Herrnstein, *I.Q. in the Meritocracy* (Boston: Little, Brown, 1973), 221.

45. Lewontin, *Biology as Ideology*, 23.

46. Henry Fairfield Osborn, preface to *The Passing of the Great Race*, by Madison Grant (New York: Scribner's Sons, 1918), ix.

47. Horsman, *Race and Manifest Destiny*, 145.

48. Gould, *Mismeasure*, 151.

49. Carl Brigham, *A Study of American Intelligence* (Princeton: Princeton University Press, 1923), 209–210.

50. William Tucker, *The Science and Politics of Racial Research* (Urbana: University of Illinois Press, 1994), 3.

51. Henry H. Goddard, "Mental Tests and the Immigrant," *Journal of Delinquency* 2 (1917):252.

52. Nicholas Lemann, "The Great Sorting," *The Atlantic Monthly*, September 1995, 84.

53. Richard J. Herrnstein and Charles Murray, *The Bell Curve: Intelligence and Class Structure in American Life* (New York: The Free Press, 1994), 270–271.

54. Ben Gose, "Test Scores and Stereotypes," *The Chronicle of Higher Education*, August 18, 1995, A31.

55. Arnold J. Toynbee, *A Study of History*, vol. 1 (Oxford: Oxford University Press, 1934), 245.

56. Elazar Barkan, *The Retreat of Scientific Racism* (Cambridge: Cambridge University Press, 1992), 343.

57. Ibid., 344.

58. Otto Klineberg, *Race Differences* (New York: Harper and Brothers Publishers, 1935), 182.

59. Ruth Benedict, *Race and Racism* (London: Routledge, 1983), 12.

60. John Middleton, introduction to *Magic, Witchcraft, and Curing*, ed. John Middleton (Austin: University of Texas Press, 1967), ix.

61. Max Weber, *Economy and Society* (New York: Bedminster, 1968), 400.

62. George Gmelch, "Baseball Magic," in *Magic, Witchcraft, and Religion*, ed. Arthur C. Lehmann and James Myers (Mountain View, Calif.: Mayfield, 1993), 277; and Ralph Schroeder, *Max Weber and the Sociology of Culture* (London: Sage Publications, 1992), 36.

63. I. C. Jarvie and Joseph Agassi, "The Problem of the Rationality of Magic," in *Rationality*, ed. Bryan Wilson (Oxford: Basil Blackwell, 1970), 192; and E. E. Evans-Pritchard, *Witchcraft, Oracles, and Magic Among the Azande* (Oxford: Clarendon Press, 1937), 63.

64. Bronislaw Malinowski, *Magic, Science, and Religion, and Other Essays* (Prospect Heights, Ill.: Waveland Press, 1992), 87.

65. Ibid., 87.

66. Ashley Montagu, *Man's Most Dangerous Myth: The Fallacy of Race* (New York: Oxford University Press, 1974), 4.

67. Malinowski, *Magic*, 84.

68. Leon Poliakov, *The Aryan Myth: A History of Racist and Nationalist Ideas in Europe* (New York: Basic Books, 1974), 7; and Alden T. Vaughan, *Roots of American Racism: Essays on the Colonial Experience* (New York: Oxford University Press, 1995), viii.

69. Malinowski, *Magic*, 84.

70. Montagu, *Man's Most Dangerous Myth*, 4.

71. Malinowski, *Magic*, 21.

72. Benedict, *Race and Racism*, 2.

Chapter Three

1. Clifford Geertz, *The Interpretations of Cultures* (New York: Basic Books, 1973), 89; and Richard J. Payne, *The Clash with Distant Cultures* (Albany: State University of New York Press, 1995), 8.

2. Anthony Giddens, ed., *Emile Durkheim: Selected Writings* (Cambridge: Cambridge University Press, 1972), 5.

3. Raymond Scupin, *Cultural Anthropology* (Englewood Cliffs, N.J.: Prentice-Hall, 1992), 63.

4. J. Hector St. John de Crevecoeur, *Letters from an American Farmer* (New York: Albert and Charles Boni, 1925), 54–55.

5. W. E. Burghardt Du Bois, *The Souls of Black Folk* (New York: Dodd, Mead, and Company, 1979), 3.

6. Ibid.

7. Martin Kilson, "Blacks and Neo-Ethnicity in American Political Life," in *Ethnicity: Theory and Experience,* ed. Nathan Glazer and Daniel P. Moynihan (Cambridge: Harvard University Press, 1975), 244.

8. C. Vann Woodward, *The Strange Career of Jim Crow* (New York: Oxford University Press, 1966), 12.

9. Janet Shibley Hyde, *Half the Human Experience: The Psychology of Women* (Lexington, Mass.: D.C. Heath and Company, 1991), 211–212.

10. Benjamin Quarles, *The Negro in the Making of America* (New York: Collier Books, 1987), 32.

11. John Edward Philips, "The African Heritage of White America," in *Africanisms in American Culture,* ed. Joseph E. Holloway (Bloomington: Indiana University Press, 1990), 232.

12. Joseph E. Holloway, "The Origins of African-American Culture," in *Africanisms in American Culture,* ed. Joseph E. Holloway (Bloomington: Indiana University Press, 1990), 16.

13. Donald D. Megil and Richard S. Demory, *Introduction to Jazz History* (Englewood Cliffs, N.J.: Prentice-Hall, 1993), 2.

14. Peter Wicke, *Rock Music: Culture, Aesthetics, and Sociology* (Cambridge: Cambridge University Press, 1987), 18.

15. Bruce Feiler, "Has Country Music Become a Soundtrack for White Flight?" *New York Times,* October 20, 1996, sec. 11, 38.

16. James Barron, "Knowing What It Means to Solo," *New York Times,* February 16, 1995, B1.

17. Amy Gutman, introduction to *Multiculturalism and the Politics of Recognition,* ed. Charles Taylor et al. (Princeton: Princeton University Press, 1992), 21.

18. Jack Citrin et al., "Is American Nationalism Changing? Implications for Foreign Policy," *International Studies Quarterly* 38, no. 1 (March 1994):9.

19. Richard Bernstein, *Dictatorship of Virtue: Multiculturalism and the Battle for America's Future* (New York: Alfred A. Knopf, 1994), 8.

20. Sandra Lipsitz Bem, *The Lenses of Gender: Transforming the Debate on Sexual Inequality* (New Haven: Yale University Press, 1993), 3.

21. Mary Cunningham, interview by author, 1994.

22. Marilyn Boyd, interview by author, 1995.

23. Sheila Welch, interview by author, 1996.

24. Kelly Keogh, interview by author, 1997.

25. Arthur C. Sanders III, interview by author, 1995.

26. Patricia Fowler, interview by author, 1995.

27. Jane Liedtke, interview by author, 1995.

28. Angela Dreessen, interview by author, 1995.

29. Donna Richter, interview by author, 1996.

30. Ruth Fisher, interview by author, 1995.

31. Linda Giles, interview by author, 1996.

32. Robert Ezra Park, *Race and Culture* (Glencoe, Ill.: The Free Press, 1950), 150.

33. Gordon Allport, *The Nature of Prejudice* (Reading, Mass.: Addison Wesley, 1954), 281.

34. Muzafer Sherif et al., *The Robbers Cave Experiment: Intergroup Conflict and Cooperation* (Middletown, Conn.: Wesleyan University Press, 1988), 200. See also C. Daniel Batson, *The Altruism Question* (Hillsdale, N.J.: Lawrence Erlbaum, 1991), 85.

35. Miles Hewstone and Rupert Brown, "Contact Is Not Enough," in *Contact and Conflict in Intergroup Encounters,* ed. Miles Hewstone and Rupert Brown (Oxford: Basil Blackwell, 1986), 19; and Norman Miller and Marilyn B. Brewer, "Categorization Effects on Ingroup and Outgroup Perception," in *Prejudice, Discrimination, and Racism,* ed. John F. Davidio and Samuel L. Gaertner (Orlando, Fla.: Academic Press, 1986), 216.

36. Jonathan Rieder, *Canarsie: The Jews and Italians of Brooklyn Against Liberalism* (Cambridge: Harvard University Press, 1985), 66.

37. John Brennan, "Race Relations in the Eighties: A Polling Review," *The Public Perspective* (January-February, 1990):12.

38. Clayborne Carson, ed. *The Papers of Martin Luther King, Jr.,* vol. 1 (Berkeley: University of California Press, 1992), 363.

39. Jimmy Carter, *Why Not the Best?* (Nashville, Tenn.: Broadman Press, 1975), 14; and Kenneth O'Reilly, *Nixon's Piano: Presidents and Racial Politics from Washington to Clinton* (New York: The Free Press, 1995), 338–339.

40. O'Reilly, *Nixon's Piano,* 408.

41. Denise Beurskens, interview by author, 1995.

42. Diana McCauley, interview by author, 1996.

43. Don Bernaducci, interview by author, 1996.

44. Kelly Keogh, interview by author, 1996.

45. Eric Welch, interview by author, 1996.

46. Linaya Leaf, interview by author, 1995.

47. Jim Pruyne, interview by author, 1995.

48. Noah Kotch, "Yale Program Is Reaching Out to the Poor Communities of New Haven," *New York Times,* August 9, 1995, B5.

49. Susan Smith, interview by author, 1996.

50. Linda Giles, interview by author, 1996.

51. Stanley Crouch, *Notes of a Hanging Judge* (New York: Oxford University Press, 1990), 10.

52. Thomas Morgan, "Many in New York Poll See Race Relations Worsening," *New York Times,* June 27, 1990, A12.

53. Jonathan Storm, "Sitcoms Yet to Match Racial Balance of Dramas," *Chicago Tribune,* May 29, 1996, sec. 2, 9.

54. Craig Barboza, "A Growing Number of Black Stars Are Shining in Hollywood," *New York Times,* October 20, 1996, sec. 11, 28.

55. Thomas E. Drake, *Quakers and Slavery in America* (New Haven: Yale University Press, 1950), 71.

56. Fernando Henriques, *Children of Conflict: A Study of Interracial Sex and Marriage* (New York: E. P. Dutton, 1975), 51.

57. Drake, *Quakers and Slavery,* 121.

58. Jason DeParle, "The Christian Right Confesses Sins of Racism," *New York Times,* August 4, 1996, E5.

59. Jack E. White, "Forgive Us Our Sins," *Time,* July 3, 1995, 29; and DeParle, "The Christian Right," 5.

60. Kevin Sack, "Burial of Mixed-Race Baby Provokes All-White Church," *New York Times,* March 29, 1996, A8.

61. Peter Applebome, "Change Is Both Sweet and Sour As Blacks Step into White Pulpits," *New York Times,* January 2, 1995, A1.

62. Sharon Stanford, interview by author, 1996.

63. Patricia Fowler, interview by author, 1995.

64. David Van Biema, "Full of Promises," *Time,* November 6, 1995, 63.

65. Jan Crawford Greenberg, "In College Sports, at Least, Racial Playing Field Is Level," *Chicago Tribune,* September 6, 1996, sec. 1, 1.

66. Greenberg, "In College Sports," 1.

67. Norma R. Yetman and Paul W. Grimes, "Racial Participation and Integration in Intercollegiate Basketball," *Sociology of Sport Journal* 10, no. 3 (September 1993):307.

68. *The Gallup Poll Monthly,* October 1993, 7.

69. E. M. Swift, "Reach Out and Touch Someone," *Sports Illustrated,* August 5, 1991, 58.

70. Bureau of the Census, *Population Projections of the United States, by Age, Sex, Race, and Hispanic Origin: 1992 to 2050* (Washington, D.C.: U.S. Department of Commerce, 1992), xviii.

71. Robert D. Putnam, "Turning In, Tuning Out: The Strange Disappearance of Social Capital in America," *PS: Political Science and Politics* 28, no. 4 (December 1995):667.

72. O'Reilly, *Nixon's Piano,* 408.

73. Peter D. Hart Research Associates, October 21, 1991; *USA Weekend,* August 18–20, 1995; and Karen S. Peterson, "For Today's Teens, Race Not an Issue Anymore," *USA Today,* November 3, 1997, 1.

Chapter Four

1. Charles C. Moskos, *The American Enlisted Man* (New York: Russell Sage Foundation, 1970), 121; and Charles C. Moskos and John Sibley Butler, *All That We Can Be: Black Leadership and Racial Integration the Army Way* (New York: Basic Books, 1996), 2.

2. Martin Binkin et al., *Blacks in the Military* (Washington, D.C.: The Brookings Institution, 1982), 12.

3. Morris J. MacGregor, *Integration of the Armed Forces, 1940–1945* (Washington, D.C.: United States Army, 1985), 3.

4. Adam Yarmolinsky, *The Military Establishment: Its Impacts on American Society* (New York: Harper and Row, 1971), 350.

5. Jack D. Foner, *Blacks and the Military in American History* (New York: Praeger, 1974), 7; and Gary A. Donaldson, *The History of African Americans in the Military* (Malabar, Fla.: Krieger Publishing Company, 1991), 14.

6. MacGregor, *Integration*, 4.

7. Donaldson, *African Americans in the Military*, 18.

8. Herbert R. Northrup et al., *Black and Other Minority Participation in the All-Volunteer Navy and Marine Corps* (Philadelphia: University of Pennsylvania Press, 1979), 8.

9. Donaldson, *African Americans in the Military*, 17.

10. Benjamin Quarles, *The Negro in the American Revolution* (New York: W. W. Norton, 1961), ix.

11. Bernard C. Nalty, *Strength for the Fight: A History of Black Americans in the Military* (New York: The Free Press, 1986), 18.

12. Russell F. Weigley, *History of the United States Army* (New York: The Macmillan Company, 1967), 211; Donaldson, *African Americans in the Military*, 42; and Bernard Bailyn et al., *The Great Republic* (Lexington, Mass.: D.C. Heath and Company, 1977), 706.

13. Donaldson, *African Americans in the Military*, 43.

14. Bailyn et al., *Great Republic*, 709.

15. Beth Bailey and David Farber, "The Double-V Campaign in WWII Hawaii: African Americans, Racial Ideology, and Federal Power," *Journal of Social History* (Summer 1993):822.

16. Richard M. Dalfiume, *Desegregation of the U.S. Armed Forces: Fighting on Two Fronts* (Columbia: University of Missouri Press, 1969), 16.

17. Graham Smith, *When Jim Crow Met John Bull: Black American Soldiers in World War II Britain* (New York: St. Martin's Press, 1987), 12.

18. Dalfiume, *Desegregation*, 20.

19. Samuel A. Stouffer et al., *The American Soldier: Adjustment During Army Life*, vol. 1 (Princeton: Princeton University Press, 1949), 507.

20. Robert W. Mullen, *Blacks in America's Wars* (New York: Anchor, 1973), 53–54.

21. Franklin D. Roosevelt, "Executive Order Reaffirming Policy of Full Participation in the Defense Program," *Federal Register* (June 27, 1941):3109.

22. Foner, *Blacks and the Military*, 158.

23. Ibid., 179.

24. Harry S. Truman, "Executive Order Establishing the President's Committee on Equality of Treatment and Opportunity in the Armed Services," *Federal Register* (July 28, 1948):4313.

25. Moskos, *American Enlisted Man*, 112.

26. Dalfiume, *Desegregation*, 101.

27. Jean Ebbert and Marie-Beth Hall, *Crossed Currents: Navy Women From WWI to Tailhook* (Washington, D.C.: Brassey's, 1993), 86.

28. Alan L. Gropman, *The Air Force Integrates, 1945–1964* (Washington, D.C.: Office of Air Force History, 1978), 9.

29. Nalty, *Strength for the Fight,* 161.

30. Gropman, *Air Force Integrates,* 87; and Nalty, *Strength for the Fight,* 248–249.

31. Binkin et al., *Blacks in the Military,* 21.

32. Mary Frances Berry and John W. Blassingame, *Long Memory: The Black Experience in America* (New York: Oxford University Press, 1982), 325.

33. Stouffer et al., *American Soldier,* 490.

34. Bailey and Farber, "The Double-V Campaign," 836.

35. Ibid., 824.

36. Smith, *When Jim Crow,* 123.

37. Brenda L. Moore, *To Serve My Country, To Serve My Race* (New York: New York University Press, 1996), 121–122.

38. Robert Dixon, interview by author, 1996.

39. Dalfiume, *Desegregation,* 76.

40. Nalty, *Strength for the Fight,* 259.

41. Stouffer et al., *American Soldier,* 586.

42. MacGregor, *Integration,* 619.

43. Department of the Army, *Commander's Equal Opportunity Handbook* (Washington, D.C.: Department of the Army, 1994), 1.

44. MacGregor, *Integration,* 620.

45. Gropman, *Air Force Integrates,* 202.

46. Richard O. Hope, *Racial Strife in the U.S. Military: Toward the Elimination of Discrimination* (New York: Praeger, 1979), 42.

47. Garian A. A. Perugini, U.S. Air Force, personal correspondence, June 16, 1995.

48. Northrup et al., *Black and Other Minority Participation,* 22.

49. Department of the Navy, *Military Equal Opportunity Assessment* (Washington, D.C.: Department of the Navy, 1994), 5.

50. Ibid., 10.

51. Gropman, *Air Force Integrates,* 216.

52. David A. Hoopengardner, U.S. Army, personal correspondence, June 14, 1995.

53. Ibid.

54. John Sibley Butler, "Race Relations in the Military," in *The Military: More Than Just a Job?* ed. Charles C. Moskos and Frank R. Wood (Washington, D.C.: Pergamon-Brassey's, 1988), 120.

55. Roger Little, "Friendships in the Military Community," *Research in the Interweave of Social Roles: Friendship* 2 (1981):226.

56. Ibid., 224.

57. Ronald Pope, 1995; James Caselton, 1994; and Michael Kinney, 1995; all interviewed by author.

58. Connie Horenkamp, interview by author, 1995.

Chapter Five

1. "Texaco Ends Bias Suit with $176 Million," *Chicago Tribune,* November 16, 1996, sec. 1, 1.

2. *"Business Week*/Harris Executive Poll," *Business Week,* July 8, 1991, 63.

3. Colin Powell, *My American Journey* (New York: Random House, 1995), 608.

4. Susan D. Clayton and Faye J. Crosby, *Justice, Gender, and Affirmative Action* (Ann Arbor: The University of Michigan Press, 1992), 3; and Harold Orlans and June O'Neill, "Preface," *The Annals of the American Academy of Political and Social Science* 523 (September 1992):7.

5. John Brennan, "Key Words Influence Stands on Minorities," *Los Angeles Times,* August 21, 1991, A5.

6. Jim Norman, "America's Verdict on Affirmative Action Is Decidedly Mixed," *The Public Perspective* (June-July 1995):49.

7. *The Gallup Poll Monthly,* August 1991, 58.

8. James R. Kluegel and Eliot R. Smith, *Beliefs About Inequality* (New York: Aldine De Gruyter, 1986), 5.

9. Howard Gardner, *Frames of Mind: The Theory of Multiple Intelligences* (New York: Basic Books, 1983), 4.

10. Daniel Goleman, *Emotional Intelligence* (New York: Bantam Books, 1995), xii.

11. Neil L. Rudenstine, *The President's Report, 1993–1995* (Cambridge: Harvard University Press, 1996), 29.

12. Ibid.

13. David K. Shipler, "My Equal Opportunity, Your Free Lunch," *New York Times,* March 5, 1995, sec. 4, 1.

14. Ibid.

15. Jamie B. Raskin, "Affirmative Action and Racial Reaction," *Howard Law Journal* 38, no. 3 (Summer 1995):551.

16. John David Skrentny, *The Ironies of Affirmative Action* (Chicago: The University of Chicago Press, 1996), 6.

17. Franklin D. Roosevelt, "Executive Order Reaffirming Policy of Full Participation in the Defense Program," *Federal Register* (June 27, 1941):3109.

18. John F. Kennedy, "Executive Order Establishing the President's Committee on Equal Employment Opportunity," *Federal Register* (March 8, 1961):1977.

19. Ibid.

20. Farrell Bloch, *Antidiscrimination Law and Minority Employment* (Chicago: The University of Chicago Press, 1994), 70.

21. Lyndon B. Johnson, "Address at Howard University's Commencement," *Public Papers of the Presidents: Lyndon Johnson,* vol. 2 (Washington, D.C.: Government Printing Office, 1965), 636.

22. Andrew Hacker, "The End of Affirmative Action," *The New York Review of Books,* July 11, 1996, 21.

23. Bloch, *Antidiscrimination Law,* 71.

24. Lani Guinier, *The Tyranny of the Majority: Fundamental Fairness in Representative Democracy* (New York: The Free Press, 1994), 23.

25. William J. Clinton, "Remarks by the President on Affirmative Action," *National Archives* (July 19, 1995):4.

26. Stanley Fish, "Reverse Racism or How the Pot Got to Call the Kettle Black," *The Atlantic Monthly,* November 1993, 130.

27. Ibid.

28. John Rawls, *A Theory of Justice* (Cambridge: Harvard University Press, Belknap Press, 1971), 4.

29. Bloch, *Antidiscrimination Law,* 85; and Fish, "Reverse Racism," 130.

30. Fish, "Reverse Racism," 136.

31. Chang-Lin Tien, "A View from Berkeley," *The Chronicle of Higher Education,* March 31, 1996, 30.

32. Fish, "Reverse Racism," 135.

33. Lynn Martin, *Pipelines of Progress: An Update on the Glass Ceiling Initiative* (Washington, D.C.: U.S. Department of Labor, 1992), 1.

34. Clinton, "Remarks on Affirmative Action," 6.

35. Nicholas Lemann, "Taking Affirmative Action Apart," *The New York Times Magazine,* June 11, 1995, 62; and Duncan Kennedy, "A Cultural Pluralist Case for Affirmative Action in Legal Academia," *Duke Law Journal* 1990, no. 4 (September 1990):712.

36. Anthony Patrick Carnevale and Susan Carol Stone, *The American Mosaic* (New York: McGraw-Hill, 1995), 48.

37. Louis Uchitelle, "Union Goal of Equality Fails the Test of Time," *New York Times,* July 9, 1995, A1.

38. Glenn C. Loury, "Why Should We Care About Group Inequality?" *Social Philosophy and Policy* 5, no. 1 (1987):256; and Gertrude Ezorsky, *Racism and Justice: The Case for Affirmative Action* (Ithaca: Cornell University Press, 1991), 15.

39. Peter T. Kilborn, "A Leg Up on the Ladder, but Still Far from the Top," *New York Times,* June 16, 1995, A1.

40. Jonathan S. Leonard, "The Impact of Affirmative Action on Employment," *Journal of Labor Economics* 2, no. 4 (1994):457; and Bloch, *Antidiscrimination Law,* 96.

41. Bloch, *Antidiscrimination Law,* 84.

42. Max Frankel, "Reaffirm the Affirmative," *The New York Times Magazine,* February 26, 1995, 22.

43. Donna Alvarado, "Study Backs Affirmative Action in Medical Schools," *The Pantagraph,* July 30, 1996, D3.

44. Lemann, "Taking Affirmative Action Apart," 63.

45. Glenn C. Loury, "Incentive Effects of Affirmative Action," *The Annals of the American Academy of Political and Social Science* 523 (September 1992):21.

46. William Bradford Reynolds, "Affirmative Action and Its Negative Consequences," *The Annals of the American Academy of Political and Social Science* 523 (September 1992):43.

47. See Stephen L. Carter, *Reflections of an Affirmative Action Baby* (New York: Basic Books, 1991), 26.

48. Clinton, "Remarks on Affirmative Action," 6.

49. Steven Yates, *Civil Wrongs: What Went Wrong with Affirmative Action* (San Francisco: Institute for Contemporary Studies, 1994), 198.

50. Stephanie N. Mehta, "Affirmative-Action Supporters Face Divisive Problem," *Wall Street Journal,* June 2, 1995, B2.

51. Andrew Hacker, *Two Nations: Black and White, Separate, Hostile, Unequal* (New York: Charles Scribner's Sons, 1992), 129.

52. Bloch, *Antidiscrimination Law,* 96. See also Julius Wilson, "The Black Community in the 1980s: Questions of Race, Class, and Public Policy," *The Annals of the American Academy of Political and Social Science* 454 (March 1981):40.

53. William L. Taylor and Susan M. Liss, "Affirmative Action in the 1990s: Staying the Course," *The Annals of the American Academy of Political and Social Science* 523 (September 1992):34.

54. Orlans and O'Neill, "Preface," 9.

55. Paul M. Barrett, "SBA Minority Set-Aside Raises Questions," *Wall Street Journal,* February 23, 1996, B12.

56. *The Gallup Poll Monthly,* August 1991, 58.

57. Dorothy J. Gaiter, "How Shoney's, Belted by a Lawsuit, Found the Path to Diversity," *Wall Street Journal,* April 16, 1996, A1.

58. David Molpus, "Birmingham, Alabama, Takes New Affirmative Action Step," *National Public Radio, Morning Edition,* May 22, 1995, 5.

59. Richard D. Kahlenberg, *The Remedy: Class, Race, and Affirmative Action* (New York: Basic Books, 1996), 83.

Chapter Six

1. Henry J. Steiner and Detlev F. Vagts, *Transnational Legal Problems* (Mineola, N.Y.: The Foundation Press, 1976), 20.

2. Lawrence H. Fuchs, "The Reaction of Black Americans to Immigration," in *Immigration Reconsidered,* ed. Virginia Yans-McLaughlin (New York: Oxford University Press, 1990), 306.

3. David M. Reimers, *Still the Golden Door: The Third World Comes to America* (New York: Columbia University Press, 1992), 92.

4. Gregory Spencer, Bureau of the Census, *Projections of the Population of the United States, by Age, Sex, and Race: 1988 to 2080* (Washington, D.C.: U.S. Department of Commerce, 1989), xviii.

5. Nina Glick Shiller, Linda Basch, and Christina Slzanton Blanc, "From Immigrant to Transmigrant: Theorizing Transnational Migration," *Anthropological Quarterly* (January 1995):48.

6. Thomas Weyr, *Hispanic U.S.A.: Breaking the Melting Pot* (New York: Harper and Row, 1988), 7.

7. Yvonne Yazbeck Haddad and Adair T. Lummis, *Islamic Values in the United States* (New York: Oxford University Press, 1987), 3.

8. William H. Frey and Jonathan Tilove, "Immigrants In, Native Whites Out," *The New York Times Magazine,* August 20, 1995, 44.

9. Jonathan Kaufman, "America's Heartland Turns to Hot Location for the Melting Pot," *Wall Street Journal,* October 31, 1995, A1.

10. Peter Brimelow, *Alien Nation* (New York: Harper Perennial, 1996), xxi.

11. Chang-Lin Tien, "A View from Berkeley," *The Chronicle of Higher Education,* March 31, 1996, 30.

12. Steven A. Holmes, "Federal Government Is Urged to Rethink Its System of Racial Classification," *New York Times,* July 8, 1994, A9.

13. Richard W. Stevenson, "Hispanic Population Grows by 70 Percent in California," *New York Times* February 26, 1991, A13.

14. Dominick La Capra, introduction to *The Bounds of Race,* ed. Dominick La Capra (Ithaca: Cornell University Press, 1991), 13.

15. Arnold J. Toynbee, *The Economy of the Western Hemisphere* (London: Oxford University Press, 1962), 36; Suzanne Oboler, *Ethnic Labels, Latino Lives* (Minneapolis: University of Minnesota Press, 1995); and Andres Torres, *Between Melting Pot and Mosaic: African Americans and Puerto Ricans in the New York Political Economy* (Philadelphia: Temple University Press, 1995), 5.

16. Pierre L. van den Berghe, *Race and Racism: A Comparative Perspective* (New York: John Wiley and Sons, 1967), 56.

17. Toynbee, *Economy,* 37.

18. van den Berghe, *Race and Racism,* 57.

19. Colin Powell, *My American Journey* (New York: Random House, 1995), 8. See also Thomas Sowell, *The Economics and Politics of Race: An International Perspective* (New York: William Morrow and Company, 1983), 98; and Sidney W. Mintz, "Can Haiti Change?" *Foreign Affairs* 74, no. 1 (January-February 1995):76.

20. Albert Hourani, *A History of the Arab Peoples* (Cambridge: Harvard University Press, 1991), 116.

21. Ibid.

22. See Joe R. Feagin and Hernan Vera, *White Racism: The Basics* (New York: Routledge, 1995), x; Philip Perlmutter, *Divided We Fall: A History of Ethnic, Religious, and Racial Prejudice in America* (Ames: Iowa State University Press, 1992), 39; and Toni Morrison, "On the Back of Blacks," in *Arguing Immigration: The Debate over the Changing Face of America,* ed. Nicolaus Mills (New York: Touchstone, 1994), 98.

23. Fuchs, "The Reaction of Black Americans," 306; and Ransford W. Palmer, *Pilgrims from the Sun: West Indian Migration to America* (New York: Twayne Publishers, 1995), 20.

24. Robert L. Bach, "Recrafting the Common Good: Immigration and Community," *The Annals of the American Academy of Political and Social Science* 530 (November 1993):165.

25. Mary H. Cooper, "Muslims in America," *CQ Researcher* 3, no. 16 (April 1993):375; and Kathleen M. Moore, *Al-Mughtaribun: American Law and the Transformation of Muslim Life in the United States* (Albany: State University of New York Press, 1995), 10.

26. Malcolm Gladwell, "Black Like Them," *The New Yorker,* April 29-May 6, 1996, 76.

27. Powell, *My American Journey,* 22.

28. Ibid.

29. Sowell, *Economics and Politics,* 104.

30. Lena H. Sun, "A Cultural Bank and Trust," *Washington Post National Weekly Edition,* February 27-March 5, 1995, 9.

31. Sharon-Ann Gopaul-McNicol, *Working with West Indian Families* (New York: The Guilford Press, 1993), 29.

32. Ibid., 55.

33. Sam Fulwood, "U.S. Blacks: A Divided Experience," *Los Angeles Times,* November 25, 1995, A30.

34. John C. Walter, *The Harlem Fox: J. Raymond Jones and Tammany, 1920–1970* (Albany: State University of New York Press, 1989), 19.

35. Jim Sleeper, *The Closest of Strangers: Liberalism and the Politics of Race in New York* (New York: W. W. Norton, 1991), 54.

36. Ibid., 55.

37. Ibid., 57.

38. Anonymous, interview by author, 1994.

39. James Baldwin, *The Fire Next Time* (New York: Dell Publishing, 1963), 76.

40. Sharon Stanford, interview by author, 1996.

41. Linaya Leaf, interview by author, 1995.

42. "Study Abroad by U.S. Students, 1993–94," *The Chronicle of Higher Education,* November 10, 1995, A41.

43. Janelle Gordon, interview with author, 1996.

44. Linda Giles, interview with author, 1996.

45. Jane Lee, interview with author, 1995.

46. Arlene Winslow, interview with author, 1995.

47. Katie Sawyer, interview with author, 1995.

48. James Baldwin, *Nobody Knows My Name* (New York: Dial Press, 1961), xiii.

49. Elaine Graybill, interview with author, 1996. See also Karen De Witt, "In Japan, Blacks As Outsiders," *New York Times,* December 10, 1995, E4.

50. Malcolm X, *The Autobiography of Malcolm X* (New York: Ballantine Books, 1964), 321.

51. Ibid., 340.

Chapter Seven

1. George Gallup Jr. and Frank Newport, "For the First Time, More Americans Approve of Interracial Marriage Than Disapprove," *The Gallup Poll Monthly,* August 1991, 60.

2. Ibid., 62.

3. Richard D. Alba and Reid M. Golden, "Patterns of Ethnic Marriage in the United States," *Social Forces* 65, no. 1 (September 1986):202–203; and Paul C. Rosenblatt, Terri A. Karis, and Richard D. Powell, *Multiracial Couples: Black and White Voices* (Thousand Oaks, Calif.: Sage, 1995), 4.

4. Richard D. Alba, *Ethnic Identity: The Transformation of White America* (New Haven: Yale University Press, 1990), 15. See also Paul R. Spickard, *Mixed Blood: Intermarriage and Ethnic Identity in Twentieth-Century America* (Madison: The University of Wisconsin Press, 1989), 15.

5. Judy Scales-Trent, *Notes of a White Black Woman* (University Park: The Pennsylvania State University Press, 1995), 7. See also Maria P. P. Root, "A Bill of Rights for Racially Mixed People," in *The Multiracial Experience,* ed. Maria P. P. Root (Thousand Oaks, Calif.: Sage, 1996), 7; and Stanley Lieberson and Mary C. Waters, *From Many Strands: Ethnic and Racial Groups in Contemporary America* (New York: Russell Sage Foundation, 1988), 163.

6. Jane Lee, interview by author, 1995.

7. Angela Dreessen, interview by author, 1995.

8. Mary Leuus, interview by author, 1996.

9. Ruth Fisher, interview by author, 1995.

10. Patricia Fowler, interview by author, 1995.

11. Fisher, interview.

12. Albert I. Gordon, *Intermarriage* (Boston: Beacon Press, 1964), 221; and Edward Byron Reuter, *The American Race Problem: A Study of the Negro* (New York: Thomas Y. Crowell, 1938), 22.

13. Reuter, *American Race Problem*, 3.

14. Jack D. Forbes, *Black Africans and Native Americans* (Oxford: Basil Blackwell, 1988), 68.

15. Gretchen Gerzina, *Black London: Life Before Emancipation* (New Brunswick, N.J.: Rutgers University Press, 1995), 5.

16. Ibid., 4.

17. Ibid., 204.

18. C. Vann Woodward, *The Strange Career of Jim Crow* (New York: Oxford University Press, 1966), 14.

19. Ibid.

20. Madison Grant, *The Passing of the Great Race* (New York: Scribner's Sons, 1918), 85.

21. Kathy Russell, Midge Wilson, and Ronald Hall, *The Color Complex: The Politics of Skin Color Among African Americans* (New York: Harcourt Brace Jovanovich, 1992), 11.

22. Reuter, *American Race Problem*, 135.

23. William Loren Katz, *Black Indians: A Hidden Heritage* (New York: Atheneum, 1986), 10.

24. Scott L. Malcomson, "Having Their Say," *The New Yorker*, April 19-May 6, 1996, 139.

25. Carl N. Degler, *Neither Black nor White: Slavery and Race Relations in Brazil and the United States* (New York: The Macmillan Company, 1971), 256; and Winthrop D. Jordan, *White Over Black* (Chapel Hill: University of North Carolina Press, 1968), 178.

26. Mary Frances Berry and John W. Blassingame, *Long Memory: The Black Experience in America* (New York: Oxford University Press, 1982), 126.

27. Naomi Zack, *Race and Mixed Race* (Philadelphia: Temple University Press, 1993), 13.

28. Bart Landry, *The New Black Middle Class* (Berkeley: University of California Press, 1987), 29–30.

29. Verna M. Keith and Cedric Herring, "Skin Tone and Stratification in the Black Community," *American Journal of Sociology* 97, no. 3 (November 1991):777; and Faye V. Harrison, "The Persistent Power of Race in the Cultural and Political Economy of Racism," *Annual Review of Anthropology* 24 (1995):61.

30. Shirlee Taylor Haizlip, *The Sweeter the Juice* (New York: Simon and Schuster, 1994), 15.

31. Michael P. Johnson and James L. Roark, *Black Masters: A Free Family of Color in the Old South* (New York: W. W. Norton, 1984), 54–55.

32. Robert Thomas, "Thyra Johnson, Symbol of Racial Distinctions, Dies," *New York Times*, November 9, 1995, B11.

33. Gregory Williams, *Life on the Color Line: The True Story of a White Boy Who Discovered He Was Black* (New York: E. P. Dutton, 1995).

34. Bureau of the Census, *Current Population Reports: Marital Status and Living Arrangements* (Washington, D.C.: U.S. Department of Commerce, 1994), 20.

35. Susan Kalish, "Multiracial Births Increase As U.S. Ponders Racial Definitions," *Population Today* 23, no. 4 (April 1995):1–2.

36. Lieberson and Waters, *From Many Strands,* 164–165.

37. Kristyan M. Kouri and Marcia Lasswell, "Black-White Marriages: Social Change and Intergenerational Mobility," *Marriage and Family Review* 19, nos. 3–4 (1993):242.

38. Lieberson and Waters, *From Many Strands,* 206.

39. Anonymous, interview by author, 1995.

40. Angela Dreessen, interview by author, 1995.

41. Lieberson and Waters, *From Many Strands,* 211.

42. Rick Bragg, "Just a Grave for a Baby, But Anguish for a Town," *New York Times,* March 31, 1996, A10.

43. Mary Douglas, "Taboo," in *Magic, Witchcraft, and Religion,* ed. Arthur C. Lehmann and James Myers (Mountain View, Calif.: Mayfield, 1993), 50–51.

44. Grant, *Passing of the Great Race,* 17.

45. Lucille Holcomb, interview by author, 1995.

46. Ruth Frankenberg, *White Women, Race Matters: The Social Construction of Whiteness* (Minneapolis: University of Minnesota Press, 1993), 104.

47. Sharon M. Lee, "Racial Classification in the U.S. Census: 1890–1990," *Ethnic and Racial Studies* 16, no. 1 (January 1993):79.

48. Steven A. Holmes, "Federal Government Is Urged to Rethink Its System of Racial Classification," *New York Times,* July 8, 1994, A9.

49. Ursula M. Brown, "Black/White Interracial Young Adults: Quest for a Racial Identity," *American Journal of Orthopsychiatry* 65, no. 1 (January 1995):127–128.

50. F. James Davis, "The Hawaiian Alternative to the One-Drop Rule," in *American Mixed Race: The Culture of Microdiversity,* ed. Naomi Zack (Lanham, Md.: Rowman and Littlefield, 1995), 129; and Jonathan P. Decker, "Florida Draws New Race Line," *Christian Science Monitor,* September 29, 1995, 3.

51. Linda Mathews, "More Than Identity Rides on a New Racial Category," *New York Times,* July 6, 1996, A1.

52. "Poll on a Multiracial Category," *Newsweek,* February 13, 1995, 65.

53. Ruth Colker, "Which Drop of Blood Should the Census Bureau Count?" *Chicago Tribune,* April 16, 1996, sec. 1, 11.

54. Mathews, "More Than Identity," A7.

55. Glen Grant and Dennis M. Ogawa, "Living Proof: Is Hawaii the Answer?" *The Annals of the American Academy of Political and Social Science* 530 (November 1993):148–150.

Chapter Eight

1. Ruth G. McRoy and Louis A. Zurcher, *Transracial and Inracial Adoptees* (Springfield, Ill.: Charles C. Thomas, 1983), 4; and Rita Simon and Howard Altstein, *Transracial Adoptions* (New York: John Wiley and Sons, 1977), 13.

2. Frederick M. Winship, "Transracial Adoptions Are Growing," *Washington Post,* July 20, 1972, D4.

3. "South Carolina Adoption Furor Escalates to Arson," *Washington Post,* October 25, 1980, A10.

4. Rita Simon, Howard Altstein, and Marygold S. Melli, *The Case for Transracial Adoption* (Washington, D.C.: The American University Press, 1994), 17.

5. Public Law 103-383 (October 20, 1994), *Improving America's Schools Act of 1994,* part E, *Multiethnic Placement Act of 1994* (Washington, D.C.: Government Printing Office, 1994), 1.

6. Department of Health and Human Services, *Guidance on the Multiethnic Placement Act of 1994* (Washington, D.C.: Office of the Secretary of Health and Human Services, 1995), 13.

7. Alissa J. Rubin, "Panel OKs Bill to Encourage Interracial Adoptions," *Congressional Quarterly,* May 4, 1996, 1226.

8. Department of Health and Human Services, *Guidance on the Multiethnic Placement Act,* 1.

9. Randall Kennedy, "Orphans of Separatism: The Politics of Transracial Adoption," *Current,* October 1994, 8.

10. Sue Anne Pressley, "The Colors of Adoption," *Washington Post National Weekly Edition,* January 13, 1997, 30.

11. Molly Davis, "Transracial Adoption," *Crisis* (November-December 1992):20.

12. Ibid., 20; and Kevin Merida and Michael A. Fletcher, "Looking for Leaders in New Places," *Washington Post National Weekly Edition,* November 27-December 3, 1995, 12.

13. Kennedy, "Orphans of Separatism," 9.

14. Elizabeth Bartholet, "Where Do Black Children Belong? The Politics of Race Matching in Adoption," *University of Pennsylvania Law Review* 139, no. 5 (May 1991):1222.

15. Kennedy, "Orphans of Separatism," 11; and Julie C. Lythcott-Haims, "Where Do Mixed Babies Belong? Racial Classification in America and Its Implications for Transracial Adoption," *Harvard Civil Rights and Civil Liberties Law Review* 29, no. 2 (Summer 1994):533.

16. Asher D. Isaacs, "Transracial Adoption: Permanent Placement and Racial Identity," *National Black Law Journal* 14, no. 1 (Fall 1995):141.

17. Joyce A. Ladner, *Mixed Families: Adopting Across Racial Boundaries* (New York: Anchor, 1977), 79–81.

18. Simon, Altstein, and Melli, *Case for Transracial Adoption,* 115.

19. Kim Forde-Mazrui, "Black Identity and Child Placement: The Best Interests of Black and Biracial Children," *Michigan Law Review* 92, no. 4 (February 1994):950.

20. Sheila Welch, interview by author, 1995.

21. Jane Liedtke, interview by author, 1995.

22. Mary Campbell, interview by author, 1995.

23. Pressley, "Colors of Adoption," 30.

24. Richard Watts, interview by author, 1997.

25. Pressley, "Colors of Adoption," 30.

26. Watts, interview.

27. Ibid.; Sheila Welch, interview; and Campbell, interview.

28. Campbell, interview.

29. Simon and Altstein, *Transracial Adoptions,* 97.

30. Eric Welch, interview by author, 1995.

31. Dick Rundall, interview by author, 1995.

32. Liedtke, interview.

33. Sheila Welch, interview.

34. Liedtke, interview.

35. Rundall, interview.

Conclusion

1. Karen De Witt, "Wave of Suburban Growth is Being Fed by Minorities," *New York Times,* August 12, 1994, A1.

2. Ben L. Martin, "From Negro to Black to African Americans," *Political Science Quarterly* 106, no. 1 (1991):91.

3. Jean Bethke Elshtain, *Democracy on Trial* (New York: Basic Books, 1995), 35; and Amitai Etzioni, ed., *Rights and the Common Good* (New York: St. Martin's Press, 1995).

4. Roger Fisher, William Ury, and Bruce Patton, *Getting to Yes* (New York: Penguin, 1981), 26–27.

5. Michel Marriott, "Another Majority, Silent and Black," *New York Times,* October 22, 1995, E3.

SELECTED BIBLIOGRAPHY

Alba, Richard D. *Ethnic Identity: The Transformation of White America.* New Haven: Yale University Press, 1990.

Allen, Theodore W. *The Invention of the White Race.* Vol. 1. London: Verso, 1994.

Allport, Gordon W. *The Nature of Prejudice.* Reading, Mass.: Addison Wesley, 1954.

Applebome, Peter. "John Hope Franklin, the Last Integrationist." *The New York Times Magazine,* April 23, 1995, 34–37.

Bailey, Beth, and David Farber. "The Double-V Campaign in WWII Hawaii: African Americans, Racial Ideology, and Federal Power." *Journal of Social History* (Summer 1993):817–843.

Baldwin, James. *Nobody Knows My Name.* New York: Dial Press, 1961.

———. *The Fire Next Time.* New York: Dell Publishing, 1963.

Bambrough, Renford. *The Philosophy of Aristotle.* New York: Mentor, 1963.

Banfield, Edward C. *Civility and Citizenship in Liberal Democratic Societies.* New York: Paragon House, 1992.

Barber, Bernard. *The Logic and Limits of Trust.* New Brunswick, N.J.: Rutgers University Press, 1983.

Bartholet, Elizabeth. "Where Do Black Children Belong? The Politics of Race Matching in Adoption." *University of Pennsylvania Law Review* 139, no. 5 (May 1991):1164–1256.

Barzun, Jacques. *Race: A Study in Superstition.* New York: Harper Torchbooks, 1965.

———. *The French Race: Theories of Its Origins and Their Social and Political Implications.* Port Washington, N.Y.: Kennikat Press, 1966.

Baumeister, Roy F. *Identity: Cultural Change and the Struggle for Self.* New York: Oxford University Press, 1986.

Bell, Linda A., and David Blumenfeld, eds. *Overcoming Racism and Sexism.* Lanham, Md.: Rowman and Littlefield, 1995.

Bellah, Robert N., et al. *Habits of the Heart: Individualism and Commitment in American Life.* Berkeley: University of California Press, 1985.

———. *The Good Society.* New York: Alfred A. Knopf, 1991.

Bem, Sandra Lipsitz. *The Lenses of Gender: Transforming the Debate on Sexual Inequality.* New Haven: Yale University Press, 1993.

Benedict, Ruth. *Race and Racism.* London: Routledge, 1922. Reprint, 1983.

Bennett, William J., ed. *The Book of Virtues: A Treasury of Great Moral Stories.* New York: Simon and Schuster, 1993.

Berk, Laura E. *Child Development.* Boston: Allyn and Bacon, 1994.

Bernstein, Richard. *Dictatorship of Virtue: Multiculturalism and the Battle for America's Future.* New York: Alfred A. Knopf, 1994.

Berry, Mary Frances, and John W. Blassingame. *Long Memory: The Black Experience in America.* New York: Oxford University Press, 1982.

Binkin, Martin, et al. *Blacks in the Military.* Washington, D.C.: The Brookings Institution, 1982.

Bok, Sissela. *A Strategy for Peace: Human Values and the Threat of War.* New York: Pantheon Books, 1989.

Bowser, Benjamin P., ed. *Racism and Anti-Racism in World Perspective.* Thousand Oaks, Calif.: Sage, 1995.

Brimelow, Peter. *Alien Nation.* New York: Harper Perennial, 1996.

Brown, Claudette E. *The Black Population in the United States: March 1994 and 1993.* Bureau of the Census, *Current Population Reports,* 20–480. Washington, D.C.: U.S. Government Printing Office, 1995.

Brown, Ursula M. "Black/White Interracial Young Adults: Quest for a Racial Identity." *American Journal of Orthopsychiatry* 65, no. 1 (January 1995):125–130.

Bunker, Barbara Benedict, and Jeffrey Z. Rubin, eds. *Conflict, Cooperation, and Justice.* San Francisco: Jossey-Bass Publishers, 1995.

Butler, John Sibley, and Kenneth L. Wilson. "The American Soldier Revisited: Race Relations and the Military." *Social Science Quarterly* 59, no. 3 (December 1978):451–467.

Carson, Clayborne, ed. *The Papers of Martin Luther King, Jr.* Vol. 1. Berkeley: University of California Press, 1992.

Carter, Stephen L. *Reflections of an Affirmative Action Baby.* New York: Basic Books, 1991.

Cavalli-Sforza, L. Luca, Paolo Menozzi, and Alberto Piazza. *The History and Geography of Human Genes.* Princeton: Princeton University Press, 1994.

Chu, Donald, and David Griffey. "The Contact Theory of Racial Integration: The Case of Sport." *Sociology of Sport Journal* 2, no. 4 (December 1985):323–333.

Clinton, William J. "Remarks by the President on Affirmative Action." *National Archives* (July 19, 1995):1–6.

Coleman, James S. *Foundations of Social Theory.* Cambridge: Harvard University Press, 1990.

Cose, Ellis. *The Rage of a Privileged Class.* New York: HarperCollins, 1993.

_____. *Color-Blind: Seeing Beyond Race in a Race-Obsessed World.* New York: HarperCollins, 1997.

Coser, Lewis A. *The Functions of Social Conflict.* Glencoe, Ill.: The Free Press, 1956.

Cox, Oliver. *Caste, Class, and Race.* New York: Doubleday, 1948.

_____. *Race Relations: Elements and Social Dynamics.* Detroit: Wayne State University Press, 1976.

Crouch, Stanley. *Notes of a Hanging Judge.* New York: Oxford University Press, 1990.

Dalfiume, Richard M. *Desegregation of the U.S. Armed Forces: Fighting on Two Fronts.* Columbia: University of Missouri Press, 1969.

Dalton, Harlon L. *Racial Healing.* New York: Doubleday, 1995.

Davis, David Brion. *The Problem of Slavery in Western Culture.* Ithaca: Cornell University Press, 1966.

Davis, F. James. *Who Is Black? One Nation's Definition.* University Park: The Pennsylvania State University Press, 1991.

Dominguez, Virginia R. *White By Definition: Social Classification in Creole Louisiana.* New Brunswick, N.J.: Rutgers University Press, 1986.

Donaldson, Gary A. *The History of African Americans in the Military.* Malabar, Fla.: Krieger Publishing Company, 1991.

Drake, Thomas E. *Quakers and Slavery in America.* New Haven: Yale University Press, 1950.

Du Bois, W. E. Burghardt. *The Souls of Black Folk.* New York: Dodd, Mead, and Company, 1979.

Ebbert, Jean, and Marie-Beth Hall. *Crossed Currents: Navy Women from WWI to Tailhook.* Washington, D.C.: Brassey's, 1993.

Edelman, Marian Wright. *The Measure of Our Success: A Letter to My Children and Yours.* Boston: Beacon Press, 1992.

Edwards, Audrey, and Craig K. Polite. *Children of the Dream: The Psychology of Black Success.* New York: Doubleday, 1992.

Eisenstein, Zillah R. *The Female Body and the Law.* Berkeley: University of California Press, 1988.

Elkins, Stanley M. *Slavery: A Problem in American Institutional and Intellectual Life.* Chicago: The University of Chicago Press, 1976.

Ellis, Richard. *American Political Cultures.* New York: Oxford University Press, 1993.

Ezorsky, Gertrude. *Racism and Justice: The Case for Affirmative Action.* Ithaca: Cornell University Press, 1991.

Fish, Stanley. "Reverse Racism or How the Pot Got to Call the Kettle Black." *The Atlantic Monthly,* November 1993, 128–136.

Fisher, Roger. "Negotiating Power: Getting and Using Influence." *American Behavioral Scientist* 27, no. 2 (November-December 1983):149–166.

Fisher, Roger, and Scott Brown. *Getting Together: Building a Relationship That Gets to Yes.* Boston: Houghton Mifflin, 1988.

Fitzgerald, Thomas K. *Metaphors of Identity: A Culture-Communication Dialogue.* Albany: State University of New York Press, 1993.

Foner, Jack D. *Blacks and the Military in American History.* New York: Praeger, 1974.

Frankenberg, Ruth. *White Women, Race Matters: The Social Construction of Whiteness.* Minneapolis: University of Minnesota Press, 1993.

Franklin, John Hope. *The Color Line: Legacy for the Twenty-First Century.* Columbia: University of Missouri Press, 1993.

Franklin, John Hope, ed. *Color and Race.* Boston: Houghton Mifflin, 1968.

Fredrickson, George M. *The Arrogance of Race: Historical Perspectives on Slavery, Racism, and Social Inequality.* Middletown, Conn.: Wesleyan University Press, 1988.

_____. "Demonizing the American Dilemma." *The New York Review of Books,* October 19, 1995, 10–16.

Fuchs, Lawrence H. *The American Kaleidoscope.* Hanover, N.H.: University Press of New England, 1990.

Fukuyama, Francis. *Trust: The Social Virtues and the Creation of Prosperity.* New York: The Free Press, 1995.

Gates, Henry Louis, Jr. *Loose Canons: Notes on the Culture Wars.* New York: Oxford University Press, 1992.

Gerzina, Gretchen. *Black London: Life Before Emancipation.* New Brunswick, N.J.: Rutgers University Press, 1995.

Gladwell, Malcolm. "Black Like Them." *The New Yorker,* April 29-May 6, 1996, 74–81.

Glendon, Mary Ann, and David Blankenhorn, eds. *Seedbeds of Virtue.* New York: Madison Books, 1995.

Gopaul-McNicol, Sharon-Ann. *Working with West Indian Families.* New York: The Guilford Press, 1993.

Gossett, Thomas F. *Race: The History of an Idea in America.* Dallas: Southern Methodist University Press, 1963.

Gould, Stephen Jay. *The Mismeasure of Man.* New York: W. W. Norton, 1981.

Graham, Hugh Davis. "The Origins of Affirmative Action." *The Annals of the American Academy of Political and Social Science* 523 (September 1992):50–62.

Grant, Glen, and Dennis M. Ogawa. "Living Proof: Is Hawaii the Answer?" *The Annals of the American Academy of Political and Social Science* 530 (November 1993):137–154.

Grant, Madison. *The Passing of the Great Race.* New York: Scribner's Sons, 1918.

Gropman, Alan L. *The Air Force Integrates, 1945–1964.* Washington, D.C.: Office of Air Force History, 1978.

Guinier, Lani. *The Tyranny of the Majority: Fundamental Fairness in Representative Democracy.* New York: The Free Press, 1994.

Hacker, Andrew. *Two Nations: Black and White, Separate, Hostile, Unequal.* New York: Charles Scribner's Sons, 1992.

_____. "The End of Affirmative Action." *The New York Review of Books,* July 11, 1996, 21–28.

Haddad, Yvonne Yazbeck, and Adair T. Lummis. *Islamic Values in the United States.* New York: Oxford University Press, 1987.

Henriques, Fernando. *Children of Conflict: A Study of Interracial Sex and Marriage.* New York: E. P. Dutton, 1975.

Herrnstein, Richard J., and Charles Murray. *The Bell Curve: Intelligence and Class Structure in American Life.* New York: The Free Press, 1994.

Hewitt, John P. *Dilemmas of the American Self.* Philadelphia: Temple University Press, 1989.

_____. *Self and Society: A Symbolic Interactionist Social Psychology.* Boston: Allyn and Bacon, 1991.

Hewstone, Miles, and Rupert Brown, eds. *Contact and Conflict in Intergroup Encounters.* Oxford: Basil Blackwell, 1986.

Hochschild, Jennifer L. *Facing Up to the American Dream.* Princeton: Princeton University Press, 1995.

Hollins, Martha L., et al. *Enrollment in Higher Education: Fall 1986 Through Fall 1994.* NCES 96-851. Washington, D.C.: U.S. Department of Education, 1996.

Holloway, Joseph E., ed. *Africanisms in American Culture*. Bloomington: Indiana University Press, 1990.

hooks, bell. *Black Looks: Race and Representation*. Boston: South End Press, 1992.

Hope, Richard O. *Racial Strife in the U.S. Military: Toward the Elimination of Discrimination*. New York: Praeger, 1979.

Horsman, Reginald. *Race and Manifest Destiny: The Origins of American Racial Anglo-Saxonism*. Cambridge: Harvard University Press, 1981.

Hourani, Albert. *A History of the Arab Peoples*. Cambridge: Harvard University Press, 1991.

Hughes, Robert. *Culture of Complaint: The Fraying of America*. New York: Oxford University Press, 1993.

Ignatiev, Noel. *How the Irish Became White*. New York: Routledge, 1995.

Isaacs, Asher D. "Interracial Adoption: Permanent Placement and Racial Identity." *National Black Law Journal* 14, no. 1 (Fall 1995):126–156.

Isaacs, Harold R. *Idols of the Tribe: Group Identity and Political Change*. New York: Harper and Row, 1975.

Iyengar, Shanto. *Is Anyone Responsible? How Television Frames Political Issues*. Chicago: The University of Chicago Press, 1994.

Jackman, Mary R. *The Velvet Glove: Paternalism and Conflict in Gender, Class, and Race Relations*. Berkeley: University of California Press, 1994.

Jacoway, Elizabeth, and David R. Colburn, eds. *Southern Businessmen and Desegregation*. Baton Rouge: Louisiana State University Press, 1982.

Jaynes, Gerald David, and Robin M. Williams, eds. *A Common Destiny: Blacks and American Society*. Washington, D.C.: National Academy Press, 1989.

Jordan, Winthrop D. *White Over Black*. Chapel Hill: University of North Carolina Press, 1968.

Kahlenberg, Richard D. *The Remedy: Class, Race, and Affirmative Action*. New York: Basic Books, 1996.

Keith, Verna M., and Cedric Herring. "Skin Tone and Stratification in the Black Community." *American Journal of Sociology* 97, no. 3 (November 1991): 760–778.

Kennedy, Duncan. "A Cultural Pluralist Case for Affirmative Action in Legal Academia." *Duke Law Journal* 1990, no. 4 (September 1990):705–757.

Kennedy, Randall. "Orphans of Separation: The Politics of Transracial Adoption." *Current* (October 1994):8–13.

King, Martin Luther, Jr. *I've Been to the Mountaintop*. New York: Harper San Francisco, 1963.

Kingwell, Mark. *A Civil Tongue: Justice, Dialogue, and the Politics of Pluralism*. University Park: The Pennsylvania State University Press, 1995.

Kinsley, Michael. "The Spoils of Victimhood: The Case Against Affirmative Action." *The New Yorker*, March 27, 1995, 62–69.

Kondo, Dorinne K. *Crafting Selves: Power, Gender, and Discourses of Identity in a Japanese Workplace*. Chicago: The University of Chicago Press, 1990.

Kouri, Kristyan M., and Marcia Lasswell. "Black-White Marriages: Social Change and Intergenerational Mobility." *Marriage and Family Review* 19, nos. 3–4 (1993):24–55.

Kuhn, Thomas S. *The Structure of Scientific Revolutions*. Chicago: The University of Chicago Press, 1970.

Ladner, Joyce A. *Mixed Families: Adopting Across Racial Boundaries.* New York: Anchor, 1977.

Landry, Bart. *The New Black Middle Class.* Berkeley: University of California Press, 1987.

Lehmann, Arthur C., and James Myers, eds. *Magic, Witchcraft, and Religion.* Mountain View, Calif.: Mayfield, 1993.

Lemann, Nicholas. "The Great Sorting." *The Atlantic Monthly,* September 1995, 84–100.

Leonard, Jonathan S. "The Impact of Affirmative Action on Employment." *Journal of Labor Economics* 2, no. 4 (1994):439–463.

Lewontin, R. C. *Biology as Ideology: The Doctrine of DNA.* New York: Harper-Collins, 1992.

Lieberson, Stanley, and Mary C. Waters. *From Many Strands: Ethnic and Racial Groups in Contemporary America.* New York: Russell Sage Foundation, 1988.

Lincoln, C. Eric. *Coming Through the Fire: Surviving Race and Place in America.* Durham, N.C.: Duke University Press, 1996.

Lippmann, Walter. *The Good Society.* New York: Grosset and Dunlap, 1936.

Little, Roger. "Friendships in the Military Community." *Research in the Interweave of Social Roles: Friendship* 2 (1981):221–235.

Loury, Glenn C. "Why Should We Care About Group Inequality?" *Social Philosophy and Policy* 5, no. 1 (1987):249–271.

_____. "Incentive Effects of Affirmative Action." *The Annals of the American Academy of Political and Social Science* 523 (September 1992):19–29.

Luhmann, Niklas. *Trust and Power.* New York: John Wiley and Sons, 1979.

MacGregor, Morris J. *Integration of the Armed Forces, 1940–1945.* Washington, D.C.: United States Army, 1985.

MacLeod, Duncan J. *Slavery, Race and the American Revolution.* Cambridge: Cambridge University Press, 1974.

Malcolm X. *The Autobiography of Malcolm X.* New York: Ballantine Books, 1964.

Malinowski, Bronislaw. *Magic, Science, and Religion, and Other Essays.* Prospect Heights, Ill.: Waveland Press, 1992.

Martin, Lynn. *Pipelines of Progress: An Update on the Glass Ceiling Initiative.* Washington, D.C.: U.S. Department of Labor, 1992.

McCrum, Robert, William Cran, and Robert MacNeil. *The Story of English.* New York: Viking, 1994.

McLaughlin, Virginia Yans, ed. *Immigration Reconsidered.* New York: Oxford University Press, 1990.

Merton, Robert K. "The Self-Fulfilling Prophecy." *The Antioch Review* 8 (1948):192–210.

Mill, John Stuart. *On Liberty.* New York: W. W. Norton, 1975.

Mills, Nicolaus, ed. *Arguing Immigration: The Debate over the Changing Face of America.* New York: Touchstone, 1994.

Montagu, Ashley. *Man's Most Dangerous Myth: The Fallacy of Race.* New York: Oxford University Press, 1974.

Moore, Brenda L. *To Serve My Country, To Serve My Race.* New York: New York University Press, 1996.

Morrison, Toni. *Playing in the Dark: Whiteness and the Literacy Imagination.* Cambridge: Harvard University Press, 1992.

Moskos, Charles C. *The American Enlisted Man.* New York: Russell Sage Foundation, 1970.

_____. "Success Story: Blacks in the Army." *The Atlantic Monthly,* May 1986, 65–72.

Moskos, Charles C., and John Sibley Butler. *All That We Can Be: Black Leadership and Racial Integration the Army Way.* New York: Basic Books, 1996.

Moskos, Charles C., and Frank R. Wood, eds. *The Military: More Than Just a Job?* Washington, D.C.: Pergamon-Brassey's, 1988.

Mullen, Robert W. *Blacks in America's Wars.* New York: Anchor, 1973.

Nalty, Bernard C. *Strength for the Fight: A History of Black Americans in the Military.* New York: The Free Press, 1986.

Noel, Lise. *Intolerance: A General Survey.* Translated by Arnold Bennett. Montreal: McGill–Queen's University Press, 1994.

Northrup, Herbert R., et al. *Black and Other Minority Participation in the All-Volunteer Navy and Marine Corps.* Philadelphia: University of Pennsylvania Press, 1979.

Omi, Michael, and Howard Winant. *Racial Formation in the United States.* New York: Routledge, 1989.

Orlans, Harold, and June O'Neill. "Preface." *The Annals of the American Academy of Political and Social Science* 523 (September 1992):7–9.

Palmer, Ransford W. *Pilgrims from the Sun: West Indian Migration to America.* New York: Twayne Publishers, 1995.

Park, Robert Ezra. *Race and Culture.* Glencoe, Ill.: The Free Press, 1950.

Payne, Richard J. *The Clash with Distant Cultures.* Albany: State University of New York Press, 1995.

Poliakov, Leon. *The Aryan Myth: A History of Racist and Nationalist Ideas in Europe.* New York: Basic Books, 1974.

Popkin, Samuel L. *The Reasoning Voter: Communication and Persuasion in Presidential Campaigns.* Chicago: The University of Chicago Press, 1991.

Powell, Colin. *My American Journey.* New York: Random House, 1995.

Pritchard, E. E. Evans. *Witchcraft, Oracles, and Magic Among the Azande.* Oxford: Clarendon Press, 1937.

Putnam, Robert D. *Making Democracy Work: Civic Traditions in Modern Italy.* Princeton: Princeton University Press, 1993.

_____. "Turning In, Tuning Out: The Strange Disappearance of Social Capital in America." *PS: Political Science and Politics* 28, no. 4 (December 1995):664–683.

Quarles, Benjamin. *The Negro in the American Revolution.* New York: W. W. Norton, 1961.

_____. *The Negro in the Making of America.* New York: Collier Books, 1987.

Rawls, John. *A Theory of Justice.* Cambridge: Harvard University Press, Belknap Press, 1971.

_____. *Political Liberalism.* New York: Columbia University Press, 1993.

Reimers, David M. *Still the Golden Door: The Third World Comes to America.* New York: Columbia University Press, 1992.

Reuter, Edward Byron. *The American Race Problem: A Study of the Negro*. New York: Thomas Y. Crowell, 1938.

Reynolds, William Bradford. "Affirmative Action and Its Negative Consequences." *The Annals of the American Academy of Political and Social Science* 523 (September 1992):38–49.

Rieder, Jonathan. *Canarsie: The Jews and Italians of Brooklyn Against Liberalism*. Cambridge: Harvard University Press, 1985.

Roediger, David R. *The Wages of Whiteness: Race and the Making of the American Working Class*. London: Verso, 1991.

Root, Maria P. P., ed. *The Multiracial Experience*. Thousand Oaks, Calif.: Sage, 1996.

Ryan, William. *Blaming the Victim*. New York: Pantheon Books, 1971.

Schollaert, Paul T., and Donald Hugh Smith. "Team Racial Composition and Sports Attendance." *The Sociological Quarterly* 28, no. 1 (1987):71–87.

Schuman, Howard, Charlotte Steeh, and Lawrence Bobo. *Racial Attitudes in America: Trends and Interpretations*. Cambridge: Harvard University Press, 1985.

Schutte, Gerhard. *What Racists Believe: Race Relations in South Africa and the United States*. London: Sage Publications, 1995.

Searle, John R. *The Construction of Social Reality*. New York: The Free Press, 1995.

Sherif, Muzafe, et al. *The Robbers Cave Experiment: Intergroup Conflict and Co-operation*. Middletown, Conn.: Wesleyan University Press, 1988.

Shriver, Donald W., Jr. *An Ethic for Enemies: Forgiveness in Politics*. New York: Oxford University Press, 1995.

Simon, Rita, Howard Altstein, and Marygold S. Melli. *The Case for Transracial Adoption*. Washington, D.C.: The American University Press, 1994.

Sinopolit, Richard C. "Thick-Skinned Liberalism: Redefining Civility." *American Political Science Review* 87, no. 3 (September 1995):612–620.

Skrentny, John David. *The Ironies of Affirmative Action*. Chicago: The University of Chicago Press, 1996.

Sleeper, Jim. *The Closest of Strangers: Liberalism and the Politics of Race in New York*. New York: W. W. Norton, 1991.

Smedly, Audrey. *Race in North America: Origin and Evolution of a Worldview*. Boulder: Westview Press, 1993.

Smith, Graham. *When Jim Crow Met John Bull: Black American Soldiers in World War II Britain*. New York: St. Martin's Press, 1987.

Smith, Robert C. *Racism in the Post–Civil Rights Era: Now You See It, Now You Don't*. Albany: State University of New York Press, 1995.

Sniderman, Paul M., and Michael Gray Hagen. *Race and Inequality: A Study in American Values*. Chatham, N.J.: Chatham House Publishers, 1985.

Sniderman, Paul M., Philip E. Tetlock, and Edward G. Carmines. "Prejudice and Politics: An Introduction," in *Prejudice, Politics, and the American Dilemma*, ed. Paul M. Sniderman, et al. Stanford: Stanford University Press, 1993.

Sonenshein, Raphael J. *Politics in Black and White: Race and Power in Los Angeles*. Princeton: Princeton University Press, 1993.

Sowell, Thomas. *Race and Economics*. New York: David McKay Company, 1975.

_____. *The Economics and Politics of Race: An International Perspective.* New York: William Morrow and Company, 1983.

Spickard, Paul R. *Mixed Blood: Intermarriage and Ethnic Identity in Twentieth-Century America.* Madison: The University of Wisconsin Press, 1989.

St. John de Crevecoeur, J. Hector. *Letters from an American Farmer.* New York: Albert and Charles Boni, 1925.

Steele, Shelby. *The Content of Our Character.* New York: St. Martin's Press, 1990.

Stouffer, Samuel A., et al. *The American Soldier: Adjustment During Army Life.* Vol. 1. Princeton: Princeton University Press, 1949.

Takagi, Dana Y. *The Retreat from Race.* New Brunswick, N.J.: Rutgers University Press, 1992.

Tannenbaum, Frank. *Slave and Citizen: The Negro in the Americas.* New York: Alfred A. Knopf, 1947.

Taylor, Charles, et al. *Sources of the Self: The Making of Modern Identity.* Cambridge: Harvard University Press, 1989.

_____. *Multiculturalism and the Politics of Recognition.* Princeton: Princeton University Press, 1992.

Taylor, William L., and Susan M. Liss. "Affirmative Action in the 1990s: Staying the Course." *The Annals of the American Academy of Political and Social Science* 523 (September 1992):30–37.

Toynbee, Arnold J. *The Economy of the Western Hemisphere.* London: Oxford University Press, 1962.

Tucker, William. *The Science and Politics of Racial Research.* Urbana: University of Illinois Press, 1994.

Turner, Victor. *Dramas, Fields, and Metaphors: Symbolic Action in Human Society.* Ithaca: Cornell University Press, 1974.

U.S. Department of the Army. *Commander's Equal Opportunity Handbook.* Washington, D.C.: United States Army, 1994.

U.S. Department of the Navy. *Military Equal Opportunity Assessment.* Washington, D.C.: United States Navy, 1994.

van den Berghe, Pierre L. *Race and Racism: A Comparative Perspective.* New York: John Wiley and Sons, 1967.

Wallace, James D. *Virtues and Vices.* Ithaca: Cornell University Press, 1978.

Walter, John C. *The Harlem Fox: J. Raymond Jones and Tammany, 1920–1970.* Albany: State University of New York Press, 1989.

West, Cornel. *Race Matters.* Boston: Beacon Press, 1993.

Wicke, Peter. *Rock Music: Culture, Aesthetics, and Sociology.* Cambridge: Cambridge University Press, 1987.

Wilkinson, Rupert. *The Pursuit of the American Character.* New York: Harper and Row, 1988.

Williams, Patricia J. *The Alchemy of Race and Rights.* Cambridge: Harvard University Press, 1991.

Williamson, Joel. *New People: Miscegenation and Mulattoes in the United States.* New York: New York University Press, 1984.

Woodward, C. Vann. *The Strange Career of Jim Crow.* New York: Oxford University Press, 1966.

Worchel, Stephen, and William G. Austin, eds. *Psychology of Intergroup Relations*. Chicago: Nelson-Hall, 1986.

Yarmolinsky, Adam. *The Military Establishment: Its Impacts on American Society*. New York: Harper and Row, 1971.

Yates, Steven. *Civil Wrongs: What Went Wrong with Affirmative Action*. San Francisco: Institute for Contemporary Studies, 1994.

Zack, Naomi. *Race and Mixed Race*. Philadelphia: Temple University Press, 1993.

INDEX